GOD AND ME
EVERY DAY . . .

MARY EMMA BRISTOW

WESTBOW
PRESS®
A DIVISION OF THOMAS NELSON
& ZONDERVAN

Scriptures taken from the Holy Bible, New International Version®, NIV®. Copyright © 1973, 1978, 1984, 2011 by Biblica, Inc.™ Used by permission of Zondervan. All rights reserved worldwide. www.zondervan.com The "NIV" and "New International Version

WestBow Press books may be ordered through booksellers or by contacting:

WestBow Press
A Division of Thomas Nelson & Zondervan
1663 Liberty Drive
Bloomington, IN 47403
www.westbowpress.com
1 (866) 928-1240

ISBN: 978-1-9736-3157-6 (sc)
ISBN: 978-1-9736-3158-3 (hc)
ISBN: 978-1-9736-3156-9 (e)

Library of Congress Control Number: 2018907142

Print information available on the last page.

WestBow Press rev. date: 06/15/2018

PRAISING GOD BLESSES US

"We praise You, God, we praise You, for Your name is near; people tell of Your wonderful deeds. As for me, I will declare this forever; I will sing praise to the God of Jacob."
Psalm 75:1,9

What a better way to start the day than praising God! May we praise Him for who He is, and for what He does. We need to stop and think about this because so much of our lives we simply take Him for granted.

He is our creator God, our loving God and our merciful God. We need to "tell of Your wonderful deeds". He separated the waters from the land, and the light from the dark. But He didn't stop there. He "holds us by His right hand", He guides us with His counsel. He is not Santa Claus, but a loving Father who wants the very best for us.

MY PRAYER: *Lord God, You are so wonderful. Only You could love us like You do, only You could forgive us for ignoring You and doing our own thing. You do so much to make our life lovely and we take and take and take with taking the time to thank You. We love You.*

MaryEmma

JANUARY 2

CREATED IN GOD'S IMAGE

"Then God said, 'Let Us make mankind in Our image… " "So God created mankind in His Own image, in the image of God He created them; male and female He created them."
Genesis 1:26-27

Yesterday I started reading at the beginning of the Bible and when I read this verse I thought, "this shows how special we are". We are not just another animal, but we are created in God's image.

We are created in God's image because He loves us. He created us and then when we love Him and accept His gift, He gives us new birth as His children. How much more could we want! The psalmist said that He "holds our hand in His and guides us with His counsel".

I want to memorize that verse. I spilled my coffee this morning and as I was cleaning up the mess, into my head flashed "this is God's will for You in Christ Jesus". It was a reminder from God: instead of being upset and angry with myself, I had peace as I cleaned it up, because of God's Help. God does hold our hand and guide us.

MY PRAYER: *Lord God, thank You for making us special and loving us so much. We love You.*

MaryEmma

OURS IS THE GREAT GOD

"Your ways, God, are holy. What god is as great as our God? You are the God who performs miracles; You display Your power among the peoples."
Psalm 77:13-14

The psalmist sounds like he is at peace with God and the world. He is praising God and remembering all the great things God has done. But the beginning of the Psalms shows a different attitude: he is depressed.

"I cried out to God for help; I cried out to God to hear me. When I was in distress, I sought the Lord; at night I stretched out untiring hands and I would not be comforted."
Verses 1-2

Here he is at the bottom of the pit. What happened between verses 1 and 2 and 13 and 14? He made a decision; where to direct his thoughts. He decided to remember the deeds and miracles of the Lord and meditate on them.

The psalmist changed his thinking. We have a choice to turn our thoughts to God or keep them on ourselves. Verse 2 says: "I will not be comforted." A choice. Verse 11 says: "I will remember the deeds of the Lord." A choice.

Jesus said that in this world we would have trouble, but in Him we would have peace. Our heavenly Father lets us make the choice.

MY PRAYER: *Lord, I pray that we will all read your word, remember what your word says, and trust You. We love You.*
MaryEmma

JANUARY 4

REJOICING BRINGS PEACE

"Sing for joy to God our strength; shout aloud to the God of Jacob!"
Psalm 81:1

Rejoicing is one step closer to God, to realizing His power and to realizing His love and presence with us. We are commanded to rejoice. We don't have to make a lot of noise, rejoicing starts in our attitude. It was an ordinance of God for Israel. But it is also a command for Christians. One of my favorite verses in 1 Thessalonians is: "Rejoice always, pray unceasingly, for this is God's will for you in Christ Jesus."

In Philippians 4, it says: "Rejoice, I say it again, Rejoice. The Lord is near." If we want to be more aware of God, to be closer to Him, we need to rejoice. He is our strength, He is our source of love, and He wants us to rejoice in Him.

This Psalm continues with telling how God blessed them and how they turned away from Him. He wanted to continue blessing them, but they wanted to do their own thing and ignored him.

Could that be the answer to the problems we have in this life?

When we start thanking God for everything, joy follows. May He bless us today.

MY PRAYER: *"Lord, help us to remember to praise you and thank you instead of being depressed and feeling alone. You are always with us, you always want our love and yet we ignore you so often. Forgive us. We love you.*

MaryEmma

JANUARY 5

OUR PROTECTION COMES FROM OUR LORD

"For the Lord God is a sun and shield; the Lord bestows favor and honor;
no good thing does He withhold from those whose walk is blameless."
Psalm 84:12

We are blessed when we trust in our Lord and Savior. He is our sun, giving us peace and joy and love deep inside us. When we trust Him, He is our shield; we know He is protecting us. We receive peace from his presence. What a wonderful God that we have!

Why do we look other places for peace, for joy, for love when is all comes from him? Why do we not trust him and allow him to lead us through this life?

MY PRAYER: *Lord God, You alone are the God of this universe. You alone give us protection. We thank You. You are wonderful and we love you. We don't deserve your gifts, but we love You and thank You.*

MaryEmma

JANUARY 6

WHEN WE CALL, HE ANSWERS

"Hear me, Lord, and answer me, for I am poor and needy. Bring joy to Your servant, Lord, for I put my trust in You."
Psalm 86:1,4

How often do we stop and think about how wonderful our Lord is? He is always with us, loving us and wanting to help us, but often we don't even think about Him. We just do it our way. He wants us to trust Him, and then He will fill us with joy.

Because God is forgiving and good, we can go to Him at any time with any problem. We never have to be alone. We are never unloved. Are we not blessed by a heavenly Father who wants us to call to Him? He is never too busy because He loves us. He loves and helps all who call to Him.

Isn't He wonderful!

MY PRAYER: *Help me, Lord, to think of You each day. Help me to be aware of Your presence in my life. Thank You for the joy you put into my heart. I love you.*
MaryEmma

UNDIVIDED HEART

"Teach me Your way, Lord, that I may rely on Your faithfulness;
give me an undivided heart, that I may fear Your name."
Psalm 86:11

These are beautiful words. It is a prayer from the heart of David to God, His heavenly Father. He had an intimate relationship with God. We can see it in his words. Is this the way we pray? Do we open up our heart and spirit to God?

What is our relationship with God? Is He some remote figure out there someplace who is powerful, or is He the one we turn to when we are happy, or when we are sad?

Do I really want an undivided heart? Do I really want to glorify God? Maybe I want Him to teach me, but do I want the rest?

Or do I just want Him to take care of my wants? Good questions to ask ourselves anytime? Who or what is God in our lives?

MY PRAYER: *Thank You, Lord for Your words to me. Help me to be a ready listener and to be quick to obey. I know You love me, Help me to learn to know You and Your will for me better.*

MaryEmma

JANUARY 8

JESUS IS OUR EXAMPLE

*"...God, for He is gracious and compassionate, slow
to anger and abounding in love...."*
Joel 2: 13b

I read this verse in my Bible class last week, and I thought, "I have read this verse before. I know it is in the Psalms." I did a word search and I found it in 9 different places in the Bible!

The first was in Exodus when God was introducing Himself to Moses and the last time in Jonah when very angrily, he accused God with it. Think about what it says about our God. Do we think of God being gracious? He is.

But there were no references in the New Testament. I thought that strange, since so many Old Testament verses are quoted in the New.

Then I realized that we don't need the words: we have the example in Jesus Christ as He worked with people like you and me. He came to show us the Father in person. As we remember how Jesus came to this earth, I pray that we will go beyond the 'babe in the manger' and think of the grown up 'babe' who by His life, showed us that God is "gracious and compassionate, slow to anger and abounding in love."

MY PRAYER: *Lord God, I pray that we will be aware of Your presence today and we will reflect You as we associate with others.*

MaryEmma

JANUARY 9

LOOK UP AND SEE OUR LORD

"He gives strength to the weary and increases the power of the weak... but those who hope in the Lord will renew their strength. They will soar on wings like eagles; they will run and not grow weary, they will walk and not be faint."
Isaiah 40: 29,31

There are times when we need to just stop and look up. Take our eyes off ourselves and ours, and see God. We like to concentrate on this verse- what wonderful things God does for us.

But we need to think about God Himself, not just what he does or doesn't do for us. May we look up today and see His majesty. May we look around at the beautiful buildings and realize that it is our God who gave men the wisdom to build them. We have a wonderful loving God.

Have we thanked Him and praised Him today?

MY PRAYER: *Thank You Lord for all You have done-and for all the marvelous things You do in our lives every day. Help me to open my eyes and see You all about me. I love you.*

MaryEmma

JANUARY 10

DO WE WANT GOD OR HIS BLESSINGS?

"I sought the Lord, and He answered me; He delivered me from all my fears."
Psalm 34:4

I like this verse, God answers when we call, but we need to remember who he is, not just what he does for us. The preceding verses were glorifying the lord and praising his name.

Why do we concentrate on what God does for us instead of him?

Why do we put the emphasis on us instead of the Lord?

In this Psalm David praised God before he asked for help.

Could it be that before we can really hear the Lord we have to get our thoughts off ourselves and onto God?

As we praise Him, our thoughts turn from ourselves to Him and we are more aware of His power. If He spoke and the world went into place, He can certainly help me with my problems.

MY PRAYER: *I pray that today we will be more aware of You, your greatness and your holiness. When we praise you instead of complaining about our problems, we receive assurance that you are with us and will help us. When we praise You we are comforted by your Spirit.*

MaryEmma

WHAT IS OUR DECISION?

> *"…redeemed…but with the precious blood of Christ, a lamb without blemish or defect. He was chosen before the creation of the world, but was revealed in these last times for your sake. Through him you believe in God, who raised him from the dead and glorified him, and so your faith and hope are in God."*
> 1 Peter 1: 19-21

Peter could be a lawyer, arguing before the jury: What decision will you make? Will it be for pleasures on this earth which are temporary, or will it be for Jesus Christ who redeemed you with his precious blood?

We can choose perishable things like silver or gold and live an empty life, or will we choose a life with temporary grief but a glorious life with God the Father that is eternal?

Peter reminds us that Christ, our Savior Lamb was chosen to be our redeemer before creation.

They were blessed and we are blessed that Jesus Christ was revealed in our times. In verse 10 he reminded them that the prophets searched intently trying to find out when Christ would appear. The Prophets even predicted the suffering that Jesus would go through and the wondrous glories that would come to us from his suffering.

We have a decision to make also.

Do we believe in God who raised him from the dead and glorified him?

Is our "faith and hope" in God?

MY PRAYER: *Lord God, my decision is for you. You have blessed me and loved me. You have helped me through the difficult times and then taught me what you wanted me to learn from those hard days. You are wonderful and I love you and I want my life to rest in you. Thank you for being my God.*

MaryEmma

JANUARY 12

HE IS OUR ROCK

"When I said, "My foot is slipping, Your unfailing love, Lord, supported me. When anxiety was great within me, Your consolation brought me joy. But the Lord has become my fortress, and my God the rock in whom I take refuge."
Psalm 94:18-19,22

This morning, when I started to pray, my thoughts kept flitting from here to there. They were all about me. That is when I picked up my Bible and started reading, to focus on God instead of me.

I read how wonderful our Lord and Savior is. He teaches us and He helps us. When we are in trouble His unfailing loves supports us. When fears overtake us, and all we can think of is "what might happen", His consolation brings us peace and joy.

I love His description as a rock. When I was a child, we vacationed in a place that had a huge rock in my swimming area. In a picture, I was just a speck standing beside it. Even my Daddy looked small. Nothing could move it. It was a wonderful thing to look at. So secure, and so is our God. We can trust Him to always be here with us.

MY PRAYER: *"Thank You Lord, for always being with us. We can always count on you to help us. We love You."*

MaryEmma

SING FOR JOY TO THE LORD

"Come, let us sing for joy to the Lord; let us shout aloud to the Rock of our salvation, Let us come before Him with thanksgiving and extol Him with music and song. For the Lord is the great God, The great King above all gods."
Psalm 95:1-3

This is a Psalm of praise: It is a call to worship. God gives us joy and salvation. We thank Him and praise Him with music, because He is the One and Only God. I read these verses and then I started reading them personally: me to Him.

As I repeated the words of God, I was more aware of His presence, and His love for me; it awakened my love for Him. The Psalm ends with a warning: don't harden your heart - and a plea: Keep our spiritual ears open.

We always want him to do things for us, but we need to do for him: to open our hearts in praise and love him.

MY PRAYER: *Lord, help us to listen for your still quiet voice and understand: Our Lord is the great God! You are not just great, you are wonderful and full of love and want the best for us.*
We love you.

MaryEmma

JANUARY 14

GOD DESERVES ALL CREDIT

*"Praise be to the name of God for ever and ever; wisdom
and power are His. He changes times and seasons;
He deposes kings and raises up others. He gives wisdom to the wise and
knowledge to the discerning. He reveals deep and hidden things;
He knows what lies in darkness, and light dwells with Him."*
Daniel 2:20-22

This is a prayer of praise and thanksgiving. Daniel was thanking God for giving him the answer to the King's dream. The king was going to have all the wise men put to death including young Daniel and his friends. They immediately went to prayer and God responded.

But it isn't just the prayer that impresses me, but the way he talked to the King. The King asked Daniel if he could tell him what he saw and Daniel replied "No". But he added "There is a God in heaven" who can.

I am afraid I would have taken partial credit. "Yes, I can with the help of God." Daniel gave God all the credit.

Do we give God the credit He deserves in our lives?

MY PRAYER: *Dear Lord help me to not be so full of myself that I cannot see You. Help me to see others You have sent who need to know You better. Thank You, God for being my God.*

MaryEmma

JANUARY 15

PRAISE SHOWS OUR LOVE

"For great is the Lord and most worthy of praise;
He is to be feared above all gods."
Psalm 96: 4

Why are we to praise the Lord? This Psalm tells us why: "Great is the Lord". We sometimes forget that. We tend to take for granted someone who is always around and always available.

Our "Lord is great and most worthy of praise". Do we tell Him how wonderful He is? Of course he knows, but as we praise him with words of admiration and love, our love and admiration grows. That blesses us.

Do we share this information with others who may not know Him?

He loves us. Do we love Him?

MY PRAYER: *Lord, You are great. I praise You for Your splendor and majesty. I thank You for Your strength and glory. You are capable of making my life wonderful and You do. I love You and thank You. No one loves us as much as You do.*

MaryEmma

JANUARY 16

JOY IS A GIFT

*"The Lord reigns, Let the earth be glad; Let the distant shores rejoice
Light shines on the righteous and joy on the upright in heart. Rejoice
in the Lord, you who are righteous, and praise His holy name."*
Psalm 97:1,11-12

Do we love The Lord for who He is, or for what He does for us? That is a good question to ponder.

The psalmist describes Him in such beautiful ways. Do we rush by those descriptions to get to what He does for us? He gives us joy and shows His love to us. We have a wonderful loving God.

When we are unhappy, do we go to him for peace?

When we are tired, do we ask for his joy?

Do we share his joy and love with others?

MY PRAYER: *Lord, You truly are wonderful. We love You and praise You for who You are, not just for what You do for us. Help us to worship You today in our Hearts.*

MaryEmma

WHERE IS OUR BELIEF?

"Do not let Your hearts be troubled. You believe in God; believe also in Me."
John 14:1

I memorized the first 6 verses of this chapter when I was in high school, and when I feel sad or lonely or just a little lost, I say them to myself. It reminds me that I am never alone. It reminds me that I will be with God forever.

We have His word to read to know God's will for us, and we have God's Spirit to guide us and direct us. He has taught us to pray. This is the same Spirit of God that hovered over the waters in Genesis 1 and the same Spirit that guided David and it is the same Spirit that Jesus left with us when He returned to heaven.

We are so blessed. How can we feel sad?

How can we be lonely?

How can we not believe and trust and rejoice?

Our God is great and worthy to be praised. May we worship Him today.

MY PRAYER: *Dear Lord, thank You for Your Spirit; thank You for His presence; thank You for Your continuous love and watch over me. I love you.*
MaryEmma

JANUARY 18

HOW DO WE FACE PROBLEMS?

> *"I thank and praise You, God of my ancestors; You have given me
> wisdom and power, You have made known to me what we asked
> of You, You have made known to us the dream of the King."*
> Daniel 2:23

When Daniel was threatened with death, he did not try to figure out a way to escape the palace and get back to Israel. He did not try to find a hiding place in the palace to hide until the King was happy again.

He immediately turned to God. He asked his 3 friends to pray. He was very specific. His prayer was not "bless me and mine. Thank You." He asked his friends to "plead with God for mercy from the God of heaven concerning this mystery."

How do we react when we face a problem? Do we go to God, or do we try to figure out what to do on our own?

Too often God is our last resort!

We will have problems in this life. That is when we discover God is real. It is also when we discover whom we trust.

Remember: Jesus said in this world we will have problems, but in Him, we will have peace.

MY PRAYER: *Lord, Help me to share your peace with all those I meet along this life's pathway. Let me see You and Your path for me. Thank You for Your love and guidance.*

MaryEmma

JANUARY 19

WE ARE HIS SHEEP

*"Know that the Lord is God. It is He who made us, and we
are His; we are His people, the sheep of His pasture."*
Psalm 100:3

"Know that the Lord is God". We need to remember that. Keep it
tucked away in our active mind, because sometimes we forget and we think
we are in charge. Our troubles begin when we think we can make our own
decisions. "We know what path to travel: we don't need God to help us."
We forget that God loves us more than anyone else in the world does and
He wants only His best for us.

"We are the sheep of His pasture". Our Lord is the good shepherd. The
good shepherd takes care of His flock. He lives with them and protects
them. If they are injured He nurses them tenderly. When we think of the
good shepherd who loves us, it is easy to have a spirit of thanksgiving and
praise.

He is great and He is good and His love endures forever!

Will we take a moment to thank Him for what He has done for us?

Will we praise Him for who He is?

MY PRAYER: *Thank You, God, for being my God. Thank You for being with
me always, and for sending Your Spirit to live in me. You are truly great, all
powerful and loving.*

MaryEmma

JOY IS THE ANSWER

"Sing to The Lord a new song, for He has done marvelous things, His right hand and His holy arm have worked salvation for Him."
Psalm 98:1

What are the marvelous things that God has done?

He has given us salvation. He has made His salvation known to the world. That is what God has done.

What is our response?

Shout and sing for joy to the Lord, tell him we love you. Thank him because he is near to us.

What is joy? It is a combination of love and thankfulness that bubbles up inside us. Even nature responds to God. The imagery in this Psalm is wonderful. "Let the rivers clap their hands, let the mountains sing together for joy".

Are we enthusiastic for our Lord and Savior?

He has given so much to us. What are we giving to Him?

MY PRAYER: *Lord, how can I allow myself to be unaware of Your presence and Your goodness to me each and every day? I am unworthy of you, but you are worthy. I pray I will keep a song of joy in my heart and in my consciousness each day.*

MaryEmma

JANUARY 21

HOLY IS OUR LORD

"Great is the Lord in Zion; He is exalted over all the nations, Let them praise Your great and awesome name--He is holy."
Psalm 99:2,3

How often do we think of God as holy? He is holy and He is sovereign. We like to think of Him as our comforter, our friend, our savior and He is that, but He is also holy.

He is perfect. He is powerful. It is easy to thank Him for His blessings,- when we remember-but hard to praise Him for who He is.

Why is it hard to concentrate on God? Could it be that his blessings are so wonderful that we can only think of ourselves? When we are in trouble, we automatically call out to him. We ask him for help, we read his word, looking for answers, but in good times we are too busy enjoying our blessing to talk to him.

A good question to ponder today: Do we love God for who He is, or for what He does for us?

MY PRAYER: *Lord, it is difficult for me to fully appreciate who You are. I truly hold You in awe, but cannot stretch my mind to understand Your almighty power, Your ever presence. Your unconditional love is always before me. Help me love You more.*

MaryEmma

JANUARY 22

GOD IS OUR COMFORTER

"Hear my prayer, Lord; let my cry for help come to You.
Do not hide Your face from me when I am in distress. Turn
Your ear to me; when I call, answer me quickly."
Psalm 102:1-2

There are times when we have all felt this way.

We need an answer, we need help, and God is slow in answering us. What are we to do?

The psalmist kept listing all his problems and finally in Verse 12 he acknowledges God and His power. It was a big pity party. It fit my mood perfectly this morning, because I was having a pity party. I have started itching from the chemicals in the swimming pool. Then I remembered God has promised to teach us and guide us. That helped. I turned to the next Psalm and here it was: "Praise the Lord, my soul; all my inmost being, praise His holy name."

That was my answer and my pity party left. I read down the Psalm and when I came to verse 5, it said: "who satisfies your desires with good things". Why can I praise God so easily when I am blessed with all the good things He gives me, and when I have one little problem, I want to beg and complain?

This was the moment of confession: 'Forgive me Lord, I have sinned'. I still itch, but I have peace and joy in my spirit, because I am aware of my great and holy God. He will show me how to handle my problem. We have a wonderful God.

Have we thanked him today?

MY PRAYER: *Lord, thank You for always being with me when I need You. Thank you for your love and help. I love You.*

MaryEmma

THE SCOPE OF GOD'S LOVE

For as high as the heavens are above the earth, so great is His
love for those who fear Him; as far as the east is from the west,
so far has He removed our transgressions from us."
Psalms 103: 11-12

Who is God? What is He like? For those who wonder, these verses give us a picture. Our Lord is loving, He is just, He is merciful. He doesn't treat us as we deserve to be treated!

How much does He love us?

How far away does He remove our sin?

This Psalm gives us the answer. As wonderful as our earthly father may have been, our heavenly Father is better. If our earthly father was a disappointment, we have a great substitute in our Father in heaven.

How can we not love Him and praise Him.

Have we thanked Him today?

MY PRAYER: *Thank You for teaching me to love You. You are wonderful and I love You. There is not other God like you. You love us and teach us; guide and correct us and you remove our sins when we confess as far as the east is from the west. How can we not love you?*

MaryEmma

JANUARY 24

HOW DO WE DESCRIBE THE LORD GOD?

"Praise the Lord, my soul. Lord my God, You are very great; You are clothed with splendor and majesty. The Lord wraps Himself in light as with a garment; He stretches out the heavens like a tent."
Psalm 104:1-2,

How would we describe God? What descriptive words would we use? This entire Psalm is a beautiful prayer of praise to our Lord. He is light. Light allows us wisdom and understanding and discernment, and it is from our Lord that we receive His light. Nothing is too big for our God. He "rides on the wings of the wind."

Isn't that a good description of His Holy Spirit?

Why wouldn't we sing praises to our Lord?

Why wouldn't we meditate on His greatness?

May we take time to read Psalm 104. We will be blessed.

MY PRAYER: *Lord, You are wonderful. We can't find the words to describe you. We can only share how you bless us to help others know you. You are our light and our wisdom and everything that is good comes from You. Thank you. I love You.*

MaryEmma

JANUARY 25

LOOK TO THE LORD

"Look to The Lord and His strength; seek His face always."
Psalm 105:4

When I read verse 4 of this Psalm, I knew this was the verse I was to meditate on today. "Look to the Lord", concentrate on Him. Think about His strength. Sing praises to Him, "tell of all His wonderful acts" and our hearts will rejoice.

What will be cluttering up our mind today? Where will our Lord be? Will He be in our mind or safely tucked away somewhere until we need Him?

We need to remember the wonders He has done.

Joseph went from a favored son to a slave, then a prisoner and then to the second highest person in Egypt.

He really had a rough life; jealous brothers and harsh treatment, but He survived because he kept his eyes on his Lord.

God had a purpose in leading him through difficult times. He saved his family from starvation. When his brothers were fearful he would take their life, he said, "You meant it for bad, but God meant it for good." He kept his eyes on God.

"Look to The Lord and His strength; seek His face always."

MY PRAYER: *Lord God, help me to keep my eyes on You today. Make our attitude today be one of praise and thanksgiving. Forgive us when we complain and remind us that it is you we are complaining against. We love you.*

MaryEmma

WHAT DO WE THANK GOD FOR?

"Let them give thanks to the Lord for His unfailing love
and His wonderful deeds for mankind, for He satisfies
the thirsty and fills the hungry with good things."
Psalm 107: 8-9

Our assignment for the day!
Give thanks to The One who loves us.
Give thanks to The One who is good.
Give thanks to The One who has redeemed us.
And remember His wonderful deeds.

When I read this Psalm, I just bowed my head and said, "Thank You Lord. Thank You for loving me and blessing me and letting me know You." What a wonderful God we have.

What are we thanking him for today? Do we need to think about it, or is it a natural flow of our thoughts?

MY PRAYER: *Thank You for being You and thank You for all the wonderful things You do for us. You are great and we love you.*

MaryEmma

JANUARY 27

WHAT IS OUR DECISION?

> *"My Heart, O God, is steadfast; I will sing and make music with all my soul. I will praise You, Lord, among He nations; I will sing of You among the peoples. For great is Your love, higher than the heavens; Your faithfulness reaches to the skies."*
> Psalm 108:1,3-4

How often do we praise God to others? How often do we praise Him in our own heart? David's heart is steadfast, because he knows God loves him. It sounds like David has it all under control with no problems, but as we read down to the end of the Psalm we see that David is fearful for his life. So how can David be so positive when He is in danger? He trusts God. He knows God and he loves God. And he knows that God loves him, because he has a relationship with God.

Joy is a decision we make. To love is a decision we make. We can trust God or we can trust ourselves and the situation we are in. It is our choice. David chose to trust God.

What is our choice for today?

Will we praise our Lord and Savior and trust Him?

Will we worry and fret?

MY PRAYER: *Dear Lord, help me to truly trust in Your love and strength for me today. Increase my love for You, help me to be Your child in word and deed. I love you.*

MaryEmma

JANUARY 28

DO WE PONDER?

"Great are the works of the Lord; they are pondered by all who delight in them. Glorious and majestic are His deeds and His righteousness endures forever. The Lord is gracious and compassionate."
Psalm 111:2-4

'Great are the works of the Lord.' Do we ponder them?

'Glorious and majestic are His deeds'. This is my verse today that I want to keep in my mind.

Now that I am in Oklahoma, I look out my window and see lots of trees and nature and we know God made them.

But when I was in Philly and looked out my window, I saw the big impressive buildings, and I knew that God was responsible for them. Without giving people the wisdom to build them, they wouldn't exist. Do we give God the credit He deserves?

When the Children of Israel were in the wilderness, and they built the tabernacle, God gave wisdom to even the weavers of cloth to make He beautiful curtains. Nothing is too small or too big for our Lord to do.

Today when we look at the people around us that God made, or nature, or buildings, let us ponder "Glorious and majestic are His deeds!"

MY PRAYER: *Lord, help me to be aware of Your presence and to see You in all the marvelous works You have done. You alone are our creator and our Lord. We love you.*

MaryEmma

JANUARY 29

A COMMAND

"Praise the Lord. Praise the Lord, you His servants; praise the name of the Lord. Let the name of the Lord be praised, both now and forevermore. From the rising of the sun to the place where it sets, the name of the Lord is to be praised."
Psalm 113:1-3

Are we obedient children of our heavenly Father? These verses sounds like a command. Praise the Lord! Sometimes we think, "Why should we?" God already knows how great He is.

He is the Lord our God. He is our father. He isn't a remote and distant Father. He created us and desires fellowship with us.

Do we desire fellowship with him?

He is always with us, helping us, teaching us, loving us, giving us peace. We are to praise Him to others, but first we must praise Him within our hearts. Praising him brings us into fellowship and we feel his love filling us and giving us peace.

Are we having a bad day? Praise him.

Do we feel unloved and unappreciated? Praise him.

Does he seem far away? Praise him.

"MY PRAYER: *I praise You, Lord, for Your goodness and mercy; for teaching me and forgiving me and helping me through my life. You are truly a mighty God. I love you.*

MaryEmma

JANUARY 30

WANTS!

"The Lord is my shepherd. I shall not want."
Psalm 23:1

I was saying this to myself prayerfully, and all of a sudden I realized that I do want! And I had to confess this sin to God. He has provided for me and I don't need anything, but--I do want--I want to go—I want to do—I want more money —I want to feel better.....

What is wrong with me? Paul said that he had learned to be content whatever the situation, whether with much or with little. There is a little spirit of discontent that pops into our minds when we allow it. Parents 'want' for their children.

Why are we not thankful with what we have?

Is it an attitude that we are unaware of, and maybe that is the reason the Bible tells us to be thankful. We need to be reminded.

Are we preventing God from blessing us because we complain or want when he has given us so much.

Are we are thanking God for what He has given us?

MY PRAYER: *I pray Lord, that we will recognize what you have given us and be thankful. If 'wants' pops into our heads help us to discuss it with You and let your wisdom direct us. You are wonderful Father. We love you.*

MaryEmma

JANUARY 31

APPRECIATION

"The Lord is my strength and my defense. He has become my salvation. He is my God, and I will praise Him, my father's God, and I will exalt Him. Who among the gods is like You, Lord? Who is like You -majestic in holiness, awesome in glory, working wonders?"
Exodus 15: 2,11

Moses and the Israelites had just been saved from slavery and death. They had just walked through the Red Sea on dry land, and then the waters came together to cover the Egyptian army chasing them.

We can hear the relief and the joy in their song of praise.

They knew that only the one and true living God had the power to save them. They recognized His work and praised Him and recognized His love. He had led them through rough times. He had provided for all their needs. He listened when they complained and he listened when they praised him.

Have we praised God this morning?

Have we told Him we love Him and appreciate Him?

Do we see the wonders He works in our life?

MY PRAYER: *Lord God, bless us today with an awareness of Your presence and Your holiness. Thank you for everything. Forgive us when we ignore You and when we don't appreciate you. We love you.*

MaryEmma

THE GREATEST GIFT

"Praise be to the God and Father of our Lord Jesus Christ! In His great mercy He has given us new birth into a living hope through the resurrection of Jesus Christ from the dead, and into an inheritance that can never perish, spoil or fade. This inheritance is kept in heaven for you."
I Peter 1:3-4

Praising God is not only found in the psalms, but throughout the scriptures. It is an example for us that we should praise our Lord throughout our life and throughout our day.

We have the greatest of all gods: The One and only true God. We praise Him for His mercy; He doesn't treat us as our sins deserve. We praise Him for our new birth. This new birth is a spiritual birth and comes because of the death and resurrection of Jesus Christ.

Jesus "was chosen before the creation of the world" (verse 20) to be the source of our salvation. This salvation comes easily for us. We only have to accept the gift that Jesus offers. This spiritual birth makes us children of God and gives us the inheritance of eternal life with our Lord.

MY PRAYER: *Thank You. Thank you for this wonderful gift. Thank you for your love and your gift of salvation. You are so fantastic! Keep us aware of this gift of love and your presence. You are great!*

MaryEmma

FEBRUARY 2

WE ARE SPECIAL!

*"But you are a chosen people, a royal priesthood, a holy nation,
God's special possession, that you may declare the praises of
Him who called you out of darkness into His wonderful light."*
1 Peter 2:9

We are God's special possession! We have been chosen! That means
we are loved. We may not feel loved by those around us, but we are always
loved by God, and He is always with us.

We have received mercy. The light of our savior Jesus Christ brought
us out of darkness into His light. This is what God has done for us.

What is our part?

We can declare His praises. We can thank Him for His blessings.
We can stop taking Him for granted. We can love Him back. We have a
wonderful loving God.

Have we given Him praise today?

Have we thanked him for calling us out of darkness into his light?

MY PRAYER: *All mighty and loving God, I praise You for saving me; for
giving me all spiritual blessings in Christ Jesus.*

*Thank You for caring for me and loving me. Help me be a blessing to others.
It is so easy to love you when we remember all you do for us.*

Mary Emma

FEBRUARY 3

HOW TO PRAY

"...We do not know what we ought to pray for, but the Spirit himself intercedes for us through wordless groans, and he who searches our hearts knows the mind of the Spirit, because the Spirit intercedes for God's people in accordance with the will of God."
Romans 8:26-27

"We do not know what we ought to pray for", but we do know we want to pray according to God's will. As we pray, let's ask God how he wants us to pray for our situation. Ask him to guide our thoughts and our words according to His perfect will.

He wants our very best for us and only our Holy Father knows what is best. As we trust him, He will "work for our good" because we love him.

Do we tell God what we want him to do?

Do we ask him what he wants us to do about the situation?

Do we ask him to show us his will?

MY PRAYER: *Lord, thank you for wanting our fellowship. Thank you for your help in daily situations. Forgive us when we tell you what to do instead of asking. We love you*

MaryEmma

MORE THAN CONQUERORS

"Who can separate us from the love of Christ? Shall trouble or hardship or persecution or famine or nakedness or danger or sword? No, in all these things we are more than conquerors through Him who loved us."
Romans 8: 35

What can we say to these loving words except thank You, Lord. What gives us confidence in these words? The fact that Jesus died for us, was resurrected and sits at the right hand of God interceding for us. Maybe we humans can love in a skimpy manner but anyone who loves us enough to go through what Jesus did, loves us a lot.

Nothing can happen that will make Jesus turn away from us. Love involves patience and forgiveness. We do fail but when we wake up spiritually, and turn back to him, he forgives because he has been waiting patiently for us.

Could this be a good definition of true love?

Do we believe that Jesus Christ loves us?

Do we love him?

His love gives us strength to persevere, to conqueror the problems that come our way.

MY PRAYER: *Thank You, Lord, for loving me, for blessing me, for letting me know You. You are truly a great and holy God and I love You. Show me the way You want me to go today and bless me with a greater awareness of Your presence and love.*

Mary Emma

FEBRUARY 5

THE SECRET OF CONTENTMENT

"I have learned to be content whatever the circumstances. I know what it is to be in need, and I know what it is to have plenty. I have learned the secret of being content in any and every situation, whether well fed or hungry, whether in plenty or in want. I can do all this through HIM who gives me strength."
Philippians 4: 11-13

Can we say this? Have we learned the secret of being content? It depends on where our thoughts are. Someone said that when we pray, we need to keep our gaze on God and glance at our problem.

Do we pray so we may know God better, or just to get answers for our problems? Our Lord and Savior is the answer for peace.

Are we content with what God has given us? Are we dissatisfied with God? The answer to peace is God, but we must keep our gaze on Him instead of the problems.

Hebrews teaches us to keep our eyes on Jesus and to keep our thoughts on Jesus. Was that Paul's secret?

How do we receive contentment?

MY PRAYER: *Lord, I pray that we may please You today with our thoughts, our love and devotion. I pray that we will be satisfied with Your plans and trust You instead of ourselves. You are a wonderful God. Thank you.*

MaryEmma

FEBRUARY 6

WE ARE LOVED!

"Praise be to the God and Father of our Lord Jesus Christ, who has blessed us in the heavenly realms with every spiritual blessing in Christ. For He chose us in Him before the creation of the world to be holy and blameless in His sight."
Ephesians 1:3-4

Are we holy and blameless in his sight? What is required for that to be true? Jesus already provided that with his death and resurrection. All we have to do is to accept.

How often do we praise God for our spiritual blessings?

We have been chosen, we are loved, and He has given us grace-the forgiveness of our sins. The list can go on and on and on. We are loved!

Let's stop and think about that for a minute. We are loved by the greatest power this world has ever known.

What does that mean to us?

Do we love him?

Jesus showed his love for us. How do we show our love for him?

Can we show our love by praising Him?

Do we?

MY PRAYER: *I pray that as we go through the day, we will remember to praise You. Thank You for blessing us with every spiritual blessing. Make us more aware of You. You are great. We love you.*

MaryEmma

FEBRUARY 7

GOD'S DOWN PAYMENT

*"And you also were included in Christ when you heard the message
of truth, the gospel of your salvation. When you believed, you
were marked in Him with a seal, the promised Holy Spirit, who
is a deposit guaranteeing our inheritance until the redemption of
those who are God's possession--to the praise of His glory."*
Ephesians 1:13-14

Who is the Holy Spirit? It is the Spirit of God. He is our down payment on our spiritual blessings; our deposit from God-a sign of His promises.

But He is also our helper today. It would have been wonderful to have known Jesus when He was on earth, but He was in the form of a man, and could only be in one place at one time. Now He is with us at all times in his Spirit.

When He left to return to His heavenly Father, He promised a comforter and a teacher who would teach us and remind us of what he had said. (John 14:26) We didn't hear those words personally but as we read the scripture prayerfully his Holy Spirit impresses us with the importance of his words.

God's Holy Spirit is with us at all times, helping us through difficult times. He is with us when we are talking to God and helps us to pray.

Are we listening for his gentle and quiet voice?

MY PRAYER: *Thank You for making us yours, thank You for teaching and reminding us of your Word, always just at the right time when we need to hear You. We love you.*

MaryEmma

FEBRUARY 8

WHY DO WE PRAY?

"One of those days Jesus went out to a mountainside to pray, and spent the night praying to God. When morning came, He called His disciples to Him and chose twelve of them, whom He also designated apostles."
Luke 6:12-13

Jesus spent the night praying--that is a long time. From the time it got dark until it was light in the morning. What did He talk about all night? How long does it take to pick out 12 men, to discuss their good and bad qualities? What did they talk about?

Have we ever spent all day visiting with a friend? What did we find to talk about? It is easy, isn't it, if we are good friends. Prayer is not just asking. I want this and give me that. Does that sound like our prayers?

Prayer is conversation between us and our heavenly Father. It is fellowship. It is sharing information. It is talking, but it is also listening; what does God want us to know and do and change?

When we focus on God instead of the things around us we can hear Him spiritually; we receive understanding or conviction or just love. We have a wonderful God.

Do we focus on God or our wants in prayer?

MY PRAYER: *Lord, thank You for wanting to spend time with me. Thank You for Your love. You are a mighty God and a loving God and you want to teach us and love us. We love you.*

MaryEmma

FEBRUARY 9

OUR GREAT TEACHER

"I keep asking that the God of our Lord Jesus Christ, the
glorious Father, may give you the Spirit of wisdom and
revelation, so that you may know Him better."
Ephesians 1:17

What do our prayers sound like? Is this the way that we pray? Could there be a better request than this? Do we really want to know God better?

Our glorious Father wants to bless us. We are in school with God and He is our teacher. He gives us homework and He gives us tests. When we fail a test, He doesn't throw us out of school, but gives us more homework and another test. He gives us a new situation and a new test.

All the problems that I have had and all the mistakes that I have made, have worked together to move me closer to God and have helped me to love Him more. Each day brings a new situation and he is there with us to help us and get to know him better as we go through the day.

Are we aware of his help?

Do we talk to him and ask for help?

Do we ignore him and trust ourselves?

MY PRAYER: *Lord, I pray this morning is that You will give us Your Spirit of wisdom and revelation, that we might know You better. We need to be more aware of you during the good times and the not so good times. We love You.*
MaryEmma

FEBRUARY 10

*"You (God) will keep him in perfect peace, whose mind
is stayed on You, because he trusts in You."*
Isaiah 26:3

This is a promise. It is so easy to be in peace and yet so hard sometimes. Why?

How do we get peace? How do we keep peace? By keeping our mind on our Lord, because we trust and love Him. When we love someone, we think of them a lot. This allows God to guide our thinking and rest in Him.

Hebrews tells us to keep our mind on God and also fix our eyes on him? We fix our spiritual eyes on what we want, so we need to ask ourselves, what are we wanting, what is our desire. That is where our eyes are fixed.

The answer to that determines our peace.

What are our thoughts today?

What are we wanting today?

MY PRAYER: *Lord, bless us today as our mind is stayed on You, our Lord and Savior. You want us be at peace because You want the best for us. Thank You. We love you.*

MaryEmma

FEBRUARY 11

HOPE!

"I pray that the eyes of your heart may be enlightened in order that you may know the hope to which He has called you, the riches of His glorious inheritance in His holy people, and the incomparably great power for us who believe."
Ephesians 1:18-19

Hope! Hope comes when we understand all the wonderful things that God has prepared for us. When we read and understand with our mind and also we understand in our hearts. Paul calls this spiritual understanding the "eyes of our heart."

We read with our physical eyes, but also with the eyes of our heart. It is the understanding of what God has done for us and what He wants for us. It is greater understanding of what God has prepared for us--both in the future and right now. The fruit of His Spirit is what He has prepared for us now-love, joy, peace, patience, kindness, gentleness, goodness, faithfulness and self control and in the future, eternal life with Him.

God is fact and we recognize His greatness, but it is with our heart that we love Him.

Do we need to pray this prayer for ourselves?

For a discouraged friend?

MY PRAYER: *Lord, I pray that we will recognize Your plans for us today. I pray that our love for You will increase as we grow in our relationship with you.*
MaryEmma

FEBRUARY 12

WHY IS LOVE IMPORTANT?

"...And I pray that you, being rooted and established in love, may have power, together with all the Lord's holy people, to grasp how wide and long and high and deep is the love of Christ, and to know this love that surpasses knowledge-that you may be filled to the measure of all the fullness of God."
Ephesians 3:17-19

Why is love so important? Why is it emphasized so much in the gospels. Even in the Old Testament we have the command to love God and love each other. Everything in Jesus' life on earth was an expression of love: Both for his father and for us.

Why is love so important?

Paul says that it is more important than knowledge. The Pharisee had knowledge, they knew the scriptures, they even knew all the prophecies about where Jesus would be born. Love was not a priority for them, their love was focused on rules and tradition. They kept adding rules on top of rules, that no human could keep.

God knew just the right time, to introduce love into religion, to take it from rules to relationships. Jesus came to show us how to live and how to love others as he loved us.

Why do we need to love? So that we may be "filled to the measure of all the fullness of God."

Is this a test for love?

Are we so filled with love that we are one with our Lord?

MY PRAYER: *Lord, we need your help to love as you do. We need your help to focus on you and to be filled with your Spirit. Help us remember that we can double check our love for you by our love for others. You are great. Thank you.*
MaryEmma

FEBRUARY 13

OUR RESPONSIBILITY!

"For you were once darkness, but now you are light in the Lord. Live as children of light (for the fruit of the light consists in all goodness, righteousness and truth) and find out what pleases the Lord."
Ephesians 5: 8-10

As I was reading this morning, verse 10 jumped out at me. We are told to 'find out' what pleases the Lord.

How do we do that?

God has given us His written word. We need to read with our spiritual eyes and ears. We listen to God speak as we read. We know we can talk to Him. We can ask for His Spirit to fill us with wisdom and revelation so we will know Him better. We can ask to know His great love for us so we can share it with others.

These are tools that God has given us and as we know Him better, we will understand how to please Him. His Spirit will guide us. Verse 17 says: "Do not be foolish, but understand what the Lord's will is" and then we have a comparison in V 18. "Do not get drunk on wine. Instead, be filled with the Spirit."

Is it our responsibility to find out what pleases our Lord?

Do we need to pray about it?

MY PRAYER: *Lord, I pray that we will search for what pleases You and live the life You want for us. Help us to know Your great love and how to share it with others. We love you.*

MaryEmma

44

HOW DO WE PRAY FOR OTHERS?

"We continually ask God to fill you with the knowledge of His will through all the wisdom and understanding that the Spirit gives, so that you may live a life worthy of the Lord and please Him in every way."
Colossians 1:9-10

This is a prayer from one Christian for another. Does this sound like our prayers? Prayers I read in the scriptures inspire me to lift my eyes above. How do we pray for others?

God tells us to ask for whatever we need, help with whatever is bothering us, but He also gives us these beautiful examples of how to pray for others.

We are God's children, but sometimes we act like teenagers. "I want to please God, but I will do it my way, not His". To know God's will for us, we need to know HIM. We need His Spirit to teach us, but we need to be teachable. We have an example how to prayer for others.

Is our love strong enough to pray for someone we see that is struggling? Why not?

MY PRAYER: *I pray that we will allow you to fill us with the knowledge of your will. Teach us how you want us to pray for others. Not what we think they need, but what you want for them. We need your help. We love you.*

MaryEmma

FEBRUARY 15

"I will praise the Lord, who counsels me; even at night my heart instructs me. I keep my eyes always on the Lord. With Him at my right hand, I will not be shaken. Therefore my heart is glad and my tongue rejoices; my body also will rest secure."
Psalm 16:7-9

Do we rest at night?

On sleepless night, what do we do? These verses give us guidance. The Psalmist praises God and then listens to him for counsel? With this closeness with our Creator we can rest secure.

Do we fuss about nights we don't sleep good?

Do we use it as extra time to spend with God, enjoying his presence?

I have written these verses on a card and sometimes, I just have to pick up the card and read them. They give me reassurance, a reminder of what a wonderful God we have. My heart fills with praise and thanksgiving for my Lord.

How can we ask for anything more than this wonderful relationship with our Lord and Savior? He is always with us. He counsels us. He doesn't force His will on us, and he is always ready to comfort and reassure us.

MY PRAYER: *Lord you are wonderful. You are always ready to shower us with love and closeness with you. You help us to love others, you remind us of their need of you. You give us special times so that we can pray to you and for others.* You are great!

MaryEmma

FEBRUARY 16

GOD PROVIDES SECURITY

*"Keep me safe, my God, for in You I take refuge. I say to the Lord,
'You are my Lord; apart from You I have no good thing.' Lord, You
alone are my portion and my cup; You make my lot secure.*
Psalm 16: 1,2,5,

When I picked up my Bible this morning, I could not leave Psalm 16. There is so much gold among the words. God keeps me safe: in big ways and in little ways. I don't like walking down the stairs, but in the morning when I go down to exercise as I glance down the stairs I whisper, 'protect me, Lord', and the little fear leaves me.

The Psalmist David had fears for his life-real fears-- he was in war and my fears are little, but we have the same God. The same God who loves both of us, is the same God who protects both of us.

Even with all the blessings God has given me through the years, the greatest is Him; Knowing Him! He gives me nourishment and He gives me security. He counsels me. He is always with me.

Are we aware of his love?

Are we aware of his protection or our fear?

MY PRAYER: *I pray that we will keep our eyes always on you. Thank You for Your protection. Thank You for Your reassurance. Thank for you peace. You are so wonderful. We love You.*

MaryEmma

FEBRUARY 17

HIS LOVE NEVER FAILS

"Because of the Lord's great love we are not consumed, For His compassions never fail. They are new every morning; great is Your faithfulness."
Lamentations 3:22-23

We like to complain. Jeremiah had plenty of reasons to complain. But as he was complaining, he became aware of God and his thoughts and attitude changed. Instead of concentrating on what he didn't have, he started thinking of what he DID have.

We always have the love of God available: He is close to us when we seek Him. He has great love for us and that love never grows cold.

It is always with us whether we take advantage of it or reject it. We are to put our hope in him, to seek him and wait for him to act. That is how we show our love for him.

We will always have something to complain about, but we will also have God's love to encourage us.

MY PRAYER: *Lord, bless us today with praise and joy when we really just want to complain! Help us to see You instead of the irritations of life. We love you and thank you.*

MaryEmma

GOD SHOWS COMPASSION

*"The Lord is good to those whose hope is in Him, to the one who
seeks Him... for no one is cast off by the Lord forever. Though He
brings grief, He will show compassion, so great is His unfailing love.
For He does not willingly bring affliction or grief to anyone."*
Lamentations 3:25,31-33

"God does not willingly bring affliction or grief to anyone." Then why
do we experience it? My mother said it hurt her more to spank me, than it
did me. I never was sure that I believed her. She spanked me to emphasize
that what I was doing was bad for me and it would create problems if she
allowed it to continue. She wanted me to have the best life possible and that
included discipline. Does our God love us any less than our earthly mother?

God does not create bad things, but he allows bad things into our lives
to help us learn and become mature Christians. When things are going
good, it is easy to trust in ourselves. When things go wrong, we turn to
God for help. Each time he helps, he teaches us more about him and what
we need to live in this world.

When we make bad decisions, or people around us make bad decisions,
it affects our lives. He uses these events to teach us; to show us the right
way to live.

Is our hope in him?

Do we seek him for our answers?

MY PRAYER: *Lord God, you love us and you allow things to happen to us
because you love us and you will teach us through the events, both good and bad.
You never ignore us, as we do you. You are on the job 100% of the time to help us
become like Jesus. Thank you.*

MaryEmma

FEBRUARY 19

"I called on Your name, Lord, from the depths of the pit. You heard my plea: "Do not close your ears to my cry for relief." You came near when I called You, and You said, "Do not fear."
Lamentations 3:55-57

We tend to think if we are doing God's work, nothing bad will happen to us. Jeremiah was God's Prophet. He was telling Judah to repent of their sins or God would punish them. Instead of repentance, they took revenge and this is how Jeremiah reacted. He prayed, "Help me" and God answered, "Do not fear".

None of us are perfect, not even those who are serving God. There is always more to teach us and by our example help us to teach other how to go through adversity.

They hunted Jeremiah, they put him into a pit and threw stones at him. He thought he was going to die. 'I can't survive this, it is over.' And then, God heard him and lifted him out of the pit.

Jesus said, "In this world you will have trouble, but in me you will have peace." It is human nature to fear, and divine to trust God.

MY PRAYER: *Lord, I pray that we will keep our eyes on You during the good time and the bad. Help us trust You when we are afraid. Guide us as we go through this day. We love you.*

MaryEmma

HOW DO WE DRESS?

"Therefore, as God's chosen people, holy and dearly loved, clothe yourselves with compassion, kindness, humility, gentleness and patience. Bear with each other and forgive one another if any of you has a grievance against someone. Forgive as the Lord forgave you. And over all these virtues put on love, which binds them all together in perfect unity. Let the peace of Christ rule in your hearts."
Colossians 3:12-15

How do we dress: Do we follow the fashion of the season or do we choose God's style? He has told us how to dress. He does not care about the length of our skirts, or the right color for our shirts.

He has been very specific; he wants others to see love and kindness and gentleness and patience when they look at us. He wants our necklace to be forgiveness, our belt to be love. This is the fashion that God had ordained for his children.

We are chosen by God. We are loved by God, and because we are loved, we can show our love to others by the clothes we wear.

As we read the gospels, we can see the compassion and kindness and humility and gentleness and patience Jesus showed to others. God in heaven is giving us the opportunity to live as he did.

How do we dress?

Whose fashion do we follow?

MY PRAYER: *Lord, help us dress according to Your style; with compassion and kindness and humility. Help us to be gentle and patient as we go through life. We need Your help. We love You and thank You.*

MaryEmma

FEBRUARY 21

"....that your love may abound more and more in knowledge and depth of insight, so that you may be able to discern what is best....."
Philippians 1:9-10

Love is the glue that binds everything together. It must be godly love. It must be wise love. When we love with God's love we also receive knowledge and insight. Foolish love can hurt others.

Sometimes it is hard to love a difficult person, but God provides the love that is needed. The secret: loving God first, then He can supply love for others through us.

As we get to know Him better, that love grows. We get to know God through reading His word and through spending time talking and listening to Him. Our quiet times with Him will be the most important time of our day.

How do we love a difficult person?

Do we need to talk to God about it?

MY PRAYER: *Lord, there are people in this world who are just not loveable, but since you love them, we must also. Give us the secret. Is it spending time with you and learning how much you love us? Is it praying for them? Teach us to pray for those who need your help. We love you.*

MaryEmma

PRAY FOR THOSE IN AUTHORITY

"I urge, then, first of all, that petitions, prayers, intercession and thanksgiving
be made for all people-for kings, and all those in authority...."
1 Timothy 2: 1-2

We have many beautiful examples of prayer in the Bible: how to pray for ourselves, how to pray for others. This verse instructs us to pray for all those in authority over us. That includes politicians. If they are in the opposite party, we may not want to pray for them. We may not want God to bless them. Remember that the King at the time written was cruel but still they were told to pray for him.

What would happen if we prayed for our elected officials to have God's spirit of wisdom and revelation, or that their love would grow in knowledge and insight; that they might discern what is best? We don't know their pressures and temptations, but we can pray that God will guide them according to his perfect will.

We have a selfish reason to pray: that we may live peaceful and quiet lives.

Will we pray for those in authority over us?

Do we believe prayer makes a difference?

MY PRAYER: *Lord, give us wisdom as we pray. Help us discern your will for ourselves and for those in authority. Help us to be obedient to you and to pray instead of criticize. We Americans have been blessed so much that we take it for granted instead of thanking you. Forgive us.*

MaryEmma

WHY SHOULD WE GLORIFY GOD?

*"Not to us, Lord, not to us but to your name be the
glory, because of Your love and faithfulness."*
Psalm 115:1

I remember singing a song with these words when I was young. The words remind us of how important God is. Our prayers are full of us; "bless me and mine", and sometimes we forget to praise the One we are praying to. Because of His love, we know how to love; because of His faithfulness, we are blessed.

Why do we not glorify our God's name more during our days? On Thanksgiving Day, we may deliberately sit and thank Him for all the blessings we can think of. We can glorify him today by praising and thank him.

Have we glorified God's name today by word or action?

MY PRAYER: *Lord, I pray that we will open our hearts to You and praise and thank you. That is the way you make us more aware of you and your love. As we thank you we recognize your faithfulness to us and we want to thank you more. You are our help and our shield. You make life worthwhile. Not to us but to You be the glory!*

MaryEmma

FEBRUARY 24

WHY DO WE CALL?

"I love the Lord, for He heard my voice; He heard my cry for mercy.
Because He turned His ear to me, I will call on Him as long as I live.
The Lord is gracious and righteous; our God is full of compassion."
Psalm 116:1,2,5

God is always ready to help us. He wants us to call on Him and trust Him.

Our problem: we need to take our eyes off ourselves and turn them to God. That is when we call out to Him: when we have stopped putting ourselves first; when we start trusting Him. Why do we need trouble before we turn to him?

Our Lord and Savior is full of compassion, He is gracious and righteous.

Do we call for him because we love him?

Do we call for him only when we are in trouble?

MY PRAYER: *Lord, we love You and we want your best for us. Please help us to worship and reverence You as You deserve. You are worthy of all praise and love. Thank you for loving us.*

MaryEmma

FEBRUARY 25

CALL ON THE NAME OF THE LORD

"What shall I return to the Lord for all His goodness to me? I will lift up the cup of salvation and call on the name of The Lord."
Psalm 116: 12-13

As I read Psalm 116, this verse jumped out at me. Yes, Our Lord is so good to us-what does He want us to do in return? Work hard? Go to Africa and be a missionary? What does He want for us to do? Call on his name is the answer.

Why does he want us to call on his name? He wants to spent time with us. Usually we are too busy to spend but a few minutes with him. True, he wants us to accept Him as Savior but then he wants us to call on Him, to praise Him, to love him.

We try to do our duty as His children. We take on a project that we choose, instead of spending time with Him and letting Him show us what to do. The psalmist seemed to think that we are to have intimate fellowship with our heavenly Father. Do we?

Most of us memorized verses to praise him and thank him as children, but I didn't get the message until I was an adult. We can honestly praise Him because we can see His love and faithfulness. Bad things happen, but God is always with us to help us through as we praise and thank Him. Our Lord loves us.

How much do we love him?

Do we love him enough to spend quality time with him?

MY PRAYER: *Thank You for Your goodness to us. Help us to praise You and love You and give You the credit for what You do instead of taking it ourselves. We love You.*

MaryEmma

FEBRUARY 26

HIS LOVE ENDURES FOREVER

"Give thanks to The Lord, for He is good; His love endures forever."
Psalm 118:1

We are loved! God, the greatest one in all the world, loves us! Sometimes we don't feel loved, so what are we to do?

First we are to believe and then we are to thank the Lord, our God, for loving us. We can start thinking of all the ways He has shown us His love by His blessings. Would He bless us if we were not loved? We are so used to His blessings that we take them for granted.

Have we confessed our sin for lack of appreciation?

Have we told him thank you?

Have we said, "Lord, I love you."

MY PRAYER: *Thank You for Your great love for us today, and thank You that Your love endures forever. We love You. You are so good to us.*

MaryEmma

FEBRUARY 27

OUR STRENGTH AND DEFENSE

"The Lord is my strength and my defense; He has become my salvation."
Psalm 118:14

The Lord is my everything! He became my salvation when I called. He gave me strength when I was weak and helpless. He is my defense and my protector when I am afraid. My God is my everything. What more can I ask for?

Why do we try to live in this world without his help?

Why do we ignore him and take on the world by ourselves?

Why do we want to be independent?

He wants his best for us. He wants to give us peace and love and joy that makes a drab world beautiful and helps us love others. He wants to make our path smooth by holding our hands.

Why do we resist?

Are we too busy with ourselves to enjoy him?

MY PRAYER: *Lord, You are wonderful, you are my strength and defense. I am helpless without you. You are my salvation. You have given me the ticket into the future world with you. I love You. I want to be more aware of You and your holiness and love. Thank you.*

Mary Emma

FEBRUARY 28

YOUR WORD--MY HEART

"I seek You with all my heart; do not let me stray from Your commands. I have hidden Your word in my heart that I might not sin against You. Praise be to You, Lord."
Psalm 119:10-12

We need our Lord to be an intimate part of our lives.

He has given us His word, so that we can know Him. He has told us how He wants us to live and how He wants us to love.

The flesh is weak, but God is strong. When we feed our spiritual soul, we receive His strength. When we neglect Him, we are weak spiritually.

When we hide His word in our hearts, He guides us through our daily lives.

MY PRAYER: *Lord, thank You for the blessings You give me when I spend time with You in Your word. Thank You for keeping me more aware of You and Your love. Thank you for your word in my heart. You are a wonderful God. I love you and need you.*

MaryEmma

FEBRUARY 29

OPEN OUR EYES, LORD

"Be good to your servant while I live, that I may obey Your word. Open my eyes that I may see wonderful things in Your law. Your statutes are my delight; they are my counselors."
Psalm 119:17-18,24

This is a beautiful prayer to pray before we open our Bibles to read. It makes us aware of the richness of his word and to be more eager to search for them.

'Open my eyes, Lord', that I may see You. I want to understand the words written to help me know God. I want to see plainly His will for me and let him become my counselor.

The more time we spend with Him in the word, the more precious He becomes. We get to know him intimately. We see him as the God of Grace, the God of Mercy, the God of Love.

Can we ask for a better gift?

Will we spend precious time with him?

MY PRAYER: *Lord, I want to love You as You love me. I want to be pleasing to You. You are wonderful. Thank You for Your guidance and directions.*

MaryEmma

MARCH 1

SEEKING GOD'S FACE

"You are my portion, Lord; I have promised to obey Your words. I have sought Your face with all my heart; be gracious to me according to Your promise."
Psalm 119:57-58

When our eyes are on God, our thoughts are about Him.

We can say with the psalmist, "I have sought Your face with all my heart;" and we realize that He is gracious to us. He gives us peace, He gives us wisdom and He gives us His joy in our hearts.

God's gifts to us enable us to live our lives trusting Him through both problems and pleasures.

Are we seeking his face with all our heart?

MY PRAYER: *Lord, you are so gracious to me, for loving me and guiding me. I need You. I want to obey You. Help me to be what You want me to be, what you created me to be. I love you.*

MaryEmma

MARCH 2

WE ARE CUSTOM-MADE

*"Your hands made me and formed me; give me understanding
to learn your commands. May your unfailing love be my
comfort, according to your promise to Your servant."*
Psalm 119: 73,76

God made us and formed us. He custom made us; he didn't make us in a factory line up. He gave individual gifts to each of us. He loves us very much. Sometimes we feel that no one loves us, but God always does. We are precious in His sight-we are his.

As we realize this love, we want to spend time with Him.

As we read and study His word, we come to a greater understanding of Him. He gives us comfort as we read His word; He gives us compassion. As we read and meditate on His word, it becomes alive.

Do we want to know him?

Do we want to know his commands?

Do we want to be more aware of his love?

That is what our Lord wants.

MY PRAYER: *Thank You for making me in your image and teaching me to know You. I receive strength from your love and compassion. Help me to know your will and obey with love.*

MaryEmma

MARCH 3

WHAT IF?

*"Three times a day Daniel got down on his knees and prayed,
giving thanks to His God, just as he had done before."*
Daniel 6:10

In my Monday Bible Study, we are studying Daniel. I have not been able to get this verse out of my mind. I am impressed, not that he prayed in spite of the fact he would be thrown into the Lion's den if he prayed, but the fact his regular routine was to get away from everything else and spend intimate time with God, 3 times a day.

I have a quiet time first thing in the morning and it is wonderful. I say sentence prayers through the day, 'Thank You, Lord', 'Help me, Lord', and 'Forgive me, Lord', but I don't remove myself from the world and just fellowship with God 3 times a day. I have been wondering, "What would my life be like if I had Daniel's habits?"

Verse 4 says: "They could find no corruption in him, because he was trustworthy and neither corrupt nor negligent". I am not putting a guilt trip on us, I am just wondering what life would be like, if our communion with our Lord was as intimate as Daniel's. Something to ponder!

MY PRAYER: *Lord, bless us today with an awareness of Your love. Help our love for You grow so we will want to spend more time with You. You are wonderful. We love you.*

MaryEmma

MARCH 4

WISDOM, INSIGHT, UNDERSTANDING!

"Oh, how I love your law! I meditate on it all day long. Your commands are always with me and make me wiser than my enemies. I have more insight for I meditate on your statutes. I have more understanding for I obey Your precepts."
Psalm 119:97-99,

This is a prayer of love for God's word. Sometimes the word, 'law' gives us a negative thought, a harsh reaction. We can use word, or God's word, when it says law, statutes, and precepts. Those are legal words. When we love God's word, it is easy to meditate on them as we go through the day.

Choose a verse each morning to meditate on. His word gives us insight and understanding and it makes our day more peaceful. The world can swirl around us, but if we are meditating -thinking-of God's word, we have that peace that passes human understanding.

Sometimes when things are going bad, I just have to grab my Bible and immerse myself in it until I receive God's peace.

Are we becoming wiser?

Do we have more insight?

Do we have a better understanding of God's way?

MY PRAYER: *Lord, bless us today as we read and remember your words of love and guidance. Thank You for Your great love for us. You are fantastic. We love you.*

MaryEmma

MARCH 5

MY LIGHT IN A DARK WORLD

"Your word is a lamp for my feet, a light on my path."
Psalm 119: 105

The Lord's word is a light that shows us the way to go. It gives us peace as we travel this world. It opens our eyes to recognize true love, and it is our source of finding wisdom and guidance.

His word protects us by helping us to recognize sin.

As we read we can communicate with God. We call that prayer or meditation. We don't read with just our head, but with our heart and head. We read the facts of life, and God's spirit gives us understanding on how to use those facts. That is the reason we can read and reread the same scriptures and it is always new.

Because our life changes, God's guidance always fits our needs at the moment. It is not ancient history. It is for our life today. Jesus says, "I have come that you may have life, and have it to the fullest".

MY PRAYER: *Lord thank You for Your guidance, for your word that lets us know what You want for us, and teaches us about Your love and forgiveness. You are wonderful and we love you.*

MaryEmma

MARCH 6

OUR SHIELD

"You are my refuge and my shield; I have put my hope in Your word."
Psalm 119:114

When we are disappointed, when we are depressed and upset, where do we go? What do we do?

We open the word of God and start reading and let those words soak into our spirit, we receive God's peace and direction. It puts us into the presence of God and He is our hope, our refuge and our shield. We have a wonderful God!

When I am afraid or fearful, God's word will often come floating into my mind and I realize that I am not trusting in him. I have put my hope in my circumstances and myself instead of him. God's word speaks to us as we read it; it is alive!

Is His word in our mind?

Have we put His word in our memory bank?

He wants to help us.

MY PRAYER: *Lord, thank You for your word, for being our shield and refuge. You have compassion and encourage us. You don't want us to be depressed and unhappy and we won't be when we allow Your spirit to fill us. We love you.*
MaryEmma

DISCERNMENT

"Deal with Your servant according to your love and teach me your decrees. I am your servant; give me discernment that I may understand Your statutes."
Psalm 119:124,125

This is a beautiful prayer to pray before we start reading God's word; give me discernment and understanding. God's word is not just an accumulation of harsh laws we are to obey, but it is to help us know God better. We read every day because we need a renewed closeness to God everyday. God deals with us in love, even when we are being disciplined. He wants closeness with us and we understand that as we read His word.

Corrie Ten Boon was asked after she visited America what she thought was lacking in Christendom here. Her answer was 'discernment'. We Americans just go breezing though life because it is so easy and we don't look for God around us. We don't listen for His "still quiet voice".

Are we listening for his voice in our daily routine?

MY PRAYER: *Lord, make us more aware of Your greatness, Your love and Your presence. We love You.*

MaryEmma

MARCH 8

"Your statutes are wonderful; therefore I obey them. The unfolding of Your words gives light; it gives understanding to the simple. Direct my footsteps according to Your word; let no sin rule over me. Make Your face shine on your servant and teach me Your decrees."
Psalm 119:129,130

As we read God's word we get understanding. It is a light for us to walk by. But to receive this blessing, we must read it prayerfully.

It is not a history book. It is a personal letter from God to us, each of us personally. Prayer is a dialogue. I talk to God and I listen to God. His spirit teaches us as we read prayerfully. Prayer is wonderful and reading His word is wonderful, but they go together. If we try to separate them, we get off balance. I can get too emotional in my prayer life and too rigid in my Bible study if I don't combine them.

When I started my spiritual journey, I remember being surprised by realizing that I pray better, if I read first; but I understand the word better, if I pray first. What is the answer? Read prayerfully!

Do we receive discernment in our reading of His word?

MY PRAYER: *Lord, direct my footsteps according to Your word and keep me from sin. Continue to teach me and bless me. Thank You. I love You*
MaryEmma

MARCH 9

I CALL, HE ANSWERS

"I call with all my heart; answer me, Lord, and I will obey your decrees. I call out to You; save me and I will keep your statutes."
Psalm 119: 145-146

Have You noticed that Psalm 119 is all personal? Some psalms are written to the congregation, but this is full of "I"'s and "You"'s.

It is intimate between God and me. I related to these verses this morning, because some mornings, I say "Thank You Lord" and other mornings I say, "Help me, Lord". What do I mean when I say "Help me"? My life is not in danger as David's was. I pondered that this morning during my prayer time. What am I asking of God?

I mean: help me to stop thinking about the activities of the day and think of You. Help me get rid of negative thoughts and replace them with positive thoughts. Help me think of how great and wonderful You are. Help me make the right decisions today. Help me be filled with Your spirit of love and joy and peace.

What are we asking God?

What do we need today?

MY PRAYER: *I pray that today we will be more aware of You and Your help. Give us the assurance we need that you are listening and we can bring anything to you, bit or little. We love You.*

MaryEmma

MARCH 10

PEACE IN THE MIDDLE OF TROUBLE

*"Great peace have those who love Your law, and
nothing can make them stumble."*
Psalm119:165

There is a lot of wisdom in these few words. How often do we search for peace when it is as close as our Bible. When I am upset about something, I find that my peace returns more quickly when I pick up the Bible and read.

If I am really upset, I turn to 1 Peter 2 where it talks about Christ's suffering: "He committed no sin, and no deceit was found in His mouth. When they hurled their insults at Him,

He did not retaliate; when He suffered, He made no threats.

Instead, He entrusted Himself to Him who judges justly."

Can we say we have ever been treated as badly as Jesus? I don't think he had a pity party as we do. He didn't call up all his friends to cry. He called on one: his heavenly Father and we have that same choice.

Are we willing to entrust ourselves to God?

Do we find peace in his Word?

Do we need to talk to God about it?

MY PRAYER: *You are the greatest God, the one and only God. Thank you for giving us your word to teach us and comfort us and prepare us for life. We love you.*

MaryEmma

MARCH 11

OUR ATTITUDE MATTERS

*"Though the fig tree does not bud and there are no grapes on
the vines ...yet I will rejoice in the Lord, I will be joyful in
God my Savior. The Sovereign Lord is my strength."*
Habakkuk 3:17-19

We can rejoice when things are going good for us, but how often do
we rejoice when things are bad? Habakkuk is in a dialogue of his questions
and God's answers.

He starts by asking God "How long, Lord, must I call for help, but
you do not listen?"

Does God respond to demands like that?

Yes, God does, and tells him the bad things that are going to happen
to his nation. They will go into captivity because of their disobedience.

Would we lose our faith if that were to happen to us?

Even through shock and fear, his response to God is trust and because
of that trust he can rejoice: "I will rejoice in The Lord, I will be joyful in
God my Savior." How can he react like that? Because he knows the Lord
is his strength and will get him through. Notice his attitude: Not, I want
to or hope to rejoice, but I will.

What is our response to God today and all that is happening around us?

MY PRAYER: *Lord, help us rejoice in You whether things are good or bad
according to us. Help us to trust your wisdom and remember your love for us.
We love you.*

MaryEmma

MARCH 12

UNDERSTANDING

"May my cry come before You, Lord; give me understanding according to your word. May my supplication come before You; deliver me according to Your promise."
Psalm 119:169-170

Here are so many things in His word that we don't understand. We don't understand everything in the Bible, but we are told to pray for understanding. God wants to teach us and to guide us into the right decisions and right relationships.

One of my favorite prayers is found in Colossians 1: 9: "We ask God to fill you with the knowledge of His will through all wisdom and understanding." It is easier to please God if we can understand, but we also need to have faith to obey when we don't understand. God will teach us what we need to know when we need it. Not too early nor too late.

Do we trust him to teach us?

Do we trust him to protect us?

It is a good prayer to start our day.

MY PRAYER: *Lord, we ask for the knowledge of Your will for us through the wisdom and understanding that the Spirit gives. We want to live a life worthy of You and please You. We love You.*

MaryEmma

MARCH 13

MAY WE...

"May my lips overflow with praise, for You teach me Your decrees. May my tongue sing of your word, for all Your commands are righteous. May your hand be ready to help me, for I have chosen Your precepts."
Psalm 119: 171-173

As we prayerfully read God's word, we get to know Him better. He teaches us and then in gratitude and love we praise him.

We want to sing when we feel his love and as we sing his praises we learn to love Him more. When we are close to Him, our hearts fill with joy and love and it is a natural response to praise and thank Him.

Many times as I am going down the stairs in the morning, I start singing a song I learned as a child at Bible Camp: the words of love and gratitude just well up and must come out.

May we start our day with praise and thanksgiving?

May we spend more time with him one on one?

MY PRAYER: *Lord, thank You for caring about us, for wanting us to know you and spend time with you. Thank You for Your help as we go through our lives. You are holy and righteous and we praise You and love you.*

MaryEmma

MARCH 14

WHERE IS OUR HELP?

"I lift up my eyes to the mountain--where does my help come from?
My help comes from the Lord, the Maker of heaven and earth. He will
not let your foot slip-He who watches over you will not slumber.
Psalm 121:1-3

From where does our help come? When we look up to the mountain do we see God and His help? Do we rely on God or do we trust ourselves? Do we say to God with our attitude: "I can handle today by myself, thank You God".

"The Lord is our shade." When we lived in humid Houston we visited Williamsburg. I was hot and tired from the sun and I was shocked when I stepped into the shade of a monument, it was cool and pleasant. I still remember that feeling because without Houston's humidity, a shade was pleasant and satisfying.

That is how our time with God is: pleasant and satisfying. He makes everything right. He gives us peace and joy as we trust Him and spend time with Him.

May we lift our eyes to the mountain to see Him?

Will we enjoy his presence as we do a peasant and satisfying shade?

MY PRAYER: *Thank You for being our "shade at our right hand". You bless us in so many ways and we take You for granted. Forgive us. We love You.*

MaryEmma

MARCH 15

LOOK UP

"I lift up my eyes to You, to You who sit enthroned in heaven."
Psalm 123:1

Where will our eyes look today? What will our thoughts dwell on today? It is so easy to forget God as we rush through our day.

Hebrews tell us to fix our eyes on Jesus, keep our thoughts on Jesus and Colossians says to set our hearts on things above. We are to think about heavenly values instead of earthly treasures; eternal rather than temporal.

God loves us so much. We are unworthy of his love, we act like babies sometimes, but he loves us as a parent, in spite of ourselves.

Where are our thoughts?

Will we show our love for Him today?

Will we lift our eyes up to him instead of on us?

MY PRAYER: *Lord, I pray that we will "lift up our eyes to You" and remember how great You are. I pray that You will help us and bless us as we fix our eyes on You. We have problems, but you are greater than any earthly problem. We love you.*

MaryEmma

March 16

WHO IS THE BUILDER?

"Unless the Lord builds the house, the builders labor in vain. Unless the Lord watches over the city, the guards stand watch in vain."
Psalm 127: 1-2

We have our plans and hopes and desires, but unless we have God's approval, they come to nothing. God loves us and He wants the best for us just as any good parent does, but sometimes we act like a two year old and insist on our own way. Sometimes God allows it and we see disaster. Sometimes we allow God to guide us and we see good.

God is our heavenly Father and He can also be our best friend. We can talk to Him and plan with Him just as we do with human friends. As we talk to Him, He will gently guide us into the best decision. Too often, we just tell Him what we want and expect Him to deliver. Prayer is not a delivery service, prayer is fellowship with our Creator. Prayer is the way we reach intimacy with our Lord and Savior.

MY PRAYER: *Lord, may we spend time with You today, talking and listening, and loving You. Forgive us when we think we are too busy for You.*

MaryEmma

MARCH 17

WE CAN TRUST HIM

"Those who trust in the Lord are like Mount Zion, which cannot be shaken but endures forever. As the mountains surround Jerusalem, so the Lord surrounds His people both now and forevermore."
Psalm 125:1-2

Isn't this a beautiful prayer? It is a prayer of faith, of trust and love. As we prayerfully repeat these words, we can feel the security that closeness with God provides. He is with us, we can trust him.

We don't have to worry about today. God is on the job. Our Lord surrounds us with His love and His protection. Our job is to trust Him.

God will help us today with whatever problem we are worrying about. He will give us wisdom and knowledge as we ask Him.

Will we trust his answer?

Will we want a second opinion from a neighbor?

Are we Mount Zion, or a shaky tree?

MY PRAYER: *We want to trust in You today, sometimes we need help with our faith. We love You but sometimes we forget your power and your love. Help us remember You are taking care of us and surrounding us with Your love. You are a wonderful Lord and Savior.*

MaryEmma

MARCH 18

HE WANTS OUR BURDENS!

"Praise be to the Lord, to God our Savior, who daily bears our burdens. Our God is a God who saves; from the Sovereign Lord comes escape from death."
Psalm 68:19-20

Our God "daily bears our burdens". Isn't that a beautiful thought? Sometimes our burdens are merely irritations; other times they are huge mountains, but either way our Lord is with us, wanting to help us.

Do we remember to ask Him, or do we try to do it in our own strength? Our God is loving and merciful, like a mother who wants to take good care of her baby. Sometimes that baby kicks and screams and cries and mom has trouble doing what is best for baby.

Could we ever act like that baby when God wants to 'bear our burdens'?

Our God and Savior is a powerful God.

Will we praise Him?

Will we remember that Jesus the Christ came to earth in the form of a baby, so He could bears our burdens as we trust Him?

MY PRAYER: *Lord God, you are so wonderful to love us and want to help us. Forgive us when we don't involve you in our lives. You want to be an intimate friend and too often we reject you. We don't mean to, but we keep thinking we are better than we really are. We love you.*

MaryEmma

MARCH 19

WALK IN OBEDIENCE

"Blessed are all who fear the Lord, who walk in obedience to Him. You will eat the fruit of your labor; blessing and prosperity will be yours."
Psalm 128: 1-2

How can we be blessed? Only fear the Lord. Fear does not mean afraid. To me, it means love and respect and a spirit of awe; that means worship. When we "fear" Him, we want to do everything to please Him. Not to escape punishment, but just because we love Him so much. God becomes the important One in our lives.

We have many examples and directions in the scriptures to show us how to obey. We obey in spirit as well as actions. Our thoughts and attitudes are so important. There is a saying, "You are what you eat". This is also true with our thoughts. "We are what we think".

Where have our thoughts been this week? We will reap the results of those thoughts. My attitude yesterday will show up today with more joy in my spirit, or less joy and peace.

MY PRAYER: *I pray that today we will reverence our Lord and Savior with our thoughts and attitudes.*

MaryEmma

MARCH 20

FORGIVENESS

"Out of the depths I cry to You, Lord; Lord, hear my voice.
Let Your ears be attentive to my cry for mercy.
If You, Lord, kept a record of sins, Lord, who could stand?
But with You there is forgiveness, so that we can, with reverence, serve You."
Psalm 130: 1-4

This is a beautiful prayer for mercy, for forgiveness of sins.
None of us are perfect, all of us sin: probably more than
we realize. David in Psalm 19 asked God to forgive the
sins he was unaware of as well as his deliberate sins.

But the wonderful thing about our Lord and Savior is that He is a
merciful God who forgives. He forgives because He loves us and wants
the very best for us.

When we confess we are acknowledging our sins and it is the first step
in growing in strength with our Lord. When we are forgiven we receive
joy in serving Him.

When we cry out to the Lord, He hears and forgives and life is good
again.

Do we make confession a regular part of our prayer life?

Do we ask God to show us our sins?

MY PRAYER: *Thank You Father, that we can come to You to confess our sins*
and receive forgiveness. Thank You that You don't keep a record of our sins. We
love You and want to serve You with reverence and joy.

MaryEmma

MARCH 21

CORPORATE PRAYERS

"Lord, the great and awesome God...We have sinned and done wrong.
Daniel 9:4

Could we, as Americans, and as Christians, pray this prayer for our country; for all the people in America?

I pray for myself and my family and friends and even the president and our government, but I have never prayed for all of us and our sins. We know we are not sinless. The scriptures tell us that we have all sinned. Daniel, who was close to God includes himself in the sins of his countrymen.

We see great sins in others but do we recognize our own sins? God has been reminding me that remembering the mistakes of others is a sin for me. He has reminded me that what I call impatience and irritation is a sin against Him.

If He is in control with His perfect will for us and we complain, are we telling Him that He is wrong?

Do we confess our sins daily?

Do we pray for our country?

MY PRAYER: *Lord, we have sinned in American. We call ourselves a Christian nation, but we just want to enjoy your blessings without obeying and glorifying you. Forgive us and remind us what is important and that is you.*
MaryEmma

MARCH 22

WHERE IS OUR CONFIDENCE?

"My Heart is not proud, Lord, my eyes are not haughty; I do not concern myself with great matters or things too wonderful for me. But I have calmed and quieted myself, I am like a weaned child with its mother; like a weaned child I am content."
Psalm 131: 1-2

It almost sounds like the psalmist is proud, doesn't it?

But notice how he has "calmed and quieted" himself?

He has accepted he cannot change the world and make everything right. Only God can do that. He has put his hope in the Lord. It is a declaration of the peace that he has in the Lord.

A toddler wants to be independent, but never gets too far away from mother. As soon as she is out of sight, he starts crying for her. When he sees her again, he is ok. His confidence is in his mother, his protector.

This is our relationship with our Lord and Savior. When we are as close and dependent on our God as a toddler is with his mom, we are content; we have hope. We are calm and quiet inside because God's Spirit is resting in us.

MY PRAYER: *Lord, you are wonderful. You are always with us, and quick to help us, to protect us. But too often we don't trust you and we are not aware of your presence and we try to take care of things ourselves Forgive us. We love you.*
MaryEmma

MARCH 23

LIVING WATERS

"Let anyone who is thirsty come to me and drink. Whoever believes in me, as Scripture has said, 'rivers of living water will flow from within them.'".
John 7:37-38

"Any one who is thirsty"! The body can't live very long without water. Our body will start shutting down without liquid. What does that mean for our Spiritual body? When we are irritable, when we are not satisfied, we need something; do we go to the refrigerator, take a walk, or turn on the TV?

Perhaps we are "shutting down" spiritually. Jesus said, "Let anyone who is thirsty come to me and drink." Jesus is the answer!

Jesus was announcing that he would give his Holy Spirit to anyone who believed in him. We don't have to be a super Christian to have to Holy Spirit. We do have to be a Christian, to believe, to accept Jesus as our Savior and Lord.

When we believe, Jesus gives us his Spirit to teach us and help us.

It would have been wonderful to have lived when Jesus walked the earth and seen His miracles and listened to Him talk. But don't we have it better now? We have access to Jesus at any moment when we wish.

Will we take advantage of his gift of "living waters?"

MY PRAYER: *Thank You Lord, for Your wonderful gift. Thank You for loving us. Help us remember you are with us and want to give us your living waters. Forgive us when we get so busy and stressed that we forget You and don't drink.*

MaryEmma

MARCH 24

TRUST ALWAYS

"God is our refuge and strength, an ever-present help in trouble, therefore we will not fear...The Lord Almighty...says, 'Be still, and know that I am God.'"
Psalm 46: 1,2,,10

Last night God was my refuge and strength and this morning, He is saying, "Be still and know that I am God." We have a wonderful loving God who is always with us to help.

My husband started having difficulty breathing and chilling, so when we got home yesterday the nurse convinced him he needed to go to the hospital. He wouldn't listen to me! His fever was high-pneumonia was the diagnosis. He was sleeping when I left the hospital. But I needed God's help in getting out of the hospital and home. I had parked on the opposite side of the hospital and couldn't find my way to my car. I kept saying, "Lord, please help me."

A nice young man (worker) showed me how to get to my car, unlocking elevators, so I wouldn't have to go outside. It was so wonderful to finally find the car. Thank You, Lord. As I drove, my prayer again was, "Lord, help me" God listens; we don't need special words. I missed a street and had to circle around on the freeway, but finally got home, thanks to my "ever-present help in trouble". God taught me once again how "He is our refuge and strength, an ever-present help in trouble".

Do we trust him in difficult times?

Do we trust him in good times?

MY PRAYER: *Lord, help us "be still" and know that you are God. Help us remember that You are with us--always. Thank You, Lord. We love you*
Mary Emma

MARCH 25

COMPLETE JOY

If you keep my commands, you will remain in my love.... I have told you this so that my joy may be in you and that your joy may be complete. My command is this: Love each other as I have loved you."
John 15: 10-12

This is the secret to 'complete joy". Joy can be elusive at times, but not when we stay connected to the vine, Jesus. Love flows through that vine down to us, the branches. That love creates joy within us.

The whole world is looking for peace, but we have the secret right here: Love plus joy equals peace. Stay connected to the vine for God's love, joy and peace to be with us.

Do we have peace in our hearts and minds?

Do we need to talk to God about this?

MY PRAYER: *Lord, help us to stay connected to You today when things gets stressful so we can have your love flowing through us. That is the secret of joy and peace. Help us remember that we do not fight our battles alone, but You are always with us. We love you.*

MaryEmma

MARCH 26

WHO DO WE TRUST?

"In You, Lord my God, I put my trust. Show me Your ways, Lord, teach me Your paths. Guide me in Your truth and teach me, for You are God my Savior, and my hope is in You all day long."
Psalm 25:1,4-5

This has been my "go to" Psalm the last few days. There is so much hope and comfort in these words. We are to trust God. We say we do, but how often do we really trust Him?

I have confidence in myself. I never once thought I would have trouble finding my car in the garage. I am good at saying, "Thank You Lord, but I can do it by myself" (Sometimes I am a good example of a spiritual 2 year old), but when I panic, I realize I need help and God always comes through.

But as I think about all the times I called for Him that night, I realized that my spiritual self was opened to God. I realized how much I needed Him. When I trust in him, he gives me peace as he guides me.

We have a wonderful God.

Do we take him for granted?

Do we trust him to guide us in our decisions?

Are we giving thanks to God for everything?

MY PRAYER: *Yes, Lord, show me, teach me, guide me. I need You I need you every day, not just when I am in a panic. Thank you for always being with me. I love you.*

MaryEmma

MARCH 27

UNITY

"How good and pleasant it is when God's people live together in unity!
Psalm133:1

Unity indicates love and joy and peace when we are together. It is good. It requires loving others as we love ourselves. Jesus said, "The world will know you belong to me by your love for one another".

We need to think about how the other person feels and consider their viewpoint and not insist on our way just because that is what we want.

How do we feel when someone objects to our plan?

How do we react when another insists on their plan?

Jesus prayed that we would be one as he and the Father were one.

Is that a description of our life?

MY PRAYER: *I pray that we will be aware of Your love for us today and we will share that love with others.*

MaryEmma

MARCH 28

PRAISE THE LORD

> *"Praise the Lord, Praise the name of the Lord; praise Him,*
> *You servants of the Lord, Praise the Lord, for the Lord is*
> *good; sing praise to His name, for that is pleasant."*
> Psalm 135:1,3

How much time do we spend praising the Lord?

How often during the day do we think of Him? When we see something beautiful, do we give our Lord the credit?

He made the beautiful mountains and valleys, but it is God who gives man the power to make a beautiful building or paint great art. He is the One who has both power and the wisdom to use His power.

He is the one who gives us strength and ability to be successful.

Have we thanked Him for what we have accomplished? It is all from Him.

Do we feel His love when we think of Him?

Do we experience his joy when we tell Him how wonderful He is?

Try it. Whatever we can give to Him, He gives us more!

MY PRAYER: *We praise You, Lord, for Your goodness and Your power and Your love. Thank You for your blessings. Forgive us when we forget who our source is. We love you.*

MaryEmma

MARCH 29

DO WE RELY ON GOD?

"I will praise, You, Lord, with all my heart... I will praise
Your name for Your unfailing love and Your faithfulness.
When I called, You answered me; You greatly emboldened me.
Psalm 138:1-3

When we are in need and we call for God's help, He answers us. We don't deserve it, but because of His love for us, and His faithfulness to His promises, He helps us. He doesn't always answer the way we want Him to, but He answers in His wisdom and what he knows that we need to learn to grow strong in him.

He knows what we need in our lives to be the people He created us to be. David fought for his life for years after he was anointed as the future king of Israel, but God knew that was what he needed to be the greatest king ever.

Do we call on God and rely on God for his help?

Have we learned to trust Him when he doesn't answer the way we wish?

MY PRAYER: *Help us to trust You when things don't go our way. Help us to love You during difficult times and remember You are always with us. We love You.*

MaryEmma

MARCH 30

REMEMBERING HIM

*"It was just before the Passover Festival. Jesus knew that the
hour had come for Him to leave this world and go to the Father.
Having loved His own who were in the world"....*
John 13:1

We are to remember Jesus' death. We know why He died: why He
was willing to die that cruel death at the hands of the Roman soldiers? He
died so that by believing, we could become the spiritual children of God,
the Father.

His body was broken, His blood was shed, for us; you and me.

His blood symbolizes the washing away of our sins, and that happens
when we believe.

I love His birth, I am happy for His resurrection, but I am impressed
by His willingness to suffer for me. He prayed three times that this cup
be taken away from Him, and the third time, He said "OK, Thy will, not
Mine". He showed us His love. Then he gave us a command to love one
another.

Do we remember why Jesus died?

Do we realize what he did for us by his death.

Do we show our love for him by loving others?

MY PRAYER: *Jesus, my Savior, you did so much for us that we take for
granted. You showed us how to live our lives. You gave us a better idea of how
loving our Father is and you sacrificed your self for us. Thank you.*

MaryEmma

90

MARCH 31

LOVE WILL FORGIVE

"... they crucified Him there, along with the criminals-one on His right, the other on His left. Jesus said, "Father, forgive them, for they do not know what they are doing.""
Luke 23:33,34

Even from the cross, Jesus was showing His love. He came for this purpose, to die for our sins, because He loves us. Because He loved, He also forgave. This is the example He has left for us: Love and Forgiveness.

They didn't deserve forgiveness; they were ruthless and cruel men. Some did it because it was their job, others did it because they wanted power and prestige.

We are to love others and we are to forgive them. Our feelings may be hurt and so we refuse to forgive. His body was hurt and He forgave. To have peace and joy in our hearts, we must love and forgive. So simple and so hard!

Are we able to forgive another who hurt us?

Will we forgive when another won't admit their wrong?

Do we love Jesus enough to forgive others who don't deserve forgiving?

MY PRAYER: *Lord Jesus, thank You for Your example of forgiving. It is difficult for us because we think of ourselves first and others second. You have given us an example of true love; forgiveness. Help us, Lord, to forgive when wronged and be what You created us to be.*

MaryEmma

APRIL 1

MERELY BY BELIEVING

"…Why do you look for the living among the dead?
He is not here; He has risen! Remember how He told
you, while He was still with you in Galilee.
Luke 24:5-6

This is the day we celebrate life! Spiritual life-eternal life, all provided for by the death and resurrection of Jesus Christ. He came to earth for one reason: to die for our sins, so we could have a relationship with our God.

All this merely by believing. The blood of the Passover lamb that saved the Israelite babies was a picture of the gift that we would someday have in Jesus. This is the day to praise Him, to thank Him and to show His love to others.

Do we praise him for who he is?

Do we thank him for what he has done for us?

Is my life an example of his love?

MY PRAYER: *Lord, thank You for giving us life; so easy for us and so difficult for You. Thank You for our life on earth and thank You for the future life we will have after our physical death. We thank You and love You.*

MaryEmma

APRIL 2

OUR GRIEF BLINDS US

"He said to them, 'How foolish you are, and how slow to believe all that the prophets have spoken! Did not the Messiah have to suffer these things and then enter His glory?'
Luke 24:25-27

The two men walking down the road were so absorbed in themselves and their grief that they did not recognize their risen Christ. How true that is of us. We keep our eyes on ourselves and our fears and disappointments so that we can't see our Lord. We need to keep our eyes on Him and just glance at ourselves, but God is so gracious; He meets us where we are.

The men were in a spiritual valley of defeat, but as they talked to Jesus they were able to take their eyes off themselves and recognize His presence. That is how we get from the valley to the mountaintop: concentrating on our Lord and Savior.

Jesus came to earth as man and died as a man, for our sins, but in His obedience, He was resurrected to His former glory; as the Son of God. Through His death we also can be resurrected to a new spiritual life as our heavenly Father's children, just by believing.

Why are we so dense that we don't recognize Jesus?

Is it because we so absorbed in ourselves?

Do we honor him?

MY PRAYER: *Lord, We need you. We thank you for all you have done for us. Forgive us when we don't recognize your actions around us. We love you.*

Mary Emma

APRIL 3

ASSURANCE

"Men of Galilee...why do You stand here looking into the sky? This same Jesus, who has been taken from you into heaven, will come back in the same way you have seen Him go into heaven."
Acts 1:11

After His resurrection Jesus spent 40 days on earth, teaching His disciples and encouraging them. When the time was right, He left to go back to the Father, but He left us with a wonderful promise. He will come again and take us with Him.

But while we are on this earth, we have His wonderful words to teach and encourage us.

When we are discouraged and down, we just need to pick up the words of God and read; let the words soak into our spirit. The disciples and women spent the next 10 days in prayer to prepare themselves for the great gift of His spirit to everyone who believes.

This is our work and our joy as we experience the blessings of our risen Lord and Savior, talking to Him and reading His word.

Do we spend time in prayer when we are waiting?

Do we look forward to his return?

Do we allow his words to encourage us?

MY PRAYER: *Help us, Lord, to trust you and be aware of your Spirit to teach us and help us. Help us to enjoy the wonderful words You left us. Help us prepare our minds to enjoy your blessings.*

Mary Emma

APRIL 4

ENEMIES

"Deliver me from my enemies, O God; be my fortress against those who are attacking me… You are my strength, I watch for You; You, God, are my fortress, my God on whom I can rely.
Psalm 59:1,9

What are our enemies? We don't have men at the door trying to kill us. But we have illnesses. We have a painful back, a tender shoulder, a headache or a rash that won't go away. How do we handle it? Maybe we have a straying child that breaks our heart or a person with an evil mouth that says painful words to us. How do we handle these enemies? Can we take the example David gives us?

David is in trouble. Saul sent his soldiers to arrest David at his house, but his wife helped him to escape.

This is the prayer of David after that experience. After he shares his fears with God, he shares his faith with God. He realizes that God is his strength and to receive that strength the easiest way is to concentrate on who God is and what He does for us.

He doesn't hide his head under the pillow, but he sings of God's strength and love. He realizes that God is his protection, both physically and spiritually.

Do we concentrate on our problems?

Are we willing to receive strength from focusing on God?

What is our choice?

MY PRAYER: *Lord, help us to trust you with our problems. Help us go to you and share our fears and then concentrate on your power and your love. Thank you.*

MaryEmma

APRIL 5

FEAR OR TRUST?

"Be merciful to me, my God, for my enemies are in hot
pursuit; all day long they press their attack.
When I am afraid, I put my trust in You.
Psalm 56:1,3

Have we ever been discouraged and then fearful?

This is where David is. He has run away from his country because King Saul was jealous and wanted to kill him. But he ran to the Philistine, the enemy, for help. There was trouble there also. What was he to do? He turned to God for help. Just like us, he turned to God as the last resort.

But his prayers gave him confidence that God was real and He was with him. What can man do to him?

Men or illness or situations can hurt us with their words and actions, They can make our lives miserable, but God is always with us to give us the confidence and hope to get us through the situation.

Do we have confidence in God?

Where will our spiritual eyes be today?

MY PRAYER: *Lord, help us keep our eyes on You today. You are our helper, and our comforter. We know that we can rely on Your faithfulness. Thank you. We love you.*

MaryEmma

THANKSGIVING

"I will glory in the Lord; let the afflicted hear and rejoice.
Glorify the Lord with me; let us exalt His name together.
I sought The Lord, and He answered me; He
delivered me from all my fears."
Psalm 34:2-4

Fears can be terrible. Sometimes we see danger, other times we sense a possibility of danger. Both times our human response is fear. What might happen?

Yesterday's prayer was for confidence as David escaped Saul, and went into the camp of the Philistines for refuge, but found that it was more dangerous than Saul. What was he to do? He asked God for help. He acted like a madman and they decided he was harmless and threw him out. This is his prayer of thanksgiving for God's guidance.

He sought the Lord and God answered him. God delivered him from his fears.

What are we afraid of today? Is it real or only a possibility?

When we are afraid do we go to God first?

Do our prayers of thanksgiving sound like David's?

When He answers, do we thank Him, or take credit ourselves?

Do we praise Him to others or just forget Him?

MY PRAYER: *Help us, Lord, like David, to glorify you and to exalt you with love and thanksgiving. You are so good!*

Mary Emma

APRIL 7

THE ANGEL OF THE LORD SURROUNDS US

"This poor man called, and the Lord heard him; He saved him out of all his troubles. The angel of the Lord encamps around those who fear Him, and He delivers them."
Psalm 34:6-7

This Psalm is so full of gratitude and love. David received the answer for his troubles, and he escaped with his life. We can receive answers today. Our problem is that we want instant answers. David waited years, but stayed faithful.

God uses our problems to help us know Him better, to grow spiritually. My prayer the last few years is that I be more aware of God's presence. We need to keep in mind that the 'angel of the Lord encamps around' us when we love and respect Him. Isn't that a beautiful thought?

So why are we ever fearful? Because we forget He is with us. We need to take David's advice. Taste and see.

MY PRAYER: *Lord, I pray that we will enjoy You and your presence, we will talk to You and listen to You. Thank You that You love us more than a mortal can ever love us. We love you.*

MaryEmma

I TRUST, I HOPE

"But I am like an olive tree flourishing in the house of God; I trust in God's unfailing love...I will hope in Your name, for Your name is good."
Psalm 52:8-9

Are we 'flourishing' in our Lord? Are we trusting in His love? Do we worry and fret; do we get discouraged?

Could it be that we are not 'flourishing' in our Savior?

How does a tree flourish? With water and food and sunshine. Our water and food comes from spending time with our Lord. Talking to Him, listening to Him, spending enough time in His word so that we will know Him intimately.

There are two paths in our lives, the path to destruction or to life eternal. The problem is there are many little paths along the way that we wander off on, until we realize that we are lost. That is the time we must call on God to help us back to Him. Daily time with God keeps us on the right path, emotionally and spiritually. Are we?

Do we fret?

Do we worry?

Do we need to spend more time with our Lord?

MY PRAYER: *Lord, You are so good to us. Thank You that You love us enough to want to spend time with us. You allow us all the time we need. You are always welcoming. We love You.*

MaryEmma

APRIL 9

"On my bed I remember You; I think of You through the watches of the night. Because You are my help, I sing in the shadow of Your wings. I cling to You; Your right hand upholds me."
Psalm 63: 6-8

This is a prayer of gratitude for protection. It is a prayer of love and appreciation. Does it sound like our prayers?

David again had escaped from Saul and was in the desert. God had anointed David to be King, so why was he in the desert, running for his life? Do you think David ever had those thoughts?

What are You doing to me, God? We have those thoughts sometimes, don't we?

God was preparing David to be the King He wanted. If God had put David on the throne immediately; from herding sheep to leading the Kingdom, it would have been like putting a fifth grader into college courses. God teaches us through all of our problems. He teaches us to trust Him and look to Him for help, instead of using our limited wisdom and human strength. Our job is to trust Him, and thank Him and praise Him.

MY PRAYER: *We do thank You and praise You, Lord. Help us in the trust department. Our human nature is to trust ourselves first. Forgive us. We love You. You are an awesome teacher.*

MaryEmma

GOD IS OUR HELP

"Save me, O God, by your name; vindicate me by Your might.
Hear my prayer, O God; ... ruthless people are trying to
kill me.... The Lord is The One who sustains me."
Psalm 54:1-4

David has just learned that the people he is living with, people he thought were his friends, have arranged to turn him over to Saul to be killed. He is disappointed; he is hurt. This is his prayer for help.

We don't have to worry about someone trying to kill us, but sometimes friends turn on us, family members disappoint us. We lose hope in our jobs and our situation. Maybe our body is the arrogant foe attacking us. What are we to do?

We can complain and judge and whine, and usually do. But we can also turn to God and have faith that He will guide us and direct us. God will show us what to do; how to handle the situation when we ask and when we follow God's guidance. Complaining is not turning it over to God. Faith that God is helping us will give us peace and joy and hope.

How do we handle the situation?

Do we complain?

Do we become angry?

Do we trust God and allow him to teach us and help us through the hard times?

MY PRAYER: *Lord, we have had bad times when we needed you to help us. We have learned that when we call on you and allow you to teach us, we have peace. You are a God of grace and peace. Thank you.*

MaryEmma

APRIL 11

OUR REFUGE

"Have mercy on me, my God, have mercy on me, for in you I take refuge, I will take refuge in the shadow of Your wings until the disaster has passed."
Psalm 57:1

There are times in our lives, when we are in despair about our situations. We are depressed and defeated and the only things we know to do is to cry out to God, as David did, "Have mercy on me".

There are times when I start my prayer time with "Help me, Lord" and God knows that I am turning it over to Him. I think, maybe, this is what God is waiting for when we feel over whelmed with our emotions, or with the way the world is whirling around us.

But when we cry out to God, He saves us, and we can feel His love creeping back into our spirit. We are comforted because we feel his presence.

Our God is so loving and gentle and He wants to give us guidance and peace.

Will we trust God to help us?

Will we call on him for help?

MY PRAYER: *Lord, you always hear and answer. You always help us when we call. We have total confidence in you because you love us and you have a plan for our lives that we may not understand. But we know you will make it right. You are our refuge in times of trouble.*

Mary Emma

APRIL 12

OUR ROCK

"I love You, Lord, my strength. The Lord is my rock,
my fortress and my deliverer; ... I take refuge, my shield
and the horn of my salvation, my stronghold."
Psalm 18:1-2

Here is a prayer of gratitude; a prayer of love to the One and only God. As I read these words, I feel my stress leaving and my faith increasing. What is stronger than a rock? He is our protection and our reassurance. He is our love. I have been reading a Bible than puts things in chronological order (my New Year's resolution) and the editor has inserted psalms into different stages of David's life. I have enjoyed it so much that I have been sharing them.

David has finally become King. Saul is dead. So all is well? No. The Philistines have decided to fight him and come in full force. But David does not rush out with his army. First he inquires of The Lord. "Shall I go and attack the Philistines? Will You hand them over to me?" God answers: "Go. I will hand them over to you."

David's relationship with God is a good example for us.

The imagery of God in this Psalm is beautiful.

How often do we inquire of the Lord before we do something?

Is he our rock?

MY PRAYER: *Lord, help us be more aware of You today. Help us to learn to trust You so that we can say, "You are my rock, I will take my refuge in You."*
MaryEmma

SING OUR PRAISES

"Sing to the Lord, praise His name; proclaim His salvation day after day. For great is the Lord and most worthy of praise.
Psalm 96: 2,4

Our Lord and Savior is great and worthy of our praise.
He is the One and only, our true and living God.
David and the people were singing to the Lord because the Ark had been returned to Jerusalem. The Ark was the presence of God. Because of their sin, it had been captured and now it had been returned. David and his people were thrilled and were rejoicing.
Do we remember to thank and praise God when He has blessed us? Too often, I fear, I take it for granted and when I am pleased, I don't give the glory to God. We praise Him because He is great. We also praise Him for the blessings He continually gives us.
Will we choose to praise Him?
Do we sing to him when we are thrilled?

MY PRAYER: *Lord, I pray that as we go through our day we will remember that You are great and MOST worthy of praise. You bless us so much. We love You.*

MaryEmma

WASH OUR HEARTS

"Search me, God, and know my heart; test me and know my anxious thoughts. See if there is any offensive way in me, and lead me in the way everlasting."
Psalm 139:23-24

"Search me"- do we want God to search our heart and mind and see what we have hidden away? Sometimes it hurts to be reminded of our shortcomings: to be reminded of how we have failed. But it is important that we confess our sins to be one with God. The psalmist said, "forgive my conscious sins and also my hidden sins." We need to ask God to show us our sins so that we can confess them. That is necessary before God can guide our lives the way He desires.

We wash our clothes and we wash our bodies. We also need to wash our heart and thoughts to be clean. By confessing we give God permission to forgive us. As we praise God and thank Him, we become aware of our failures to please God. He is on standby, waiting to forgive.

Are we willing to let Him search our hearts?

Will we let him test our thoughts?

He wants us to be pure and clean inside and out.

MY PRAYER: *Lord, I pray that we will open our hearts to You and allow You to search us. Make us aware of whatever is keeping us from you. Show us what is displeasing to You. We love you.*

MaryEmma

APRIL 15

PURE HEART

"Create in me a pure Heart, O God, and renew a steadfast spirit within me. Do not cast me from Your presence or take Your Holy Spirit from me. Restore to me the joy....."
Psalm 51:10-12

David has confessed his sin and now he wants to renew his fellowship with his Lord. He realizes that his heart has become self centered instead of God centered and he is asking for cleansing and renewal. "Restore to me the joy of Your salvation" is important to him. It is also important to us.

The joy we feel when we are one with God is precious. When the joy is not present, it is a warning sign. Joy and peace mean that we are in agreement with God. Our God is so gracious. He forgives and He restores. It is our choice.

Are we willing to submit our will to God?

Will we be obedient?

Are we willing?

MY PRAYER: *Lord, we thank You that You want to create in us a pure heart. We want fellowship with You. We want the joy that only Your presence can give us. We love You.*

Mary Emma

APRIL 16

OUR SHIELD

"Lord, are a shield around me, my glory, The One who lifts my head I call out to the Lord, and He answers me ... the Lord sustains me. I will not fear."
Psalm 3: 3-5

David is on the run again. Not from King Saul, but from His son Absalom, who wants the throne. David's heart is breaking, his son is trying to kill him, and people who he thought were his friends are betraying him. What is he to do?

He calls out to the Lord. His Lord is a shield around him.

Sometimes we feel like our family or friends or maybe a boss has turned against us. We can feel the hurt in our hearts. God has given us an example of how we can handle it. We trust God, but sometimes our faith needs to be strengthened.

God gives us strength as we need it when we call out to Him. God always answers our prayers. Sometimes He says yes, sometimes it is no, and sometimes He says wait.

Do we call out to the Lord for help?

Do we accept his answer that allows us to sleep?

Will we keep our eyes on God instead of the situation?

MY PRAYER: *Lord, the peace You give us is wonderful. You are the shield that protects us. Thank You. We love you.*

Mary Emma

*"Wash away all my iniquity and cleanse me from my sin.
For I know my transgressions.... Against You, You only,
have I sinned and done what is evil in your sight."*
Psalm 51:2-4

When we sin, it is always against God. Our sin will hurt others, but it is God that we are dishonoring.

David had just been reminded of his sin with Bathsheba. It is a beautiful story. He had not considered it sin, but his due as King to do as he pleased. But Nathan, the prophet, came to him with the truth. "You have sinned against God who has blessed You in every way."

We usually get into trouble when we have too much time on our hands, as David did.

But do we recognize our sins? It doesn't have to be adultery. We all sinned. Our sins start in our thoughts. When we choose our way instead of God's way.

Do we choose God's way or ours?

Do we ask him to show us our sins, when we can't think of any?

MY PRAYER: *Lord, You are faithful. You forgive us our sins, when we confess. We are unworthy, but You are worthy. We thank You and love You.*

MaryEmma

APRIL 18

"And You, my son Solomon, acknowledge the God of Your
Father, and serve Him…If You seek Him, He will be found by
you; but if you forsake Him, He will reject you forever."
1 Chronicles 28:9

Is God a remote God or is He a personal God? David tells us that God searches our heart to see who we really are. He understands our desires and our thoughts. We can hide a lot of our inner thoughts from others, but God knows what we are thinking and what we want to do. How do we feel about this? Does it scare us or does it make us feel loved?

If I didn't know God loved me I think I would try to run away from Him. But why would we want to keep a distance from The One who does love us so much. It means that we are never alone. God's presence is always with us, helping us and guiding us. He wants us to loves Him with all our heart and soul and strength-just as He loves us.

Do we acknowledge God's presence?

Do we praise Him and thank Him?

MY PRAYER: *Lord, we know we sin more often than we think, and we thank You for Your forgiveness. We want You to search and help us. Thank You for loving us.*

MaryEmma

APRIL 19

GOD IS GREAT

"David praised the Lord in the presence of the whole assembly, saying, 'Praise be to You, Lord, the God of our father Israel, from everlasting to everlasting. Yours, Lord, is the greatness...."
1 Chronicles 29:10-11

This is a prayer of praise and thanksgiving. David wanted to build a temple for God, but God said, "No. You have blood on your hands. Your son, Solomon, will build it." David accepted that, but he assembled all the materials needed and the people gave generously. This is his prayer. Does it sound like us when God has answered our prayers?

He acknowledges God's greatness: All power and strength come from our Lord; wealth and honor come from Him.

Do we give Him thanks?

Do we want to praise His name?

MY PRAYER: *Lord, I pray that today we will think of Your power and glory and enjoy You for who You are; not just for what You do for us. You are great and we love you,*

MaryEmma

APRIL 20

GOD IS MY ROCK

*"I will proclaim the name of The Lord. Oh, praise
the greatness of our God! He is the Rock."*
Deuteronomy 32: 3

This is the song that Moses taught the children of Israel before they entered the promised land. He did not want them to forget God, and they were to sing this song with their children.

He is a faithful God, a perfect God for them and for us. I love the symbolism of calling God my Rock. When I read that God is a Rock, I feel secure. Rocks don't disappear and leave you alone. They are strong and I think they are beautiful.

Do You have a word that reminds you of God? Here are so many words used in the scriptures to try to describe Him, to give us a better understanding of Him. Words go through our minds, but some words stop in our heart and become special.

MY PRAYER: *Lord, I pray that You will bless us today with special thoughts of You, remember that You are faithful and do no wrong. We love You.*

MaryEmma

APRIL 21

DISTRESS

> *"You, Lord, are forgiving and good, abounding in*
> *love ... Hear my prayer, Lord; listen to my cry for mercy. When*
> *I am in distress, I call to You, because You answer me."*
> Psalm 86:5-7

A prayer of David: He is asking for help from his enemies. He is asking for mercy. What are our enemies? Our emotions, our health, our fears? We don't have physical enemies who are trying to kill us, but there are many enemies in our lives attacking our peace and our joy. It may be He people around us, a job that we dislike or it could just be our pride that wants everything to go our way and God will not allow it.

David gives us He answers for a life that is not all peace and joy. "Hear me, Lord, and answer me." We may not like He answer, but God loves us and wants He best for us. "He is forgiving and good and abounding in love" but we must call on Him.

Do we call on Him?

MY PRAYER: *Lord, Help us to remember to call on You and not keep trusting ourselves when You are the true help. We love You.*

MaryEmma

APRIL 22

HE KNOWS US

"You have searched me, Lord, and You know me. You know when I sit and when I rise; You perceive my thoughts from afar... Before a word is on my tongue, You, Lord, know it completely."
Psalm 139:1-5

I love this Psalm. It makes me feel good as I read it. I tried to decide why and I decided that if God knows me that well, and still likes me, He must really love me!

He loves you and me. We are special. No matter what troubles we have, we have His presence and His love with us helping us through He problems. As we go through this day, let's remember how special we are in God's eyes. He has His arms around us. Sometimes we struggle to get out of His loving arms, but He doesn't let us get far. Why? Because He loves us.

Do we trust Him?

Do we love him?

MY PRAYER: *Lord, You are great and You are special. You know us and You still love us. Thank You. We love You.*

MaryEmma

APRIL 23

HE IS WITH US

"Where can I go from Your Spirit? Where can I flee from Your presence? If I go up to the heavens, You are there… Your right hand will hold me fast."
Psalm 139: 7-10

God is always with us. We can try to run, we can feel lost and alone, but God is with us. It is a wonderful promise that God will 'guide' us and 'hold us fast'.

We may try to run away from Him, but His Spirit will always pull us back to Him. He doesn't let his children stray far. He loves us too much.

Will we look for Him and His Spirit to guide us?

Do we want him?

MY PRAYER: *Lord, You are so wonderful. We don't deserve You. We don't deserve Your love and Your care. You are always with us and we thank You and love You.*

MaryEmma

WISDOM

*"We have not stopped praying for you. We continually ask
God to fill you with the knowledge of His will through all
He wisdom and understanding that the Spirit gives."*
Colossians 1: 9

Paul prayed for specifically for the Christians in Colossae. Not a general "bless them," but He was asking God to give them a knowledge of God's will for them. We may pray that when we are in trouble, but do we ask for that help today when things are going ok?

He was also specific in asking for the wisdom and understanding that the Holy Spirit gives us. Knowledge is desirable, but knowledge with God's wisdom is great. If we have understanding how to use God's knowledge and wisdom we can make our life so much better and help others.

Knowledge, wisdom and understanding that comes from God is a precious gift.

Do we ask Him for that gift?

Do we ask for that gift for others ?

Will we pray this prayer for ourselves and our family?

MY PRAYER: *Lord God, thank You that You want only the best for us. I pray for each person who reads this verse today. I pray that they will understand Your will for them and that You will give them the wisdom and understanding to do what You want for them. Thank You. We love You.*

MaryEmma

APRIL 25

INCENSE

"I call to You, Lord, come quickly to me; hear me when I call to You. May my prayer be set before you like incense; may the lifting up of my hands be like the evening sacrifice.
Psalm 141: 1-2

This is a prayer for help: not for protection from violence, but for spiritual growth. Sometimes when we start to pray, we feel our words aren't going past He ceiling. We are not conscious of God's presence. It is ok for us to cry out to God for help. He Bible tells us our prayers are like incense to God; a sweet savor. He loves us and wants us to talk to Him.

He wants our worship and love.

David refers to lifting his hands 'like He evening sacrifice'. We love seeing a toddler lifting his arms to mother, asking to be picked up as though everything is just too much trouble for him and He needs Mom to take over. That is what David is saying in this prayer. "I need You, Lord. Take over, please". It isn't the words but the condition of our hearts that God is interested in.

Where are our thoughts when we pray?

What is the condition of our hearts when we pray?

MY PRAYER: *God, protect our hearts today so that our mouth will not make us sin. We lift our arms to You in love and trust.*

MaryEmma

APRIL 26

HELP

"I cry aloud to The Lord; I lift up my voice to The Lord for mercy. I pour out before Him my complaint; before him I tell my trouble.... it is you who watch over my way
Psalm 142:1-3

We would think that David was having a big pity party, if we didn't know that his life was in danger. He was afraid. He needed help and He knew that only God could help him. He gives us an example of what we are to do when we are in despair. Tell God all about it. Of course, He knows already, but for some reason, God wants us to speak the words to Him. It helps us clarify our thoughts and gives us the strength to trust Him.

When we are upset, what do we do?

When we are in despair who do we talk to?

MY PRAYER: *Lord, sometimes we think we are alone, that no one cares for us, but we forget that You are always present, wanting to help us through the difficult times. Thank You. We love You.*

MaryEmma

APRIL 27

SHOW ME, TEACH ME

"for I have put my trust in You. Show me the way I should go. Teach me your will... my God; may your good Spirit lead me on level ground."
Psalm 143: 8,10

Show me, teach me, lead me is our prayer today. It is a model for the days that don't go as planned. We must call to God who loves us. We must trust Him.

When we feel we are alone, we need to "meditate on all His works and consider what His hands have done" and then we will know that we are never alone. God is listening, and loving and teaching us. He never leaves us alone.

Are we asking him to help us, to answer us?

Have we put our trust in him?

MY PRAYER: *God, You are always with us, waiting to hear us call. Show us the way we should go; teach us to do Your will. We love You and thank You.*

MaryEmma

APRIL 28

MY LOVING GOD

"Praise be to The Lord, my rock. He is my loving God and my fortress, my stronghold and my deliverer, my shield, in whom I take refuge ."
Psalm 144:1-2

This is a beautiful prayer of love and relationship. Change the 'He is' to 'You are' and it becomes a personal prayer to our Lord.

Sometimes we feel alone, even when we aren't, and making our scriptures personal prayers helps us remember we are never alone. Our Lord is always with us.

I love He last line of this Psalm: "blessed is the people whose God is The Lord".

Is He our Lord?

Do we visit with him?

MY PRAYER: *Lord, Help us remember we are never alone; that You are always with us. You are our stronghold and deliverer and shield and we love You.*
MaryEmma

APRIL 29

SO WORTHY

"I will exalt You, my God The King; I will praise Your name....Great is The Lord and most worthy of praise, His greatness no one can fathom."
Psalm 145:1-3

We do have a wonderful God, don't we? And so worthy of praise! This is our job as His children - to praise Him.

What does He do? As we read through the Psalm we are reminded of many ways he blesses us. He is gracious, he doesn't treat us as our sins deserve. He is compassionate: He is so loving that he guides and corrects us gently. He is trustworthy, He is righteous and faithful.

Read through this Psalm and make it a personal by replacing "He" with "You"

How can we not praise Him when we consider who He is and all He does for us. We can praise Him in our hearts and also with our mouths. He is worthy!

How often do we praise our Lord?

Could we use this Psalm as a guide to praising our Lord?

MY PRAYER: *Lord, I ask that we will have a great awareness of Your presence with us today. Help us to praise you as we go through our day. You are so great! We love you.*

MaryEmma

APRIL 30

WHERE IS OUR HOPE

"Do not put your trust in princes, in human beings, who cannot save. Blessed are those whose help is the God of Jacob, whose hope is in the Lord their God."
Psalm 146:2,3,5

Where is our hope today? Is it in our job? Is it in our family or our activities? Is it in our talents or our money?

It is so easy to get "puffed up" with the blessings God has given us instead of thanking Him for those blessings. Maybe that is the reason we are told to praise God so often: so we will remember it is God who blesses us and not just our effort. Four times we are told to praise God in this Psalm.

Where will we put our hope today?

Will we praise our Lord and Savior?

MY PRAYER: *Lord, You are wonderful. You have created a beautiful world. You have power and strength but you are also loving and compassionate. You are wise and just. We love you.*

MaryEmma

MAY 1

WHY DON'T WE PRAISE HIM?

"Praise the Lord…. Young men and women, old men and children,
let them praise the name of The Lord, for His name alone is
exalted. His splendor is above the earth and the heavens."
Psalm 148: 1,12-13

We are to praise our Lord. This Psalm tells us that nature praises God. Maybe we humans are the only creation of God that doesn't continually praise Him.

As I meditated on this Psalm, I thought about Psalm 144, and wondered why my heart was more moved by reminding me of what God does for me, rather than being reminded of who He is.

Is my God too small? Can I only relate to Him when I think about how He helps me, rather than how great He is?

I think I need to make this a matter of prayer. We are to praise God for who He is, not just for what He does for us. He is a glorious wonderful God. He shows us how to love others. He makes the world beautiful for all to see. He has made His greatness known to us through nature, and through people as well as through that 'small quiet voice' within us.

Will we look for His greatness today?

Do we love enough that we want to praise Him?

MY PRAYER: *Lord, help me to see Your hand around me today and be reminded to praise You for The great God that you are. We love You.*

MaryEmma

MAY 2

TRUST

> *"In You, Lord my God, I put my trust. I trust in you; do not*
> *let me be put to shame, nor let my enemies triumph over me.*
> *No one who hopes in you will ever be put to shame."*
> Psalm 25:1-3

"In You, Lord my God, I put my trust." What a beautiful way to start our prayer time. Sometimes we have trouble praying. Our mind is cluttered with "what if's" or with yesterday or what will happen today, but when we open our mind to God and just tell Him "I trust You", it help us to focus on Him.

Whatever our fears or trouble, if we trust Him, we know that He will take care of it. He will go with us through the problem when we put our trust in Him.

What is keeping us from trusting him today?

Will we trust him with whatever?

MY PRAYER: *Lord, we do trust You. We want to. Forgive us when we don't and help us increase our faith by keeping our thoughts on you and your love*

MaryEmma

MAY 3

WONDERFUL COUNSELOR

"For to us a child is born, to us a son is given, and his government will be on His shoulders. And He will be called Wonderful Counselor, Mighty God, Everlasting Father....
Isaiah 9: 6-7

This is a message of hope in the middle of condemning them and forecasting captivity for their sins. We all need hope in bad times, and Isaiah was using encouragement to get God's people to return to Him. He was promising a messiah to give them hope, to make them look up to see God and realize they had turned away from him.

God would send his Son and his kingdom will be greater than David's kingdom because it would be a spiritual kingdom.

This beautiful verse that we read at Christmas tells us what he will be to us. His power is supreme; when we are in need, he is our counselor to guide and direct us. He is the source of peace in our hearts and most wonderful of all, He is our loving Father.

Do we love him?

Is our trust in God's love and power?

Could we celebrate the birth of Jesus Christ everyday in our hearts?

MY PRAYER: *Thank You, Lord, for your gift to us. Jesus brought us not only salvation, but your encouragement and your hope and your peace. We love you.*
MaryEmma

MAY 4

GOD WORKS FOR OUR GOOD

"And we know that in all things God works for the good of those who love him, who have been called according to his purpose."
Romans 8:28

When I was a young adult, this was my "go to" verse when I was fearful or uncertain. It got me through a lot of hard times. I just trusted that God would take care of me somehow.

It wasn't until later, that I connected verse 29 with verse 28.--He would conform us to the image of his son. From my blind faith, I went to better understanding. Everything, good or bad, that happened was to make me more like Jesus. That was really good!

Not that I have arrived, but when we keep our eyes on Jesus during problems and disappointment, we have his peace and his directions.

What is our part?

Do we love him?

Do we obey him?

Do we trust him to make things right in our life?

Isn't our God good!

MY PRAYER: *Lord, we want to please you. We want to be more like Jesus, to follow the example he gave us. Help us remember you are in charge when we go through difficult times. Thank you. We love you.*

MaryEmma

MAY 5

MY TEACHER

"Show me Your ways, Lord, teach me Your paths. Guide me in Your truth and teach me, for You are God my Savior, and my hope is in You all day long."
Psalm 25:4-5

This prayer says, "I want to know You, God. I want to be closer to You and understand what You want me to do and to be". It is a cry from the heart of one who really loves God. Can we say that?

Verse 1 says "I trust you" and verses 4-5 are step 2 of growing closer to God, "Guide me in Your truth and teach me". A good prayer as we open our Bible, asking God to open our heart to understand. "My hope is in You", could also say "my trust is in You". Hope and trust seem to be interchangeable in this prayer.

MY PRAYER: *Lord, we put our trust in you and that means that we hope in You. Not a 'maybe' but a confidence that you mean what You say. Help us to increase our trust. We love You.*

MaryEmma

MAY 6

HE DELIGHTS IN US

"In my distress I called to The Lord....He reached down from on high and took hold of me, he drew me out of deep waters. ... He rescued me because He delighted in me."
Psalm 18:6,16,19.

When I read that God delights in me. I can only say, "Thank You, Lord". It is hard to believe that he does, but I believe it because the scripture says so. It thrills my heart. God delights in me. I would think that would be so for some super Christian like David or Paul, but not for an ordinary Christian like me.

Can we remember this?

When we hurt, do we call on the Lord?

Do we believe that he delights in us?

MY PRAYER: *Thank you, Lord, for the reassurance of Your love for us. We know you love us, but that you delight in us is extra special. We love you. Thank You.*

MaryEmma

MAY 7

A GUARD

"Set a guard over my mouth, Lord; keep watch over the door of my lips. Do not let my heart be drawn to what is evil"
Psalm 141;3

Do we have trouble with our mouth? Do we need to make this a verse a daily prayer? Do we "open mouth and insert foot"? We criticize the Apostle Peter for speaking before he thinks, but what about us?

When we study his life we see a different Peter in Acts than we did in the gospels. Why? In the gospels Peter was using his natural personality. In the book of Acts, we see a Peter who was filled with the Holy Spirit and allowed him to direct his thoughts and words. In the flesh, we speak what is in our mind. When God's Spirit is in control, we speak his words.

I wish I could take back many foolish words I have spoken. I have wasted so many opportunities to witness for my God.

Does our mouth need a guard over it?

Will we talk to God about this and ask for his help?

MY PRAYER: *Lord God, you know our trouble. We live too much of our lives in the flesh instead of relying on your Spirit. It all depends on our heart condition and our thoughts. Help us keep our thoughts and eyes on you. We love you.*
MaryEmma

REJOICING COMES IN THE MORNING

"Sing the praises of the Lord...For His anger lasts only a moment, but His favor lasts a lifetime; weeping may stay for the night, but rejoicing comes in the morning."
Psalm 30: 4-5

God gives us wonderful promises. We go through bad times, but God promises us help and recovery. We are told to call on Him for help. We are told to praise Him, and that will help is to recognize him..

Praising Him takes our eyes off ourselves and turns our thoughts to our Lord. He promises rejoicing after a bad situation when we trust him. He is always with us and will help us, but He is also teaching us to know Him better. We do want to know Him better and to enjoy Him.

MY PRAYER: *Thank You, Lord, for Your wonderful promises. You are really special and we love You. Help us to turn to you and rejoice in you.*

MaryEmma

MAY 9

OUR GUIDE

"Great is The Lord, and most worthy of praise for this God is our God forever and ever; He will be our guide even to the end."
Psalm 48:1,14

How often do we think about how great our God is?

How often do we think about His love and His great blessings He has given us? I plead guilty to taking God for granted for not recognizing His blessings.

We have troubles, but He is there to guide us through and give us peace. When we don't know what to do, He is there to guide us and give us direction.

We are so blessed to know our Lord and Savior! God is great and worthy of praise. We can make verse 14 into a personal prayer to God.

Do we think often about how great he is?

Do we allow him to be our guide?

MY PRAYER: *Lord, thank You for being our guide, thank you for loving us and always being with us. You are great. We love You.*

MaryEmma

REJOICE AND SING

"For The Lord takes delight in His people; He crowns the humble with victory. Let His faithful people rejoice in this honor and sing for joy....may the praise of God be in their mouths."
Psalm 149:4,5,6

We are so blessed. He takes delight in us, He loves us and enjoy us.

We are to sing, and dance and rejoice in him. We are to praise Him with our mouth and in our hearts. Why? It pleases our Lord. He takes delight in us. Twice we are told to rejoice in Him. Do we enjoy God? Do we rejoice in Him?

We should rejoice because the Lord is near. We are never alone! He loves us and cares for us.

Shouldn't we praise our God?

Shouldn't we thank him?

Shouldn't we enjoy our Lord?

MY PRAYER: *Lord God, You are wonderful. We do rejoice in you and thank you. You are always with us. Help us to praise You as we go through our day. Make us more aware of your presence and your love. We love you.*

MaryEmma

MAY 11

GOD'S SPIRIT

*"They raised their voices in praise to the Lord and
sang: 'He is good; His love endures forever.'
Then the temple of the Lord was filled with a cloud... for
the glory of the Lord filled the temple of God."*
2 Chronicles 5: 13-14

This was the dedication of the temple of the Lord that Solomon built. The people were praising God, They praised Him with music and singing and the Lord's Spirit filled the temple.

Is that what happens in us when we praise the Lord?

Does our Lord's Spirit become one with our Spirit when we praise Him? Corinthians says that our bodies are God's temple. He loves us and He is with us in his Spirit.

I am sure that there are times when we disappoint the Lord, but also times when we please Him.

If we are honest, could we say we are pleasing our Lord?

Do we sing of his love?

Are we aware of the presence of his Spirit?

MY PRAYER: *I pray that today we will please you. We praise you and love you. We want to be more aware of you. You are a great and holy God.*

MaryEmma

MAY 12

HUMBLE OURSELVES

"...If my people, who are called by my name, will humble themselves and pray and seek my face and turn from their wicked ways, then I will hear ....I will forgive their sin and will heal their land."
2 Chronicles 7:12,14

God knows us and loves us. He knows that we will sin. He has prepared a way for us to be restored to Him, through confession and prayer.

God is holy and perfect and we cannot fellowship in our sinful nature. That is the reason He sent Jesus Christ to be our savior and die for us. His blood covers our sinfulness and we become His child when we accept Him.

Why is the first step to humble ourselves? If we go to God in our pride, it creates a barrier between us and He doesn't hear our prayers. The first step is humility and prayer, but the prayer must be to seek God, not to bless us, and to turn from our self-centered ways.

Is our first desire to seek God?

Will we confess our sins to be closer to him?

MY PRAYER: *Lord, we need you. Help us to remember to humble ourselves and confess our sins to you. Help us to remember your blessings we receive when we humble ourselves and pray. You are so wonderful. We love You.*

MaryEmma

MAY 13

OUR GREAT GOD!

*"Praise be to the Lord God... who alone does marvelous
deeds. Praise be to His glorious name forever; may the whole
earth be filled with His glory. Amen and Amen."*
Psalm 72:18-19

Solomon is celebrating his blessings. He is King. He has finished the building of the temple and his palace and he is known as the wisest man on earth.

He is praising God: The God who does wonderful deeds. God does wonderful deeds for us also. Do we even realize it is God who is blessing us? Solomon was blessed because he asked for wisdom to do his job instead of wealth. He wanted wisdom to help others instead of being blessed himself.

What do we pray for?

Do we pray for wisdom for our work?

Do we ask God for guidance for today?

Do we praise Him for what He does and for what He is going to do?

MY PRAYER: *Lord, give us a special awareness of how great You are and what You want us to do for others. We love you. Thank You.*

Mary Emma

MAY 14

TRUST, SUBMIT, ACKNOWLEDGE

"Trust in the Lord with all your heart and lean not on your own understanding; in all your ways submit to Him, and He will make your paths straight. Do not be wise in your own eyes."
Proverbs 3:5-7

Trust in The Lord and not in yourself. I "discovered" this verse when I was in my early 30's. At the time, I had a great desire to grow as a Christian and get to know the Lord better.

If I was to trust the Lord and not myself, I had to ask His advice more often. In addition to my morning prayers, I started asking God's advice on little things I wanted to do. Shall I go here; shall I buy this? It was a wonderful discipline that made me more aware of God.

Then I realized that I needed to start acknowledging God. It is hard to talk about God with people who are not interested, so I asked God to help me speak of Him in casual conversation just as I would mention Bob. I asked for help in giving God the credit for helping me without it being an effort on my part.

I wanted my references to God to be natural without being planned. I didn't want to sound phony. I wanted to please God. To share what he has taught me.

God has blessed me so much. I am not totally there yet. I still trust in myself too much and God too little, but He is helping me to grow in Him.

Who did we trust when we made that decision?

Do we give God the credit for our accomplishments?

Is He our partner through the day?

MY PRAYER: *Lord, I pray that we will trust You with all our heart and not just in our common sense. Guide us and direct us. Thank You. We love you.*
MaryEmma

DISCIPLINE

"My son, do not despise the Lord's discipline, and do not resent His rebuke, because the Lord disciplines those He loves, as a Father the son He delights in. Blessed are those who find wisdom, those who gain understanding."
Proverbs 3:11-13

Why do parents discipline their children? To correct, but also to teach. God has the same reason.

The Lord disciplines us to give us wisdom and understanding. I am of the age when discipline meant spanking. But my mother also disciplined me by giving me something to do to keep me busy. Her favorite was "sweep the dining room, kitchen and back porch." By the time I had finished that job I had forgotten what my problem was and peace was restored.

I learned what was acceptable and what wasn't. God is even wiser than my mother and He loves us more. He knows how to teach us and how much discipline we need to learn to learn the lesson. God disciplines us because we are His children and He loves us. He wants the best for us.

Do we resent His discipline?

How do we react to God's discipline?

Do we rebel? Are we defiant and angry?

MY PRAYER: *Lord, help us remember that You discipline us to help us find wisdom and understanding. Help us to cooperate with You and learn your perfect will for us. We love You.*

MaryEmma

MAY 16

TRUST TO PRAISE

"Praise the Lord. Praise God in His sanctuary; praise Him in...
Praise Him for... praise Him with...Let everything that
has breath praise the Lord. Praise the Lord."
Psalm 150: 1,6

We have to trust God to be able to praise Him. Trust is really important in our relationship with Him and praising Him helps us to trust Him. Praise comes from the heart, not from the head. When we are aware of the love of God, we praise and thank Him.

The psalmist praised Him "in" and then praised Him "for" and then praised Him "with". I thought that was interesting. We are to praise Him with all our being. When I am thanking God, the emphasis is on myself and him. When I am praising God, the emphasis is on God. Praising keeps God on the throne of our lives.

Have we praised Him today?

Do we love him enough to praise him?

Do we trust him enough to praise him?

MY PRAYER: *Lord, we praise you for Your greatness. You are worthy of all praise for you made all things and have Their being in you. You are wonderful. We love you.*

MaryEmma

MAY 17

LOVE ONE ANOTHER

"As the Father has loved me, so have I loved you. Now remain in my love…. My command is this: Love each other as I have loved you."
John 15:9,12

Love one another is our command. How well do we obey?

On a recent trip, I saw a man whose appearance I was critical of. My reaction was not love! And God immediately reminded me that I was wrong. I felt guilty and did not forget that feeling of shame. Guess what the lesson on Sunday was?

Love one another! God wasn't finished with me.

It is so important that we love one another. That is the way the world will know we are Christians, "by our love for each other".

The most important commands in the entire Bible are summed up in two: Love the Lord and love your neighbor.

1 Corinthians 13 even gives us a checklist on the quality of our love.

What am I to do about my critical attitude?

Do I need to pray about this?

Do we need to pray about the love for others in our hearts?

MY PRAYER: *Lord, make my heart right. Fill my heart with an awareness of you and your love. Help my love for you be so great that it overflows into love for my neighbor.*

MaryEmma

DISTANT OR INTIMATE

"Why, my soul, are you downcast? Why so disturbed within me? Put your hope in God, for I will yet praise him, my Savior and my God."
Psalm 42:5

Is our God a distant God? Or is He an intimate God?

Do we thirst for fellowship with Him? Can we skip a day of prayer, a day of reading His word without feeling empty at the end of the day? Our God is a loving and intimate Lord.

Why are there days when we are depressed or feel negative or are stressed?

Could it be that we have pushed God away?

Could the solution be to praise our Lord and Savior?

Have we put our hope in our God?

MY PRAYER: *Lord, we need you. We try to go without you until we are in trouble or depressed, and then you remind us that we have not been with you enough to feel your hope and your love. Help us to praise you for who You are. We love you. Thank you for always being here for us.*

MaryEmma

MAY 19

CRY FOR HELP

*"You are my strength, I watch for You; You, God, are
my fortress, my God on whom I can rely...."*
Psalm 59:9,10

This Psalm opens with a cry for help. He is worrying about his life, and he tells God all about his fears. As he talks to God his fears turn into hope and he remembers how strong and capable God is. As he realizes the greatness of God, his fears turn into praise. At first he may be reassuring himself, but his heart takes over from his mind and he just starts loving God.

This is praise. It is loving God. At first we may be repeating words, but as we continue to praise God, our Spirit joins God's Spirit and we know that he is in control.

Is this how we pray when we are needy?

How do we show our love for God?

Do we share our needs with him?

MY PRAYER: *Holy God, we love You. You are our strength, You are our fortress and refuge when we are in trouble. Thank You for all you do for us. You are wonderful and we love you.*

MaryEmma

MAY 20

KING OF GLORY

"Who is this King of glory? The Lord strong and mighty,
the Lord mighty in battle. Who is He, this King of glory?
The Lord Almighty--He is The King of glory."
Psalm 21:8-10

The Lord is mighty in battle. We are not running for our lives or in active combat, but we do have our battles. We battle our emotions, our physical pain, our relationships with others.

What do we do when we are having a bad day?

We need to let The King of glory come in. Only our Lord can give us true peace; only our Lord can show us the way out of the battle.

What do we do when we feel the world is against us:

Do we allow The Lord Almighty to fight our battles for us?

Do we trust him to help us?

MY PRAYER: *We thank you and praise you, Lord Almighty.* You are The King of glory! You are strong and mighty. Help us to trust you and love you and worship you.

MaryEmma

MAY 21

MOVED BY THE SPIRIT

"Moved by the Spirit… the child Jesus…Simeon took Him in his arms and praised God, saying: Sovereign Lord, as you have promised, you may now dismiss Your servant in peace….for my eyes have seen your salvation."
Luke 2:27-30

First the shepherds, and now an old man in the temple.

What is going on in the minds of Mary and Joseph? Were they bewildered?

God was confirming His message to them. We can think we know what God is telling us to do, and then we start having doubts, 'maybe I misunderstood'. God is in control of our lives and will teach us when we allow Him. What are we to do when we start having doubts about our choices?

We can open our Bible and read and pray, asking for guidance, and God always responds at the right time. Sometimes we need more time to understand what He says.

Are we listening?

Do we read his word for worship and information?

Do we ask him for guidance?

MY PRAYER: *Lord, we pray for guidance and understanding. We pray for wisdom to help us be obedient to you. Thank you for your love and your presence. We love you.*

MaryEmma

MAY 22

HE IS OUR TEACHER

"This is what the Lord says—Your Redeemer, the Holy One of Israel: "I am The Lord your God, who teaches you what is best for you, who directs you in the way you should go."
Isaiah 48: 17

We are blessed to have a God who loves us. We are so blessed to have a God who wants to be a part of our lives, not be a remote God.

He doesn't want us to struggle or get lost in the process of living. He wants to teach us, not just information, but what is best for us. He wants to show us the way so we will walk his way and not to get lost.

Are we willing to allow God this much access to our lives?

Will we let him guide us?

Do we have an humble Spirit?

MY PRAYER: *Lord, Show us the way we should go. Teach us to do your will, for you are our God. We want your spirit to lead us. We love you.*

MaryEmma

NASTY PRIDE

"There are six things the Lord hates, seven that are detestable to Him: haughty eyes....,"
Proverbs 6:16

What does God want from us? How are we to act? He has given us a list.

Most of them sound bad and we avoid them, but the first one doesn't sound so bad, does it? Haughty eyes would be pride. How can pride be as bad as murder? Is pride thinking: "I am great" or "I am better than others" or is it "Thank You, God, I can do this myself. I don't need Your help"?

I discovered a verse in Habakkuk that surprised me: It said that an evil person is puffed up, is full of pride. A righteous person is humble and faithful.

Pride is being 'puffed up' and is the opposite of faith.

Should we examine ourselves to see if we are puffed up?

Are we prideful?

Should we talk to God about pride?

MY PRAYER: *Lord, help us to recognize when our pride is pushing you out of our lives. Make us more aware of your presence and your love. We want to please you.*

MaryEmma

MAY 24

"Dear friends, if our hearts do not condemn us, we have
confidence before God and receive from Him anything we ask,
because we keep His commands and do what pleases Him."
1John 3:21,22

Do we please God? How often do we think about pleasing God? Is that a priority for us or do we think only about Him pleasing us? If that is a condition of having our prayers answered, maybe we need to think about it.

Could we start by showing our love for Him? Spending time with Him in prayer, meditating on His word, and just enjoying Him. How often do we take time to just visit with Him, telling Him how great He is, confessing our sins to Him and thanking Him?

We need to listen as well as talk. Have we ever had a friend who talks so much it is difficult to say anything? Sometimes that is what our prayers sound like. God speaks often through His word. He answers by giving us peace and joy in our spirit. God is always with us, loving us and wanting the best for us.

Do we love Him?

Do we enjoy Him?

MY PRAYER: *Lord, we do love You and want to please You. Give us a greater awareness of You and of Your commands. We want to spend more time with You, but sometimes we get busy and we forget You. Forgive us. Thank You.*

MaryEmma

MAY 25

THE WORD IS FLAWLESS

"Every word of God is flawless; He is a shield
to those who take refuge in Him."
Proverbs 30:5

The word of God is written down for us and is very special. We are blessed to have it in printed form. Early Christians were not that fortunate. It truly is a shield. When I am upset, lonely or afraid, that is where I turn and it gives me peace and comfort. It assures me that God is in control and everything is ok, no matter what may happen. He is in control and He loves me.

How can we worry and fret when God is in control?

Do we believe God's word is flawless?

Is He our shield?

MY PRAYER: *Lord, thank you for your word. Thank you it is so easy to have your book in our hands to read and feel your protection. I am afraid that we take it for granted and don't appreciate it as we should. Forgive us and continue to be our shield. We love you.*

MaryEmma

MAY 26

ACKNOWLEDGE AND SUBMIT

"In all your ways acknowledge Him, and He will make your paths straight."
Proverbs 3:6

I have always connected this verse with the one above, but recently I have been thinking of it alone. I always thought it meant to acknowledge God to others, to witness, but maybe it means acknowledge God to ourselves!

How often do we go through the day without thinking of Him? We are so busy, being and doing, that God is ignored? He is not our highest priority. Is He disappointed?

We let little sins pile up without confessing them because we are not close enough to Him to hear His promptings. One translation uses the word submit instead of acknowledge.

Are we willing to submit?

Will we acknowledge God to ourselves and others?

Is He important in our lives?

MY PRAYER: *Lord, we want to submit our way to you, but our will gets in the way. Please help us be more aware of you and your perfect desires for us.*

MaryEmma

ALARMED

"Alarmed, King Jehoshaphat resolved to inquire of the Lord... 'Lord, the God of our ancestors, are you not the God who is in heaven?
... Power and might are in your hand, and no one can withstand you....
For we have no power...but our eyes are on You.'"
2 Chronicles 20:3,6,12

An army was coming to attack Judah, so they had a prayer meeting. What do we do when we are fearful? When we worry about our health, our jobs, our family, what do we do? We have limited power, but God doesn't. Do we go to Him in prayer to ask for help? Do we ask others to pray with us? Or do we keep our pride and fret?

God answered them. He told them to not be afraid or discouraged, He would take care of it. God told them that the battle was not theirs but His.

They were faithful and God was faithful. The battle is always in God's hands.

Will we allow God to fight our battles for us?

Do we prefer to fight them our way?

Do we need to talk to God about this?

MY PRAYER: *Lord, you are always faithful. We thank you and love you. You always answer when we call to you. Forgive us for thinking if you don't say yes, that you haven't answered. You are in control. You are great!*
MaryEmma.

SPLENDOR OR HIS HOLINESS

"Have faith in the Lord Your God and you will be upheld; have faith in His prophets and you will be successful.' After consulting the people, Jehoshaphat appointed men to sing to the Lord and to praise Him for the splendor of His holiness...."
2 Chronicles 20:2

They were in despair until they turned to God for help. The message was to have faith in God and you will be upheld.

To increase that faith they began to praise Him and sing His praises.

God acted! He saved them from the enemy. All they did was to praise their God. He started setting ambushes against the enemy and they were defeated. God is powerful. He can take care of us.

Did you notice that they praised Him for the "splendor of His holiness"? Maybe we could add that to our prayers. Praise Him for the splendor of His holiness! God is holy.

We have a wonderful God.

MY PRAYER: *Lord God, you want us to praise you and give thanks to you instead of worrying. We want to do that, but we need your help to remember how to handle fear. We love you.*

MaryEmma

HE IS WATCHING FOR US

"Listen to me…The Lord is with you when you are with Him. If you seek Him, He will be found by you, but if you forsake Him, He will forsake you."
2 Chronicles15: 1-5

This is wonderful advice for us today and we need to remember it. The Lord is with us always, but when we turn away from him, it puts a distance between us. We move away from our Lord and God.

Asa was the grandson of Solomon. Because of Solomon's sins of turning to other gods, the Kingdom was torn apart. The prophet met Asa and gave him encouragement and truth. Asa knew and loved God and his heart was pure and he destroyed the detestable idols and repaired the altar of the Lord.

Whenever we seek the Lord, we will be found by him. He never leaves us alone, He is always watching and waiting for us to call on him.

Isn't that simple? We don't have to do hard and difficult things to find the Lord. Just call him.

Will we reach out to Him in faith and trust Him?

Will we confess our sins so He can make us white as snow?

MY PRAYER: *Lord, we love you and we want you in our lives. Help us to be more aware of your presence and spend time with you. Thank you for your watchful eye.*

MaryEmma

MAY 30

BE STILL

"He says, 'Be still, and know that I am God; I will be exalted among the nations, I will be exalted in the earth."
Psalm 46:10

When we are too busy, we become tense and detached from God. He tells us to be still. When we are quiet, we can hear his words. We can understand what He wants. That is when we recognize him as our God, close and loving, not remote and uninterested.

When I read these words of this verse, I can almost feel the tension leaving my body and peace coming in. He wants us to know him, to enjoy him. He wants to protect us. We are his children.

We are so busy. Even when we don't have anything to do that is important, we keep our minds busy-cluttered with unimportant stuff, and it crowds out God. We need to make time in our day to stop, still our mind, and know God. Let His Spirit dwell in our hearts and minds.

MY PRAYER: *Lord, we want to be more aware of you and your presence. Help us 'be still', and think of you instead of trivial things. You are our Lord and Savior and we love you.*

MaryEmma

MAY 31

OBEDIENCE

*"Go from your country, your people and your Father's household to the land
I will show you. I will make you into a great nation, and I will bless you*
Genesis 12:1-2

Abraham was obedient. He did what God told him to do and left his
home that he knew to follow God's direction without really knowing where
God would lead him. Would we do that?

He tells very few people to leave their home and family, but He tells
all of us to follow him, to follow His directions. To know His directions,
we have to listen for that quiet voice that His Spirit whispers to us. To hear
that voice, we must spend time with Him. We need a three-course meal
with Him, not just a quick snack.

Do we spend time with Him?

Do we think, "bless me and bless mine," an adequate prayer?

Are we obedient to Him?

MY PRAYER: *I pray that we will be aware of you today: Aware of your love
and power and wisdom. We obey when we trust. Help us to trust. We love you.*
MaryEmma

JUNE 1

WALK STEADFASTLY

"Jotham ...did what was right in the eyes of the Lord,
just as his father Uzziah had done...
Jotham grew powerful because he walked
steadfastly before the Lord his God."
2 Chronicles 27:1,2,6

God blessed the King because he "walked steadfastly before the Lord". God blesses us when we walk with Him.

Only God sees our heart and knows our attitude and motives. That is what He looks at, not our actions but the condition of our heart that controls our actions.

God blesses us according to what we need. The King was blessed with influence and wealth and respect and hopefully with love in his family. God may bless us that way. The best blessing we can receive is peace and joy in our hearts from God our Father plus love in our family and love for others.

This is what is important to God and as we grow in our love for God our love for others grows. We become less self-centered and more concerned for others.

MY PRAYER: *Lord God, keep us close to you. As we walk through the day, help us to keep our eyes on you. Help us to be aware of your presence, both in good times and in not so good. You are great and we love you.*

MaryEmma

JUNE 2

LAST DAYS

"In the last days....
*"Come, let us go up to the mountain of the Lord... He will teach us
His ways, so that we may walk in His paths."....He will judge ...will
settle disputes...Nation will not take up sword against nation."*
Isaiah 2:3-5

There is turmoil all around us, in the world and in our communities. Sometimes it is good to look ahead and see the peace that we will have in the last days, when we allow God to be in control of our lives.

Isaiah was trying to get God's children to return to Him, to love Him and worship Him, so He was showing them what the future would look like so they could remember this promise when things got worse.

The world is not at peace yet, but we can be when we spend time with God, when we allow Him to "teach us His ways", so that we can "walk in His paths". It is the inner peace and joy that God gives us when we walk with him.

Are we at peace?

Do we have joy in our lives?

Are we walking close to the Lord?

MY PRAYER: *Lord God, we want to be close to you, we want to walk with you. Forgive us when we get too busy to have time for you. Only in you can we have overflowing peace and joy. Thank you for your wonderful gifts. We love you.*

MaryEmma

JUNE 3

WHAT IS GOOD?

"He has shown you, O mortal, what is good. And what does the Lord require of you? To act justly and to love mercy and to walk humbly with Your God."
Micah 6:8

What is the condition of our heart? This verse tells us what our Lord wants it to be. God is fed up with the empty worship of His people. He sounds like the frustrated parent of a rebellious teenager: "My people, what have I done to you?

He reminds them He brought them out of slavery in Egypt, He gave them a home. What do they want?

He doesn't want sacrifices of burnt offering; He wants our heart. God does not want empty worship that our bodies go through; He wants worship that comes from the heart. I am not sure we Christians from the 21st century are any better at worship than the children of Israel. It is more fun to "do something" than to be still let God tell us what to do.

Are we walking humbly with him?

Do we spend time alone with him?

Do we share out needs and love?

MY PRAYER: *Lord God, you are the greatest. You give us so much that we become puffed up and full of ourselves. In our hearts we really want to be filled with your Spirit, but we just go with the flow of this world. Forgive us.*
MaryEmma

JUNE 4

"There are six things the Lord hates seven that are detestable to him:...
False witness who pours out lies and a person who
stirs up conflict in the community."
Proverbs 6: 19

Why would God detest gossip? What is so terrible about a lie?

Could it be because the first and second commandments are to love? We don't show love to a person when we lie to them. We are trying to lead them astray, to fool them into believing something that is not true.

Because we love one another, we are to offer peace to those around us. One who deliberately creates unrest is one who doesn't love, but is angry or resentful. He wants the opposite of love for another. What is the condition of the heart of a person who lies and creates conflict? Isn't it filled with hate and resentment ?

What is the answer for this problem?

The only answer for hate is to allow God into our hearts and mind: A checklist for us:

Do we act justly?

Do we love mercy?

Do we love God?

MY PRAYERS: Lord, forgive us when we act unjustly. If we want to lie or create problems for another, give us a reminder of who you are and what you want for us. You are a God of Love. You gave your life for us. Help us to love as you love.

MaryEmma

JUNE 5

WOE TO ME

> *"... I saw the Lord, high and exalted, seated on a throne...*
> *'Woe to me!' I cried. 'I am a man of unclean lips, ... and*
> *my eyes have seen the King, The Lord Almighty.'"*
> Isaiah 6 1,5

When we come into the presence of God, we become very aware of our sins. I realized that fact this morning when I was reading my devotional about this verse. I found myself thinking that 'I can't think of any sins I committed yesterday', Then I was just struck in the heart with a spiritual arrow. "Yes, I did sin!" I was very impatient and irritable. This is a sin I know from reading 1 Corinthians 13.

Love is not irritable and love is not impatient. I have been both with Bob, the person I love most in all the world. I have been praying about this a lot and thought I was ok.

Yesterday at lunch, I sat down to be served and Bob went to the stir-fry bar. No one came to take my order. No water, no breadbasket, I was just ignored. I was thinking "Bob will be here with his food, before I even give my order!" and I was becoming very irritable and impatient. Finally, someone came and she was very nice and I was nice—on the outside! I was very impatient and irritable inside. God knew and he was displeased. My attitude was wrong.

Do we trust God with the use of our time?

Do we forget that He is always in control?

Do we want to please God?

MY PRAYER: *Lord, I want to be aware of your presence, but yesterday at lunch, I pushed you into the closet, and ignored you! I ask for forgiveness, and for cleansing of my heart. Help me to be more aware of you and less self-centered. I love you.*

Mary Emma

JUNE 6

"How you have fallen from heaven, morning star, son of the dawn! …
You said…"I will ascend to the heavens; I will raise my throne above
the stars of God; … I will make myself like the Most High."
Isaiah 14:12-14

This is the definition of pride. Making ourselves important, wanting to be in control. Theologians think this passage refers to Lucifer, and angel of God, who decided to overthrow God. We call him Satan, or the devil. But isn't it a good example of what happens within us sometimes?

We make our plans without regard to God's plans for us. We don't want to "bother Him" with little things-- but what is 'big' to God? We are to tell Him about anything that makes us anxious and not to use our common sense. We think we can handle it without God's help.

Pride slips into my life too often, too easily. I was walking down the hall recently; I can walk faster than many residents here and I caught myself thinking, "I am in better shape than most people here," and then I realized what I was doing! I was taking credit for my ability instead of thanking God. The sin of pride slips into us so easily!

Do we give God credit for his gifts?

Do we want to be important in other people's eyes?

Do we thank God for his blessings?

MY PRAYER: *I pray that today we will be aware of this sin of pride that pops into our hearts without warning and ask God's help to thank Him instead our taking credit for the abilities that God has given us. "Lord, make us aware of the sin of pride that is within us."*

MaryEmma

JUNE 7

SEEK THE LORD

> "... *Hezekiah ... doing what was good and right
> and faithful before the Lord His God.
> In everything ... he sought His God and worked
> wholeheartedly. And so he prospered.*"
> 2 Chronicles 31: 20-21

Do we seek the Lord in everything we do, or just the spiritual things?

Our Lord and Savior loves us more than anyone in the world and wants only the best for us. Why do we not confer with Him about our plans?

Some questions to consider:

How important is God in our daily life?

Do we include God in our plans for the day?

Do we discuss our decisions with Him?

MY PRAYER: *Lord, we love you and we don't plan to neglect you. We just get busy and forget what is important. Please give us a greater awareness of your presence with us. Thank You.*

MaryEmma

JUNE 8

PRAISE GOD

"... Hezekiah prayed...: "You alone are God over all ... listen to the words Sennacherib has sent to ridicule the living God....Now, Lord our God, deliver us ... so that all ...may know that You alone, Lord, are God."
2 Kings 19:14-19

Judah was in trouble. The Assyrian kings were coming to attack. What is Hezekiah to do? He can turn to God for help or he can make his own decisions. He has done both during his reign, just as we have made both good and bad decisions in our lives. This time, he goes straight to God for help.

Notice his prayer. He starts with praising God, not with asking for help. Why is he so slow in getting around to what he wants?

Praising God is concentrating on God. We find it easier to thank Him than to praise Him. Why? When we thank Him the emphasis is on us. When we praise Him all the emphasis is on Him, our great and glorious God. As we praise God and review His great powers and what He has done in the past and present, it gives us confidence. Our hearts move from fear to confidence. It changes the emphasis from me to God. I can't do anything, but God can. In verse 35 it says: "That night the angel of The Lord went out" and destroyed the enemy! Wow!

Do we praise God?

When do we praise God?

MY PRAYER: *We praise you, Lord. You are great and holy. You are love. With your love and power, you created the world and us. You did it without our help. Forgive us for thinking that we are so important. Our job is to love and praise you.*

MaryEmma

JUNE 9

PERFECT PEACE

"You will keep in perfect peace those whose minds are steadfast, because they trust in You. Trust in the Lord forever, for the Lord, the Lord Himself, is the Rock eternal."
Isaiah 26:3-4

What a beautiful promise we have from God. Peace. Some people search the world over and spend money trying to find peace when it is available to all.

It is a two-way deal: we trust and God gives peace. He gives peace to those whose thoughts are centered on God.

God-centered thoughts + trust = peace.

Is it easy to trust God in difficult times? We have to love Him to trust Him, and we have to know Him to love Him. We have to spend time with Him to know Him. But again, God makes that easy. He has given us His written word, He encourages us to talk to Him, and His presence is always with us.

Other people create problems for us but God promises to 'make all things work out for good' when we love Him. Can we believe Him? It is a beautiful promise God has given us: peace in exchange for trust.

MY PRAYER: *Thank You Lord, for Your promise of peace when we trust You. Help us remember that worry means we are not trusting You. We love You.*
MaryEmma

JUNE 10

PERFECTION

"Lord, You are my God; I will exalt You and praise Your name, for in perfect faithfulness You have done wonderful things, things planned long ago."
Isaiah 25:1

When we are in perfect peace, we can open our hearts and minds to God and just love Him.

We can show our love by praising Him and remembering all the wonderful things He has done. We can look out the window and see the nature He created and look at buildings and marvel at the wisdom and talent He has given man.

What do we praise God for most often?

Do we praise him for his plans?

Do we praise him for what he has done?

MY PRAYER: *Lord, You are so wonderful. You do so much for us today as well as preparing a beautiful world to live in. You give us peace; You give us unconditional love. You are worthy of all love and glory and praise.*

MaryEmma

JUNE 11

WE LONG FOR GOD

"Lord, be gracious to us; we long for you. Be our strength
every morning, our salvation in time of distress."
Isaiah 33:2

This is a beautiful prayer for those going through a time of distress, or for those who are having a perfect day.

It comes from a heart that longs to be close to God.

Do we long for Him, or are we too busy to even think of Him through the day? Is our mind so filled with activities and busyness and entertainment that God get pushed aside?

It happens to all of us from time to time! Perhaps we should ask God to make us long for Him, to increase our desire to be aware of His presence, to enjoy Him.

God wants to have fellowship with us. The president made a trip to Oklahoma recently. I would be impressed if the president of the United States wanted to spend a few minutes with me, just to know me better, but do I want to spend time with the great God, the one and only true and living God, the Creator of the Universe?

Do we long for God?

Do we want to spend time with him, one on one?

Is he our strength and salvation?

MY PRAYER: *Give us a great awareness of You and help us to realize all that You do for us, things that we take for granted. Give us a desire to spend more quality time with you. We love You.*

MaryEmma

JUNE 12

TRUST INSTEAD OF FEAR

"Say to those with fearful hearts, 'Be strong, do not fear;
Your God will come ... to save you... the eyes of the blind be
opened ... lame leap like a deer... mute tongue shout for joy."
Isaiah 35:4-6

Sometimes when we watch the news and see what is happening around the world, we become fearful.

God is telling His children not to fear, to trust Him. Isaiah is reassuring Judah with prophesies about the last days. God will punish the wicked and gather His people to Himself and all will be wonderful. Isaiah is telling them what the world can be and will be when all sin is eliminated.

They are watching their brothers in Israel become prisoners because of their sinful ways. During Hezekiah's reign, they have turned back to worshiping God, but when a new king comes, they turn away from God again and they will be sent to Babylon as prisoners.

Bad things happen in the world and bad things happen to us, but we have a heavenly Father who watches over us and helps us keep our eyes on Him. He gives us the strength we need until the world is perfect.

Do we trust our Lord to watch over us?

Do we look to him for strength?

Do worship him?

MY PRAYER: *Lord, thank You that we can trust You. You promise us better times, safe times. Thank You for Your reassurances in difficult times. We love You.*
MaryEmma

JUNE 13

POWER

"Rejoice always, pray unceasingly, in everything give thanks...."
1 Thessalonians 5:16-18

These are favorites verses. God "gave them to me" when we first moved to Philly and it helped me adjust to the changes in our lifestyle.

It continues to bless me. This morning my devotional was on obedience. When I finished reading, I asked God, "Have I been disobedient?" and immediately "rejoice always" popped into my mind. I did not rejoice during the weekend. I didn't feel good and I laid around and napped and changed channels on TV trying to find something to interest me. I did not have peace but didn't recognize it. I wish my body and my mind didn't work together, but I do have power over my mind when I rejoice. I immediately started thanking God this morning and the joy started creeping in, in spite of the tiredness of my body. Those three little phrases bring me out of myself and into the presence of God so often. But the verses are really backward. I can't rejoice until I start praying and thanking God, Then the joy joins them.

MY PRAYER: *Thank You, Lord, for these words that give me such joy and hope because they turn my mind to You. Thank You for Your love and protection.*
MaryEmma

PAY ATTENTION

"... I am the Lord your God, who teaches you what is best ... directs you. If only you had paid attention to my commands, your peace... like a river, your well-being like waves of the sea.'"
Isaiah 48: 17-18

If we had only paid attention to His words how much better off we would be. Why don't we pay attention to God's commands? He only wants the best for us. When we ignore him we create problems for ourselves. We do not know what is best for us. We only trust ourselves.

He gives us the beautiful promise of teaching us what is best for us, and He will show us the way to go.

Could we ask for anything any better?

We have His written word, we have his Spirit who teaches us how to talk and listen to Him in prayer.

What more could we ask of the Creator of the universe?

Could we ask for a better Savior?

What more do we want from the creator of the universe?

Why don't we listen?

MY PRAYER: *Thank you for teaching us. Thank you for the peace like a river flowing through us. We love you.*

MaryEmma

JUNE 15

PIERCED FOR US

*"But He was pierced for our transgressions, He was crushed
for our iniquities; the punishment that brought us peace
was on Him; and by His wounds we are healed.*
Isaiah 53:5

Isaiah was prophesying of Jesus and what would happen to Him, many years before it happened. The entire chapter tells what He will do for us and what was done to Him because of God's love for us.

It is good to stop and think about the blessings we have received because of God's love. We don't deserve his love. We are selfish and insist on our own way and yet God continues to teach us and guide us when we let Him. Why does he put up with us?

He loves us so much he died for us.

Do we love him?

What are we willing to do for him?

Will we allow him access into our lives?

MY PRAYER: *Lord God, thank You for Your blessings. You show us love each day and continue to forgive us when we don't show our love for You. You are wonderful.*

MaryEmma

JUNE 16

GOD IS # 1

""As the heavens are higher than the earth, so are my ways higher than your ways and my thoughts than your thoughts.
Isaiah 55: 9

This is our God talking to us. He knows everything and He knows all about us.

Proverbs tells us to trust God, not our own common sense. This is what God is telling us. Talk to Him, find out what He wants for us. Let Him teach us and guide us. Why are we so stubborn and prideful? All that we have is a gift from our Lord and God. He loves us and wants the best for us.

At the time this was spoken, the children of Israel were turning away from Him to worship the world.

Do we worship our Lord?

Do we talk to him and listen to him?

Will he praise him for his power?

MY PRAYER: *I pray that our heart and mind will stay true to you. Give us the knowledge of Your will for us with all the wisdom and understanding that Your Spirit gives. Thank You.*

MaryEmma

JUNE 17

GOD'S ARM

*"Surely the arm of the Lord is not too short to save, nor His ear too
dull to hear. But your iniquities have separated you from your God;
your sins have hidden His face from you, so He will not hear."*
Isaiah 59:1-2

Does it seem strange that God is not answering our prayers? Could it be that we have been disobedient? Many times I don't recognize my sins until I specifically ask God, "Have I sinned?" and the answer is always yes, with a reminder of what I have done. It may be a thought or a word. Usually it is an attitude.

I love these verses because they make me smile. It is almost tongue in check. Is His arm too short to reach you? Is God hard of hearing? I don't expect that in the Bible, but it does get the point across that it is not God, but us that needs a checkup.

Will we ask him to show us our sins?

Do we feel separated and distant from our God?

Do we need to talk to God about our sins?

MY PRAYER: *Lord God, we don't like to admit, even to ourselves than we have sinned. We have excuses, like we are busy, or I have to pay the rent, someone needs me. Help us to recognize that we need you, for love, forgiveness and leading. We love you.*

MaryEmma

JUNE 18

DELIGHT GREATLY

"I delight greatly in the Lord; my soul rejoices in my God.
For He has clothed me with garments of salvation and
arrayed me in a robe of His righteousness...."
Isaiah 61:10

Don't we have a wonderful God? He has done so much for us. Only in him do we have salvation. Only through him do we have righteousness. His love and blessing are unbelievable but true.

We can make this verse into a prayer of thanksgiving and praise. How often do we stop to thank our Lord and Savior for salvation?

I am guilty about taking our Spiritual Father for granted. He has blessed us in so many ways! It is good to stop and think about our blessings and enjoy him.

We always find time to complain about blessings we don't have at the moment! Do we thank Him for the ones He has given us?

Do we delight in our Lord?

Do we rejoice in him?

Do we allow him to fill us with his joy?

MY PRAYER: *Lord, bless us today as our hearts rejoice with gratitude at knowing you, our great God. You are wonderful and we love you and thank you for all you do for us.*

MaryEmma

JUNE 19

GOD'S PLANS

"See, I will create new heavens and a new earth. The former
things will not be remembered, nor will they come to mind.
Be glad and rejoice forever in what I will create...."
Isaiah 65: 17-18

God told Isaiah centuries ago that someday he would create a new heaven and new earth. When we read the last 2 chapters of Revelations, we see that promise again, but this time, he has given us details of the new city and our life in it.

I am amazed and thrilled as I read through the Old Testament to see how the old and the new compliment each other. Jesus came to fulfill the law given in the Old Testament, and both are filled with His love for us and His desire for us to love Him and worship Him. He is not selfish, He just wants the very best for us and that is only through Him.

Isaiah is still trying to get the children of Israel to repent. He has told them that God will punish them by taking them into captivity until they repent. Then he will restore them. Now he is telling them of the final times; the last days when our Lord will return and there will be only good in the world; all who love Him will be with Him.

Do we need to repent as the Israelites did?

What do we require to humble ourselves before the Lord?

Do we look forward to the new city?

MY PRAYER: *Thank You for the promises of our future time with you. We are so glad that you are with us now on this present earth. You always want the best for us. Thank you. We love you.*

MaryEmma

JUNE 20

CONTRITE

*"These are the ones I look on with favor: those who are humble
and contrite in spirit, and who tremble at my word."*
Isaiah 66:2

Who does God favor? What can we do to please God?

Be humble; realize that we are not god and we are not in charge of the events in our lives. What is contrite in Spirit? It is awareness that we need God to guide us through life- dependence on Him; it is humility.

How do we treat His word? I hope with awe and respect and love, because He is teaching us about the life He wants us to live.

This is the last chapter in Isaiah and he has preached his heart out to his people but they won't listen. They go through the rituals of sacrifice and worship, but their heart isn't worshipping, only their bodies. Their heart wants to get back into the world and indulge in the worship of the idols of the day.

Where is our heart and mind as we sit in church?

Where is our heart and mind the other six days of the week?

Are our eyes fixed on Jesus?

MY PRAYER: *Lord, help our hearts to be humble and open to your spirit. We love you and thank you for Your love.*

MaryEmma

172

JUNE 21

FEET LIKE A DEER

"Yet I will rejoice in the Lord, I will be joyful in God my Savior.
The Sovereign Lord is my strength; He makes my feet like the
feet of a deer, He enables me to tread on the heights."
Habakkuk 3:18-19

What does it mean to have feet like a deer? They have to be sure footed; not to fall on the rocks and rough places of the mountains. We need to walk securely in this world; to be safe during adversity.

This little letter from the prophet Habakkuk tells us how we are react to adversity.

God is disciplining His people for worshipping things other than himself. Times are bad; how are we to act?

This is a formula for life during hard times: rejoice, not because things are good, but because God is with us. He is our Savior; He is our strength. That strength is compared to the feet of a nimble deer, which can exist high in the mountains where humans couldn't. That is why we can rejoice when things go bad. We have our Lord and Savior with us.

Do we rejoice when times are difficult?

Does the thought of God's presence help us?

Can we rejoice because he is near?

MY PRAYER: *Lord, you are great. You provide every thing we need for this life. Forgive us for not recognizing it, for not trusting. You always give us what we need at the moment; neither too early or too late. Thank you.*

MaryEmma

WISE DISCIPLINE

> *"...Because You have not listened to my words.... will*
> *serve the King of Babylon seventy years....*
> *But when the seventy years are fulfilled, I will punish*
> *the King of Babylon and His nation...."*
> Jeremiah 25:8,12

God disciplines us, but with love. The children of Israel had started worshipping things of the world instead of the one true and living God. The ten tribes had been sent into captivity to Assyria. Now Judah was being sent to Babylon. God knew how long it would take for them to realize the truth of who He was. He didn't send them with out hope. He told them they would be there 70 years and He told them to "bloom where they were planted;" to makes lives for themselves.

It is like God took a willful rebellious child, turned him over His lap and spanked him. But He did it with love as an earthly father would do.

It gives us hope today because when God disciplines us, we know that He is doing it "for our own good" as my mother used to say. He is wise and loving; he knows what is best for us.

What is God trying to teach us today?

Have we talked to him about our difficulty?

Have we asked him what he wants us to do?

MY PRAYER: *Lord, you are so wonderful. You discipline us but with love, not to punish us, but to teach us. You want to bless us and give us the best. Thank you.*
Mary Emma

JUNE 23

UNDERSTANDING

"He made the earth by His power; He founded the world by His wisdom and stretched out the heavens by His understanding."
Jeremiah 51: 15

I started my prayer time this morning with this praise verse. I changed the 'He' to 'You' and made it personal. As I prayed the words to Him, I felt His love fill me.

This verse tells us so much about our God. He has power and He has wisdom. We expect that, but a third virtue is mentioned: understanding.

Power and wisdom we expect from a great God; He could be great but remote, but understanding means that He is special. He is involved; He cares about us!

How many people with power can relate to a poor hurting individual? Yet our God does. He knows us and loves us. He cares about us and wants to give us guidance and direction so we won't make mistakes. He gives us comfort and love.

When we hurt, do we turn to God for help?

Do we turn to food or entertainment, when we feel empty?

Do we turn to an understanding God?

MY PRAYER: *Lord God, we love you. We thank you that you are involved in our lives and you understand our needs and worries. We can trust you for the help we need. You are wonderful to us.*

MaryEmma

COMPASSIONS

"Yet this I call to mind and therefore I have hope:
Because of the Lord's great love we are not consumed,
For His compassions never fail.
Lamentations 3:21-22

I never failed to be amazed by the faith and love of the great people of the Bible! In the middle of His lamentation over the destruction of Jerusalem and His own mistreatment by the city's leaders, Jeremiah remembers God's great love and it gives him hope. It reminds me of David when he would be full of self pity and fear and then somewhere in the Psalm he would remember God was in control, and start praising God.

They remembered God's love, His compassion and His faithfulness.

Why do I have trouble remembering God's love when I am hurting or in trouble? When I am thinking about myself, I push God out, and I forget to rejoice. We seem to have a choice in our lives: complain or rejoice! Too often I chose the wrong one.

Do we complain?

Do we tell God he is making a mistake?

Do we remember God is in control and loves us?

MY PRAYER: *Lord, help us remember that you love us and you are also in control of everything that happens. You allow us free will and we make mistakes, but you will use them to teach us and help us to grow in you. We love you.*

MaryEmma

JUNE 25

KNOWING GOD

"You said, 'Listen now, and I will speak; I will
question You, and You shall answer me.'
My ears had heard of You but now my eyes have seen
You. Therefore I despise myself and repent."
Job 42:1-6

Job never knew why he had gone through such a hard time, but he trusted God through them. God never tempts us, but He does allow things to test us. Job never lost his faith, but through the pain his faith grew. There is a difference in 'knowing about God' and in 'knowing God'.

Hearing about God and knowing God are not the same. Knowing God means we fellowship with Him. The result: We are blessed. Job was blessed more in the second part of his life than in the first. We are too because after it is all over, our relationship with God is much more precious.

Do we know God or just about him?

Do we keep our eyes on God during difficult times?

Do we trust him enough to say, "Thy will be done?"

MY PRAYER: *Lord, thank You for the lessons you teach us. Forgive us for wanting to know why, to understand, instead of just trusting you. We love you.*
MaryEmma

JUNE 26

PRAISE AND REQUEST

"But may all who seek you rejoice and be glad in you... But as for me, 'I am poor and needy; come quickly to me, O God, You are my help and my deliverer; Lord, do not delay.'"
Psalm 70:4-5

This is a statement of faith followed by a statement of need. The Psalmist is saying to the Lord, "You are great and your arms are always open to the needy. I am one of the needy. I need your help. Help me rejoice and be thankful and take my mind off myself and turn it to You."

Does this sound like our prayers?

Do we praise him first and then ask for help?

Do we trust his love?

This is one of our greatest problems. Concentrating on me instead on the greatness of God. Our emotions can be our greatest enemy.

MY PRAYER: *Lord, we always need you even when we don't realize it and we want to rejoice with you. It is wonderful that we have a God who loves us and helps us. Thank you.*

MaryEmma

JUNE 27

LOOK TO GOD

"I was ashamed to ask the King for soldiers and horsemen to protect us from enemies on the road, because we had told the King, "The gracious hand of our God is on everyone who looks to Him."
Ezra 8:21-23

I love this verse: a great man of God felt fear in his heart and knew he needed to pray. He asked the others to fast and pray. It was dangerous to travel in those times and he had no soldiers for protection. He had bragged to the King that their God would protect them, and his faith was wavering. He felt doubt and fear and he knew the way to handle it was to honor his God. The prayer and fasting made them all more aware of God and his power?

How do we handle doubt and fear?

Do we turn to God and pray?

Is anxiety a gift from God to remind us that we need Him?

MY PRAYER: *Thank You, Lord, for reminders. When we feel fear or anxiety, help us recognize it is a nudge from you to check in with you. Calm our hearts and minds. Thank you for the peace and faith you give us during difficult times.*
MaryEmma

JUNE 28

IS PRAYER NECESSARY?

"The King said to me, 'What is it you want?'
Then I prayed to the God of heaven, and I answered the King, 'If
it pleases the King and if your servant has found favor...
Nehemiah 2:4-5

The King is waiting for an answer: Am I going to take time to ask God what I should say? Or answer the King with my common sense?

I am so impressed by Nehemiah's prayerful attitude. He rebuilt the wall by prayer and trusting God. He asked what to do and he obeyed. When the enemy tried to distract him, he turned to God for help.

The entire book of Nehemiah is a study of prayer. We could all learn a lot by studying this book. The problems are common to all of us and he never loses hope. He just turns to God.

Could we rely on God as he did?

Is it a matter of trust that we don't consult God more?

Do we believe he will help us?

MY PRAYER: *I pray that we will be so aware of your loving presence today that our words will be from you. Help us to trust you and consult you as we go through the day. Thank You, Lord, for Your help.*

MaryEmma

PRAYER IS PRACTICAL

"They all plotted together to come and fight against Jerusalem
and stir up trouble against it. But we prayed to our God and
posted a guard day and night to meet this threat."
Nehemiah 4:8-9

Again we see Nehemiah praying, turning to God to ask for help and wisdom. There is opposition to Nehemiah's plans to rebuild the wall. First they ridiculed him to discourage him. What was he to do? Nehemiah prayed. He asked for God to take care of the situation. The people who despised him, also despised God. The answer was to continue working. They were doing what God told them to do.

Now there were threats. Were they in danger? What should he do? First he prayed for guidance, then he posted a guard day and night.

They divided up the group and 1/2 guarded with their spears and the other half worked. All men stayed inside the walls at night and kept guards posted. There was opposition to building the wall, but because prayer came before the planning, the walls were completed.

How do we handle opposition and conflict?

Do we pray or do we plan first?

Do we discuss it with God or with another person?

God honors prayer. When we pray with both heart and mind, God sends us the answer.

MY PRAYER: *Lord, help us remember this lesson of trusting you and relying on you. Forgive us for praying so little. You are wonderful and we love You.*
MaryEmma

YET!

"Yet I will rejoice in the Lord, I will be joyful in God my
Savior. The Sovereign Lord is my strength; "
Habakkuk 3:18

Notice the prophet starts this verse with 'yet'.

"Yet" there are problems and there will always be problems, yet I will rejoice because I know who my savior is.

He doesn't protect us from problems, but He gives us strength through the problems.

Just as God helped Habakkuk, He helps us. When there are problems and worries, He is with us, wanting to help us, if we will only call on Him. If we will only praise and rejoice in Him and recognize His strength.

Our God gives us joy and faith to trust Him when we need Him. However great the problem, He has the solution.

What are our worries?

Are they real, or just fears and possibilities?

Will we rejoice that we can take them to our Lord?

MY PRAYER: *Lord, You are our strength. Help us remember that and rejoice in you. Help us to rejoice that we know you and can trust you to take care of any problem we have. We thank you and love you.*

MaryEmma

COINCIDENCE

"So Joseph also went up from the town of Nazareth in
Galilee to Judea, to Bethlehem the town of David...
While they were there, the time came for the baby to be...."
Luke 2: 4, 7

Centuries earlier, Micah had prophesied that the Messiah would be born in Bethlehem, and now it has happened. Isn't it interesting that the King had ordered a census be taken at just the right time for Jesus to be born in Bethlehem? A coincidence?

God is able to make what He wants happen. When He makes a plan or a promise, He is able to produce. We cause accidents but God always knows what will happen.

God is in control of our lives and it is our job to find out what He wants us to do and how He wants us to live.

What circumstances are we fighting right now?

What is our biggest worry?

Have we talked to God about them and asked His advice?

We need to keep our fellowship with our Lord active and loving. It reassures us and keeps us in peace.

MY PRAYER: *Lord, I don't understand why I worry and fret about what is happening or may happen, when I have you taking care of me. Help us to trust you more as our love for you grows.*

MaryEmma

JULY 2

THE GREATEST GIFT

*"In the beginning was the Word, and the Word
was with God, and the Word was God.
The WORD became flesh and made His dwelling among us."*
John 1:1-4,12

How often do we stop and think about the blessings of God? Blessings not just for ourselves, but the whole world.

God loves us so much that He sent his Son to teach us about Him. So we could have a better idea of the character of our invisible God. God lived among us, and now He lives in us by His Spirit, when we receive Him.

When did we last thank Him for this wonderful blessing?

Do we take the gift of our Savior for granted?

Do we read of Jesus' life and see our heavenly Father?

MY PRAYER: *Lord, we confess our sin of not appreciating all You do for us. Thank You for forgiving us. We love You.*

MaryEmma

JULY 3

SUBMISSION

"... For my eyes have seen your salvation, which you have
prepared in the sight of all nations: a light for revelation to
the Gentiles, and the glory of your people Israel."
Luke 2:28-32

Christ Jesus came to reveal to us gentiles--the rest of the world-- the God that the Israelites knew. Jesus is the light shining in the darkness for all who want to know God. He is the King Israel has been promised, although He is a spiritual king instead of a physical king.

We have been reading about Old Testament prophets and we could call Simeon a New Testament prophet. His last words to Mary were: "A sword will pierce your own soul, too." (Verse 35)

We know that Mary's heart ached as she watched people ridicule her son, hurt Him and finally kill Him. She had told the angel in the beginning that she was willing to do whatever he wanted.

Can we say those words to God when our hearts ache as we watch a loved one hurt?

When we hurt physically?

Can we submit to God's will as Mary did?

MY PRAYER: *Lord, Help us to trust you when we hurt. Help us to be patient with you as you make us into the persons you created us to be. Help us submit to you. We love you.*

MaryEmma

JULY 4

THE WORD

"Then Jesus was led by the Spirit into the wilderness to be tempted by the devil… Jesus answered, 'It is written: 'Man shall not live on bread alone, but on every word that comes from the mouth of God.'"
Mathew 4:1,4

When Jesus was hungry and at His lowest point physically, temptation came calling. That is when temptation hits us. How do we handle it? Jesus gives us the example. Respond to our human nature with His divine word.

Three times Jesus was tempted. Satan would not leave Him alone and each time Jesus responded with a bible verse.

It is interesting that Satan also quoted scripture in the second temptation.

We need divine help to live this earthly life and we can only get it from our Lord and Savior. But to truly know Him, we must know His word. We must know Him.

Do we fast from His word?

Do we recognize our temptations?

Do we know how to respond?

MY PRAYER: *Lord, help us to know both your word and your voice. Help us to turn to you in times of temptation–whatever it might be. Thank You. We love You.*

MaryEmma

JULY 5

WORKING OF GOD

"Your whole self .... circumcised by Christ... buried with
Him in baptism, in which you were also raised with Him
through our faith in the working of God....
Colossians 2:11-12

This is a beautiful picture of our Christian experience. Inside us, Christ cut off our sinful self and put His Spirit inside us. No one can see that except us but the baptism he describes is a symbol what Jesus did in us. When we are under the baptismal waters, it pictures our death and burial of the old self and when we are raised out of the water, it represents our new life of faith. It happened because of our faith in him.

God looks at our dead flesh and makes us alive in him. He forgave us our sins and nailed them on the cross. What a wonderful God and Savior that we have!

Do we thank him for making us new?

Do we live a life of faith?

Do we appreciate our Savior?

MY PRAYER: *Lord God, You are so wonderful to love us so much. You want to make our lives perfect in you. Thank you. We love you.*

MaryEmma

JULY 6

PRAYER OF LOVE

*"To Him who is able to keep you from stumbling and to
present you before His glorious presence without fault and with
great joy—to the only God our Savior be glory...."*
Jude 24-25

This is a beautiful prayer of love to God our Savior.

It is good to just stop and think about how wonderful and loving He is. He can keep us from stumbling and making mistakes when we fix our thoughts on Him; when we remember how wonderful He is and to think about His glorious presence.

Just think about what this praise says about our God. Think about His glory and majesty and power and authority. Think about how this great, great God loves us in spite of our failures.

Do we tell our Lord that we love him?

Do we enjoy thinking about his glory and majesty?

Do we say thank you for keeping us from stumbling?

MY PRAYER: *Lord, you are majestic and glorious and great. Forgive us when we only think about how you help us; help us remember your power and authority. We love you and praise you.*

MaryEmma

TREASURE AND PONDER

"Why were you searching for me?' He asked. 'Didn't you know I had to be in my Father's house?' But they did not understand what He was saying to them…But His mother treasured all these things in her heart."
Luke 2:49-51

This is all we know of Jesus' childhood. We often wish we knew more and many stories are made up. God tells us what we need to know in His word but sometimes we are not satisfied. Mary took what she knew and "treasured all these things in their heart". She "pondered" what the shepherds had told her.

After the shepherds told her what the angels told them in verse 19, "Mary treasured up all these things and pondered them in her heart".

When we read God's word, do we ponder them in our hearts?

Do we just read and forget?

Do we treasure them in our hearts?

MY PRAYER: *Thank You Lord, for sharing so much to us through your word. Forgive us when we want to know things that we don't need to know. Help us to "ponder" more and treasure more. You are the greatest! We love you.*
MaryEmma

JULY 8

"One of those days Jesus went out to a mountainside to pray, and spent the night praying to God. When morning came He called His disciples to Him and chose twelve of them, whom He also designated apostles."
Luke 6:12-13

Jesus prayed all night before he selected his disciples. Did he make a mistake? One of the twelve was Judas Iscariot, who not only stole from the group, but who later betrayed Jesus.

When we pray about things and then things don't go the way we want them to, we think we made a mistake. Maybe we did, but God knows better than we do what is best for us. He has a plan for us just as he had a plan for Jesus.

God is our spiritual parent and He is guiding and molding us, sometimes bending us to make us into the person He created us to be. God sends us pop quizzes and tests along life's highway, to help us understand where we are. We should not be discouraged when things go bad, but realize that God has a plan for us.

Jesus did not make a mistake in selecting Judas. It was planned at the beginning of creation and prophesied in the Old Testament that the Messiah would be betrayed. God does not make mistakes with us either!

Do we trust him when things don't seem to go right?

Have we asked God what his plan is?

Do we ask him "how" he want s us to pray?

MY PRAYER: *Lord, thank You that we can trust You. You are in charge all the time. Help us remember that. We love You.*

MaryEmma

LOVE THE UNRIGHTEOUS?

"love your enemies and pray for those who persecute you...children of your Father in heaven. He causes His sun to rise on the evil and the good, and sends rain on the righteous and the unrighteous."
Mathew 5:43-45

I have always thought this was an interesting insight that God allows both the evil and the good to be blessed, but this is our Lord. He is patient in His return because He doesn't want anyone to perish. He loves us all and wants all of us to love Him, but we are not to hate those who do not love Him.

In this time of world turmoil, we need to pray for the wicked. We need to pray that they will turn their hearts and minds to the One and only true God.

I was once in a group where one person was always agitating and creating unrest—to the point I felt attacked. When I got home I would get my Bible and read it until I felt peace. I learned that it was the only way I could keep my peace; to pray to God to bless the agitator. Then I had to ask God to help me mean the words I prayed.

How are we to handle people who create turmoil?

How do we keep our peace in difficult times?

Do we love those who are unrighteous?

MY PRAYER: *Lord, when we encounter unpleasant people, Help us remember that we are sometimes unpleasant to you, but you continue to love and bless us. Help us to treat others as you treat us. We love you.*

MaryEmma

JULY 10

HARSH WORDS

"For if you forgive men when they sin against you, your heavenly Father will also forgive you. But if you do not forgive men their sins, Your Father will not forgive your sins."
Mathew 6:15

Wow! That is harsh language, isn't it? Why is it so important to God that we forgive? Maybe because He loves us so much that He wants our best for us.

When we harbor a grudge or a hurt, we are unhappy. When we are unhappy, we are not healthy, physically or spiritually. Some of us have had our feelings hurt; others have had their life impacted by hurt. The answer is the same for both: we must forgive.

How? Only with God's help! We must ask Him for help. We must ask Him what we must do to be able to forgive.

I don't know the definition of forgiveness, but I think it means when we remember a situation, the feeling of hurt is gone.

Is there is a memory of anything that brings pain?

How do we handle it?

Do we need to talk to God about it?

MY PRAYER: *Lord, you forgive us and we need your help to forgive others. Give us the humility and compassion we need to forgive. Give us to love to be able to forgive. Thank you for the love that you give us..*

MaryEmma

DO WE JUDGE?

"Do not judge, and you will not be judged. Do not condemn, and you will not ... Forgive, and you will be forgiven. Give, and ....For with the measure you use, it will be measured to you."
Luke 6:37-38

I think this is the hardest command for us to obey.

Why do we like to judge others? Does it make us feel better to point out someone's mistakes? Do we see in others what we see in ourselves and try to change them?

This is a command, not a suggestion from our Lord.

When we judge or condemn, we are trying to do God's job.

He is the true judge who knows everything about the person. We judge without that wisdom.

Will we talk to God about fault finding?

Are we so used to judging that we don't notice our judging?

Do we need to be forgiven?

MY PRAYER: *Lord, forgive us when we judge another. Forgive us for finding fault with others. Help us to see our own faults and ask for your help to correct them. Thank you. We love you.*

MaryEmma

JULY 12

THE MOUTH

"Listen and understand. What goes into someone's mouth does not defile them, but what comes out of their mouth, that is what defiles them.....
Mathew 15:11,

It is so hard to control the thoughts of the mind! One unpleasant word can send our mind into turmoil, create emotions of anger and resentment or jealously. Our good mood is broken and we may speak sharply to another, messing up their good thoughts. When this happens there are two people not allowing God's Holy Spirit to be in control.

When we become aware of unpleasant thoughts, we also feel guilt and this should be a clue that we need to turn things over to God. This is difficult if we are really enjoying planning retribution on the offender. What are we to do?

Prayer is the first step. Maybe a Bible verse will pop into my mind or we can open the Word and just read until we have peace. We must allow God to take over our emotions and restore the control of His Holy Spirit.

Do we have trouble with word coming out of our mouth?

Does our mouth reflect what is in our heart?

What is our remedy for selfish thoughts?

MY PRAYER: *Lord, we have trouble with our emotions and our thoughts because we do not have our minds centered on You. I am afraid they are on ourselves. Please forgive us.*

Mary Emma

JULY 13

A CHOICE: ME OR HIM

"Come near to God and He will come near to you."
James 4:8a

Isn't this a beautiful promise? All we have to do to be close to God is to open our arms and heart to God. We open our heart to God when we pray or when we read His word prayerfully. When we think of Him in love, we are drawing near to God.

It is so simple. Why do we try to make it hard?

I remember an old diagram of a throne. We can put Christ on that throne, or we can put ourselves on the throne. The choice is ours. Verse 7 says; "submit yourselves, then to God. Resist the devil, and he will flee from you". It is so easy to put ourselves on that throne and push Christ off. We either concentrate on ourselves or on God.

I had a sore throat that made my whole body uncomfortable. I kept thinking about how I felt and I lost the joy of God. I wanted Him, but I wouldn't get off the throne! I kept my mind on how I felt. I chose me and lost my joy of being close to God. God allows us to have these experiences, so He can teach us.

Do we listen?

Do we think about him?

Do we put him first?

MY PRAYER: *Thank you, Lord, that you want us to be close to you. Thank you for giving us your word and prayer to help us. We love you.*

MaryEmma

JULY 14

WHERE IS THE POWER?

"Very early in the morning, while it was still dark, Jesus got up, left the house and went off to a solitary place, where He prayed."
Mark 1:35

It had been a busy week. Jesus had healed many and more were coming. The disciples were excited and enjoying his popularity and suddenly he disappeared!

When they awoke in the morning, He was gone, people were coming and there was work to do. Why wasn't He here?

Doesn't that sound like us and our Christian work?

Jesus knew where the power was. Jesus knew that His refreshment came from His heavenly Father, not sleep or food. His communication with God was of first importance!

How often do we inconvenience ourselves to talk to God? An extra 30 minutes of sleep sounds much better.

The busier we are, the more necessary is prayer. We think what we do for God is important. Jesus thought his fellowship with the father was the most important.

How seriously do we take our fellowship with our heavenly Father?

How high on our agenda is our prayer time?

Do we make time for prayer when it isn't convenient?

MY PRAYER: *Lord, help us to be more concerned about our fellowship with you rather than our activities. Our strength comes from you, the time we spend with you. You have taught us to pray and you have given us your written word so we can know you better. Thank you.*

MaryEmma

CONSTANTLY PRAY

"We constantly pray for you, that our God may make you worthy of His calling, and that by His power He may bring to fruition your every desire for goodness and your every deed prompted by faith."
2 Thessalonians 1:11

How do we pray for others? "God bless them, or heal them, amen". This verse gives us wonderful guidance on how to lift up another to God. We can pray for their spiritual health, not just their physical life. We can pray that their choices will bring them closer to you; that they will grow in faith.

Is there someone in your life who would benefit if you prayed this prayer for them?

Will you take the time to pray for them?

Will you pray for their faith to grow?

MY PRAYER: *I pray that you, God, will make us worthy of you Help us want your goodness, to want to know you better and be closer to you. Help us to pray for others, to pray that will be blessed spiritually. Forgive our selfish prayers. Thank You. Lord. We love You.*

MaryEmma

PRAY IN THE SPIRIT

"But you, dear friends, by building yourselves up in your most holy faith and praying in the Holy Spirit, keep yourselves in God's love as you wait...."
Jude 20-21

How do we grow in our faith? By activities in our daily life, by praying and by loving God and one another.

What does it mean to pray in the Holy Spirit? Don't we always pray in the Spirit? No, only when we are talking to God, only when our Spirit is open to his. There are times when we say we are praying but we are just saying words. They don't come from our heart; they just sound good

The words of true prayer come from a child like faith. Not an argument to get God on our side. We can't fool God. He knows when we are sincere.

When I was younger, out of duty I read my Bible and prayed, at least for 3 minutes. I am not sure what that benefited except my church pride. I was doing what I felt I was supposed to do. How much of it came from my heart I am not sure, except it did start a habit and eventually I prayed and read my Bible because I loved God and wanted to know him better. God blesses every effort; even when we don't deserve it.

Are we praying in God's Spirit?

Are we growing in love?

Are we growing in our faith?

MY PRAYER: *Lord, thank you for taking my habit of duty and turning it in to love. You are so wonderful to help us, to do what is best for us. Help us desire to grow in you by spending time with you. We love you.*

MaryEmma

COME

"Come unto me, all you who are weary and burdened, and I will give you rest. Take my yoke upon you and learn from me, for I am gentle and humble in heart, and you will find rest for your souls."
Mathew 11:28-29

I think this is one of the sweetest messages we have.

How often we are weary, tired, and heartsick and we can't get peace. This is the answer! Accept his invitation and go to him.

The catch is that we have to release our emotions and our desires to Him. We have to surrender and ask for help. Clear our mind of everything but God.

He says His yoke easy, but it sounds heavy! It isn't because He shares that yoke. Think of 2 oxen yoked together. Neither of them has to pull the full load, but it is shared. Together it is light. This is what Jesus is saying to us. "Come to me and let me help you."

Do we want him to help us?

Do we want to take all the credit for what we do?

Do we want a comforter to make it easy for us?

MY PRAYER: *Lord, thank you for wanting us to come you. You want to make our job easy by helping us. You are a partner and too often we think we are your boss. You are our helper and our comforter. Thank you for your great love.*

MaryEmma

JULY 18

PRAYER SHOWS

"One day Jesus was praying in a certain place. When He finished, one of His disciples said to Him, 'Lord, teach us to pray, just as John taught His disciples.'"
Luke 11:1

The disciples saw Jesus praying. Often He went away by Himself to pray, but sometimes He prayed when they were around.

They saw Him talking to His heavenly Father, and they wanted to do that. Why? Did they see something special in Jesus after He prayed? Why do we need to be taught to pray? Isn't it automatic, talking to God?

Maybe, sometimes, and the most effective prayer is the One that comes from the heart spontaneously. But that type of prayer usually is only wanting help and a conversation with a friend is more than asking for help. We need to talk to God about many things in our lives.

They wanted to copy Jesus habit. Is there someone in our life who wants to improve their fellowship with God because they see our prayer life?

Is there a difference in us after we pray?

Do we feel more love for others after a prayer time?

Do we want fellowship with our Lord?

MY PRAYER: *Lord, It is wonderful when we spend time just visiting with you, our Lord and Savior. You are a wonderful God. Thank you for your love.*
MaryEmma

A CONVERSATION

*"He said to them, "When you pray, say: 'Father, hallowed
be Your name, Your kingdom come. Give ... . . Forgive ...
we also forgive and lead us not into temptation.'"*
Luke 11:2-4

This is called the model prayer: we call it the 'Lord's Prayer' or 'Our
Father'. This is how Jesus taught his disciples to pray when they asked. We
can use it is a guideline for us to model our prayers.

First is an acknowledgement of God and His greatness.

This is what we call praise. We praise Him for who He is and what
He is. Why do we have so much trouble praising when it is a description
of what we think about Him?

After acknowledging who we are praying to, he says to ask for our daily
bread. Whatever we need we are free to ask for. Then comes forgiveness
and a promise to forgive those who have harmed us. We are to ask for
protection from temptation so we can remain true to God.

This is the outline of prayer that Jesus gave us. This is a good way
to start a visit with God. As we get comfortable talking to God with a
formula, then can then start sharing ourselves with him. He doesn't want
a list, He wants a visit.

Is this the way we pray?

Do we tell God what we want him to do?

Is our prayer time a worship time?

MY PRAYER: *Lord Jesus, thank You for showing us how to talk to you. We can
talk to you about whatever we want and you listen. Thank you. We love You.*
MaryEmma

JULY 20

BELIEF

"Even after Jesus had performed so many signs in their presence, they still would not believe in Him. This was to fulfill the word of Isaiah the prophet....
John 12: 37

Do we believe? Do we trust God? Do we acknowledge our faith to others?

Jesus is the powerhouse of our lives. We need to make Him the center of our life. His is the power and glory and He gives that to us as we acknowledge Him and praise and thank Him. As I watched the horror that occurred in 9/11, I kept thinking they, we, needed to turn to God. We needed Jesus in their lives. We need Jesus in our lives today.

We Americans turned to God after 9/11; the churches were full but it was only temporary. Soon we were worshiping ourselves and our desires again, instead of our creator.

Who or what do we worship?

Do we acknowledge His power and His greatness?

Why is it so hard to believe in Jesus, our Savior?

MY PRAYER: *Lord Jesus, help us make You the center of our lives today. You have all the power we need, and all the love that is available. You are the greatest! We love You.*

MaryEmma

JULY 21

EXAMPLE OF OBEDIENCE

"For I did not speak on my own, but the Father who sent me commanded me to say all that I have spoken. I know that His command leads to eternal life. So whatever I say is just what the Father has told me to say."'
John 12:49-50

We are so blessed to have the words of God written down for us so that we do not have to wonder what God wants: it is in black and white.

God loves us so much that He sent His son to encourage us to love Him back. We can read His words in the gospel and understand what God wants for us and get a glimmer of how great He is.

Do we say "thank You, Lord, for loving and blessing us?"

Do we say, "thank You Lord, for teaching us about you?

Do we realize He is teaching us how to live and think?

MY PRAYER: *Thank You, Lord, for teaching us, for loving us and sharing God's word with us. You teach us about God our Father when we read your words . You are a God of love. We love you.*

MaryEmma

JULY 22

PURCHASED

"...because you (the lamb) were slain and with Your blood
You purchased for God persons from every tribe and ... .
to serve our God... and will reign on the earth."
Revelation 5:9-10

This morning I stood at the window and thanked God for the pretty gold and red trees I saw. I raised my eyes to the top of the hill where the sky meets the earth and thanked God for the beauty and serenity He has given me. Then I thought, but the most wonderful thing He has given me is being made a part of God's family!

This verse has been rolling around in my head the last two weeks and I am in awe of what God has done for me; how much He loves me.

God sent His son from the comfort of heaven to dirty earth to be the lamb for us. The lamb, a helpless animal, is the sacrifice of sin for God's people. He was slain and with His blood He "purchased for God" me, all of us. All we have to do is believe. This is what my heart tells me to be thankful for today.

How often do we tell God thank you?

Do we see him in nature?

Do we desire to serve our God?

MY PRAYER: *Thank You, Lord, for purchasing me with Your blood and making me part of Your family. You are mighty and holy. We are unworthy of you but you love us anyway.*

MaryEmma

JULY 23

AUTHORITY

"I urge, then, first of all, that petitions, prayers, intercession and thanksgiving
be made for all people—for kings and all those in authority...."
2 Timothy 2:1-2

During this week, I pray that we will give thanks for our government and our country. We like to complain and criticize about our government, and it isn't perfect, but maybe it would be if we spent more time praying for those in authority.

Maybe it would be better if we thanked God for them instead of complaining about them.

Notice we are to offer petition, prayers, intercession as well as thanksgiving. Our prayers may determine if we live peaceful lives. We don't have to like our president or congressional person, but we do have to pray for them or we are in sin.

How often do we pray for those in authority?

Did we pray for our president today?

Did we pray for our governor?

MY PRAYER: *Lord, we pray for godly wisdom to be given to each person in our government. Thank you for giving us this government. Help our leaders to love you and listen to You. Forgive us when we don't pray for them. We are hurting ourselves as well as them. Help us to pray.*

MaryEmma

PRAISING GOD IN A LOUD VOICE

"One of them, when he saw he was healed, came back,
praising God in a loud voice. He threw himself at Jesus'
feet and thanked Him—and he was a Samaritan.
Luke 17:15-17

Jesus encountered ten men who had leprosy and when they asked for healing, He told them to go show themselves to the priest. They were healed as they went, as they obeyed. But one man when he saw he was healed, came back to thank Jesus. He was a foreigner!

We are so busy with our lives we forget to thank God. In the days of Noah, "they were eating and drinking; marrying and giving in marriage", which is okay but they were leaving God out of their lives.

As I was reading this verse this morning, I realized I had not thanked God for a safe trip in the rain yesterday when we were on the road travelling.

I had asked for a safe trip before we left, but when we got home, I was busy with other things.

How often do we take God's blessings for granted?

What else have we forgotten to thank God for?

MY PRAYER: *Lord, Forgive me when I forget to thank you. Ignoring you and not making you an intimate part of my life is a sin. I want you to be a special part of my life. I love you.*

MaryEmma

JULY 25

LOVE IS THE SECRET

"...remain in his love. I have told you this so that my joy
may be in you and that your joy may be complete.
My command is this: Love each other as I have loved you."
John 15: 10-12

This is the secret to 'complete joy". Joy can be elusive at times, but not when we stay connected to Jesus, the vine. Love flows through that vine, from the gardener God to the vine down to us, the branches. That love creates joy within us.

The whole world is looking for peace, but we have the secret right here: love plus joy equals peace.

Why do we go around with a long face?

Why do we worry and fret?

Why are we dissatisfied with our life?

The secret to real happiness is to stay connected to the vine. It provides love, joy and peace.

MY PRAYER: *Lord, help us to stay connected to You today when things gets stressful so we can have your love flowing through us that makes joy and peace. Help us remember that we do not fight our battles alone, but you are always with us.*

MaryEmma

ETERNAL LIFE

"Now this is eternal life: that they know you, the only true God, and Jesus Christ, whom You have sent. I have brought you glory on earth by finishing the work you gave me to do.
John 17:3-4

At Christmas time we spend time shopping for gifts, but we have already received the greatest gift of all.

At Christmas, all children have to do to receive their gifts is by reaching out their arms to receive it. All we have to do to receive this greatest gift of God, is to reach out by believing.

As we celebrate this greatest of all miracles, lets remember why we have Christmas. We pay for our gifts as we buy them. God paid for His gift with the death and resurrection of His son long before you and I received our gift. Every day we celebrate Christmas by taking the time to remember our greatest gift that helps us get through our day.

MY PRAYER: *Lord, thank You for the most wonderful gift of all times. Thank you that we can know you, thank you we can have fellowship with you and thank you that we know that we are loved by you. Thank You for blessing us.*

MaryEmma

MY SHIELD

"Bring to an end the violence of the wicked and make the righteous secure –You, the righteous God who probes minds and hearts. My shield is God Most High, who saves the upright in heart."
Psalm 7:9-10

When I read this verse, I thought "this is what we should be praying for our country; bring an end to the violence".

The opposite of violence is righteousness. Are there as many righteous as there are violent? If we outnumber the violent, why aren't our prayers making a difference? Do we even think about praying for this?

God protects us with His shield around us and it is comforting, but could we make it a practice to pray for the violent people? Could we pray that they would come to our God Most High for His righteousness?

David ends His request with praise and thanksgiving.

Do we praise Him for our righteousness?

Do we thank Him for saving the upright in heart?

Do we thank Him for being our shield?

MY PRAYER: *Lord God, direct our prayers today. Help us pray according to your will. Help us replace violence with your righteousness. We love you.*
MaryEmma

JOHN THE BAPTIST

"...You are to call him John. He will be a joy and delight to you, and many will rejoice because of his birth, for he will be great in the sight of the Lord.... he will bring back many of the people of Israel to the Lord their God.
Luke 1: 13-16

God always prepares us for things that will happen. It was time for the Messiah to come, but first God had promised Zechariah that this son born to parents too old for natural child birth, was to come in the Spirit and power of Elijah.

He was to make the people ready for Jesus. He was to remind people of their sin and their need to turn back to God. John would introduce his people to the Messiah.

John was born for a specific purpose. God also has a purpose for our lives.

Have we asked Him what His plans are for our lives?

Are we praying for his wisdom and understanding?

Do people today need to be brought back to the Lord their God?

MY PRAYER: *Heavenly Father, I thank you are your gift of salvation. I thank you for your presence y with me. Help us to understand your plan for our lives and then guide us and direct us as we make our decisions. Thank you for all your blessings for us.*

MaryEmma

ANGELS

"....the angel said to him, 'I am Gabriel. I stand in the presence of God, and I have been sent to speak to you and to tell you this good news.'"
Luke 1:11,19

The Bible mentions angels often. They are messengers for God. We don't know what they look like, but our artists have made them look like beautiful creatures. They do God's bidding. They usually give good news, but sometimes it is uncomfortable news.

Gabriel is chief messenger, and Archangel Michael, is our protector and fights against Lucifer's demons in the spiritual world. There are only 3 books in the Old Testament and 2 in the New that do not mention angels. They are very important in God's creation.

In heaven there are thousands and thousands of angels surrounding God. They sing praises to Him. We do not worship angels, but we can admire them for their love and obedience. We can use their words to praise God.

We do not become angels when we die, but maybe we can join in their singing when they praise our Lord and Savior.

Are we as faithful to God as they are?

Do we praise God as readily as they do?

MY PRAYER: *Lord, help us to see angels for who they are: creatures who love you and praise you and obey you. Help us to be as faithful as they are to you. We love you.*

MaryEmma

MERCURY

*"For I desire mercy, not sacrifice, and acknowledgment
of God rather than burnt offerings."*
Hosea 6:6

God desires mercy from us. He gives us mercy and we are to pass it on to others. This is one way we reflect God in our lives, by being merciful; to each other of course, but the scripture tells us to be merciful to the poor, to orphans, widows and the alien.

We don't sacrifice burnt offerings any more, but a sacrifice God desires is praise or acknowledging His name. Do we give God credit for what He does? God wants us to acknowledge Him to others and one way to do that is to be merciful to others. The second way is to praise him with our lips and mind.

How do we acknowledge our Lord?

How do we show mercy to others as God shows to us?

MY PRAYER: *Lord, I thank you for my friends this morning as I pray for them. Bless each of us with an awareness of your mercy and your love. Help us to praise with our lips and show your mercy to others. We praise you and love You.*
MaryEmma

JULY 31

THE SHIELD

"My shield is God Most High, who saves the upright in heart.
I will give thanks to the Lord because of His righteousness; I
will sing the praises of the name of the Lord Most High."
Psalm 7:10,17

Do we realize how great our God is and how much He does for us? He is our shield, our savior, our protector? Where would we be without His love for us?

Do we thank Him for His righteousness? Do we even think about His righteousness and what it means?

There are times when we need to put other things aside and just praise our Lord for his greatness. May we praise Him today, the Lord Most High. He is great and holy and He loves us even when we are not loveable.

Do we sing the praises of God?

Do we thank God for being our shield?

Do we give thanks to him for his righteousness?

MY PRAYER: *Lord, we praise you and love You. Thank you for loving us, for being our shield, for blessing us when we don't deserve it. You are merciful and wonderful. You are powerful and great and yet you have time for us. Thank You.*
MaryEmma

AUGUST 1

HE REVEALS HIS THOUGHTS

"...and who reveals His thoughts to mankind, Who turns dawn to darkness, and treads on the heights of the earth--the Lord God Almighty is His name."
Amos 4:13

We know we have a God who loves us. How often do we think about God Himself? How mighty He is? He is the One who made the mountains and the wind--and everything, and yet He reveals His thoughts to us when we listen.

Are we listening?

Or do we do all the talking?

Are we reading His word?

We have a mighty God who wants our fellowship.

MY PRAYER: *Lord God who formed the mountains and created the winds, thank You. You never forget us Forgive us when we are too busy to think about you or talk to you. We love You and praise You.*

MaryEmma

THE LORD IS OUR ROCK

"I love You, Lord, my strength. The Lord is my rock, my fortress and my deliverer; my God is my rock, in whom I take refuge, my shield and the horn of my salvation, my stronghold."
Psalm 18:1-2

God is my rock, David said, when he was fleeing from Saul who wanted to kill him. Is God our rock? Do we turn to Him when we are in trouble, or do we try to take care of it ourselves?

David trusted God. He praised God. Do we? If we trust Him, God will be our rock, our fortress, our deliverer, our shield and our salvation.

When God helps us, do we take it for granted?

Do we praise Him to others?

Can we praise God like David did? Will we?

MY PRAYER: *Lord God, You are wonderful! You are my rock, my strength, my safe spot. Thank You for always being with me and providing for me. I love You.*
MaryEmma

LOVE FOR GOD

> *"As for God, His way is perfect. The Lord's word is*
> *flawless; He shields all who take refuge in Him....*
> *It is God who arms me with strength and keeps my way secure."*
> Psalm 18:30-33

As we read these words we can feel the love David has for God. Not just love, but faith and trust in Him. None of us would want to live the life David lived between His anointing and becoming king. But this time of hardship strengthened David's faith and made him into the man we admire.

When we have trouble, we can read this Psalm and it helps us trust God.

Can we say that it is God who arms us with strength?

Do we trust Him who keeps us secure,?

Are we still trying to trust ourselves?

May He bless us today as we praise Him.

MY PRAYER: *Lord, You are wonderful. Just as you protected and stretched David, so do you protect and stretch us. Help us to trust You in difficult times as well as the good days. We love You.*

MaryEmma

AUGUST 4

GOD IS GRACIOIUS

"Turn to me and be gracious to me, for I am lonely and afflicted.
Relieve the troubles of my heart and free me from my anguish.
Look at my affliction and my distress and take away all my sins."
Psalm 25:15-18

Do we ever think of God as being gracious? My idea of gracious is being gentle, kind, loving and generous. Isn't this what our Lord is? We all have problems in our lives, but when we keep our eyes on the Lord, we are helped.

Our enemies don't have to be people, but emotions, illness or relationships. We all have them, but we have a helper! He will guard our lives and rescue us as we put trust in Him as David did.

"My eyes are ever on the Lord."

Are ours?

Where do we turn in trouble?

Is our God gentle and kind?

MY PRAYER: *Lord, You are my refuge and I thank you. Thank you for fighting our battles for us. Help us remember you are always with us and to trust you. We love you.*

MaryEmma

AUGUST 5

"The Lord lives! Praise be to my Rock! Exalted by God my Savior!
Therefore I will praise You among the nations, O Lord.
I will sing praises to Your name."
Psalm 18: 46,49

Can we praise God as David does in this Psalm?

Do we even realize how much God has helped us?

As David thinks about how God has helped Him, he breaks out in praise.

And then he tells God, his Rock, that he will sing praises to all nations. He will tell everyone how wonderful his God is. This is a wonderful example for us.

I pray that we will be aware of God today and the help He gives us through this day.

Are we telling others about God's help?

Do we praise him to others?

Have we said "thank you" today?

MY PRAYER: *Lord, You are helper and our comforter. We love You and praise You. Thank You.*

MaryEmma

AUGUST 6

THE GLORY OF GOD

"The heavens declare Your glory, O God, the skies
proclaim the work of Your hands.
Day after day they pour forth speech; night
after night they display knowledge.
There is no speech or language where their voice is not heard."
Psalm 19:1-3

God communicates with us in many ways. We have His written word that gives us knowledge, but we can also see Him in nature, even in high-rise buildings. God had to give man the knowledge to build. There is no place that we cannot see God and worship Him in our world.

The first verse can be a prayer from our heart to God. Have we talked to Him today?

Have we told him how wonderful we think He is?

MY PRAYER: *Lord, You show yourself everywhere and to everyone. Forgive us when we ignore you. Help us to recognize you in the heavens and the sky; not to worship nature, but we see your hand working. We love you.*

MaryEmma

AUGUST 7

CONFESSION

"Who can discern his errors? Forgive my hidden faults.
*Keep your servant also from willful sins, may they not rule over
me. Then I will be blameless, innocent of great transgression.*"
Psalm 19:12-13

This is a prayer of confession, a call for help-to be right with God. I love this prayer: that my words and my thoughts may please Him. But first David confesses his sins; the ones he is aware of and the ones he is not aware of, but he knows that God knows.

Sin is not wrong doing, it is wrong being. It is us doing our own thing instead of listening to God. That is the reason David ends his prayer with a request: help me with my thoughts, because the words that come out of our mouth come from our heart.

MY PRAYER: *Lord God, we confess our sins to you when we remember them. Make us aware of our unconscious sins. The ones you recognize but we are so used to them that we think they are ok. We love You and want to be right with You.*
MaryEmma

AUGUST 8

BELIEF IS AS

"After this, the word of the Lord came to Abram in a vision: 'Do not be afraid, Abram, I am Your shield, Your very great reward." Abram believed the Lord, and He credited it to him as righteousness.'"
Genesis 15:1,6

This verse is repeated several places in the scriptures, because it is so important. We must believe God; we must trust God. We call that faith. Here is a difference in believing *in* God and believing God.

Believing God is personal. Faith means that we believe God will do what He says He will do. Some believe faith means God will do what we want Him to do, but it doesn't work that way. That is trying to make Him our Santa Claus.

We have read many beautiful promises that God has given us as His children.

Do we believe God? He promises us peace. He promises us wisdom.

Do we believe Him? When we don't believe His promises, we must get on our knees and find out why we don't believe.

Righteousness and salvation come from believing God.

MY PRAYER: *Lord, help us believe Your promises and trust You. Forgive us when we try to make You Santa Claus and get unhappy when You don't perform. We love You.*

MaryEmma

AUGUST 9

TRUST WHO?

"Some trust in chariots and some trust in horses, but
we trust in the name of the Lord our God."
Psalm 20:7

I wonder if this verse were written today, what would be in place of horses and chariots? I trust in money, I trust in the military, I trust in guns.

Where is our trust? The world is in turmoil now, with terrorists and diseases. We have problems closer home- in our own families. Who do we trust?

Our God knows all. Our God has all power. He can help us if we trust Him. Abraham believed and he didn't have the written scriptures.

Where is our trust?

What are we afraid of?

Will we will trust God today.

MY PRAYER: *Lord, we do trust you. We love you. Help us when doubt creeps in. Forgive us when we don't trust you. You are my mighty God. We know you are trustworthy.*

MaryEmma

AUGUST 10

OUR WANTS

*"The Lord is my shepherd, I shall not be in want. He makes
me lie down in green pastures; He restores my soul. He guides
me in paths of righteousness for His name's sake.*
Psalm 231-3

We all know and love the 23rd Psalm. We recite it and use it
almost like a tranquilizer, but do we ever think about what it
really says? It tells us all the wonderful things God does for us. Do
we stop and really think about them? They are all the blessings
of life: rest, protection, comfort, love, and an eternal home.

But what is our role? The second line says I shall not want. I am afraid
I spend more time wanting than thinking about what I have been given.
Modern advertising makes sure that we want something else; a newer car,
another house, more clothes, the next new restaurant or the next trip.

Nothing is wrong with this, except that when we are wanting something
we don't have, we aren't thinking about our God. We aren't thanking Him
or praising Him.

Is Jesus our Shepherd?

Do we thank him for his gifts?

Do we love him or what he gives us?

MY PRAYER: *Thank You for being our shepherd. You are so wonderful to us,
you give us what we need and satisfy our desires with good things. We love you.*
MaryEmma

AUGUST 11

MERCY AND LOVE

"Remember, Lord, Your great mercy and love, for they are from of old. Do not remember the sins of my youth and my rebellious ways; according to Your love remember me, for You, Lord, are good."
Psalm 25:6-7

Our Lord is good.

When we realize how good God is and we trust Him, our natural reaction is humility. I realize how unworthy I am when I am in the presence of God, and my natural reaction is confession.

The psalmist remembers His rebellions and asks God for His mercy and love. Confessing our sins to God is like a spiritual bath. It washes away the obstacles we have put between us and God.

God understands and wants to help us. His word tells us what he wants us to do. He promises to guide us and teach us.

Do we thank him for his mercy, for not treating us as we deserve?

Do we confess our sins to him?

Do we accept his forgiveness ?

MY PRAYER: *Lord, help us have a humble spirit. We want oneness with You. Forgive us our sins. You are perfect and good and you love us. We love you.*
MaryEmma

A SHIELD AROUND US

"But You, Lord, are a shield around me, my glory, the One who lifts my head high. I call out to the Lord, and He answers me from His holy mountain. I lie down and sleep; I wake again, because the Lord sustains me. I will not fear."
Psalm 3: 3-6

Our Lord is a shield around me. Not just a shield in front of me, but around me. Our Lord protects us completely. I think of a round plastic shield surrounding me. I can see out, but nothing can penetrate that shield unless I step out of it.

We do step away from God at times, don't we? When we want our will instead of God's will. That is when we fear. But a prayer of praise and confession brings that shield around us again.

David trusted God so completely that he could lie down and sleep, even though the enemy was trying to kill him.

Can we trust God when our world is in confusion?

When things aren't going right?

Do we want his shield around us?

MY PRAYER: *Lord, You are our shield around us. We call out to you. We will not fear. Forgive us when we do and help us to trust you. We love you.*
MaryEmma

OUR VISIT WITH GOD

"Hear my cry for help, my King and my God, for to you I pray. In the morning, Lord, you hear my voice; in the morning I lay my requests before you and wait expectantly. Lead me, Lord..."
Psalm 5: 2,3,8

In the morning I share with God my needs and wants for the day. Some mornings it is a quiet adoration of God and thankfulness, but other times, it is "These are my problems, Lord, help me".

We ask for help to stay focused on God because of our enemies. We don't have people trying to kill us, but we have health problems, family situations, or money needs.

Whatever our fear is, we can agree with David, to make our paths straight in the way He wants us to go. David had a lot of trouble but he also had perfect confidence in God.

Do we?

Do we take the time to get acquainted with him?

Do we ask him to show us to way to walk?

MY PRAYER: *Lord, I pray you will give us peace today as we keep our eyes on you. We want your guidance and you help to live this day the way you know is best for us. We love you.*

MaryEmma

AUGUST 14

OUR PROTECTOR

"But let all who take refuge in you be glad; let them ever sing for joy. Spread your protection over them, that those who love your name may rejoice in You.
Psalm 5:11

What does it mean to take refuge in God? It means we are trusting Him with the situation He allows us to be in. It means that we don't have negative thoughts because they separate us from God. We feel safe and protected.

I was on a spiritual high after a Bible study and somehow I started thinking about something I didn't like, and suddenly I realized I was almost depressed. The joy was gone from my heart. I know there are valleys with every mountaintop, but I was shocked how quickly I got into the valley.

We can't be negative and focus on God at the same time. Negative thoughts means that we are not trusting God. David had all sorts of problems but he handed them over to God. He even told God his opinion on what God should do, but he ended his prayer with praise.

When we take refuge in our God there is joy. We are in God's circle of protection. Negative thoughts are the enemy.

Do we take refuge in our Lord during troubles?

Do we have his joy in our spirit?

Do we keep our minds focused on God?

MY PRAYER: *Lord, help us keep our thoughts centered on you. When something bothers us, let us share it with you. You are our peace and love and joy; all else is counterfeit. We love You and need You.*

MaryEmma

AUGUST 15

PRAYER OF LOVE

*"I say the Lord, "'You are my Lord; apart from you I have no good thing.
Lord, You alone are my portion and my cup; you make my lot secure.
I will praise the Lord....*
Psalm 16:2,5,7

This is David pouring out his heart to God. He acknowledges that without God, he is nothing. If someone were listening to our conversation with God, I wonder what they would hear? Would they hear us sharing words of love to God, or would we be asking him to do something?

These are good verses to memorize and say back to God when we are quiet, when we are fearful, when we are uncertain about the future.

What do we say to God when we aren't asking for something? These words are words of love to God.

Do we love Him?

Do we share how great he is with others?

I pray that our quiet time with God will be this intimate.

MY PRAYER: *Lord, forgive us when we don't realize You are "everything" we need. You make our life secure. You are the best blessing in our lives. We praise You and love You.*

MaryEmma

OUR GATE:

"Therefore Jesus said again, 'Very truly I tell you, I am the gate for the sheep...I am the gate; whoever enters through me will be saved....I have come that they may have life, and have it to the full."
John 10: 7, 9-11

We all want a life of peace and joy. We want 'abundant life'. We want "life to the full". That is what Jesus is promising us when we trust Him. He is our protector and our teacher. He is our comforter and our refuge.

It is so important that we remember that He loves us and wants only the best for us. Our job is to trust Him and fellowship with Him. Only in Him do we have true peace.

Why don't we have peace and joy?

Why don't we have abundant life?

Why don't we turn to him first in troublesome times?

MY PRAYER: *Lord, I pray that we will enjoy your presence today. We want to trust you and have your joy and peace. Forgive us when we trust others before you. Help us to trust you and fellowship with you. You are our gate to unbelievable peace.*

MaryEmma

AUGUST 17

NEW COVENANT

I will put my law in their minds and write it on their hearts. I will be their God, and they will be my people.....I will forgive their wickedness and will remember their sins no more."
Jeremiah 31: 31-33

The day has come when God has done what He promised. When Christ Jesus was on earth He took our sins to the cross and God not only forgave but forgot our sins. When Jesus ascended to heaven He sent back his Spirit to live with us and in us and teach us and remind us of what He had said. This is what Jesus did for us. He fulfilled the law of God and replaced it with two. Love God and love our neighbor.

We have a wonderful God and Savior.

Have we thanked Him for our blessings, for our forgiveness and for His indwelling Spirit?

Have we thanked him for his wonderful gift?

Have we thanked him for replacing the law with love?

MY PRAYER: *Thank You for everything; for replacing the law with love, for including the things we don't like because we know that you are teaching us. You know what we need to be closer to you. You always do what is best for us. We love you.*

Mary Emma

AUGUST 18

"Hear me, Lord, and answer me, for I am poor and needy. You are my God; have mercy on me, Lord, for I call to You all day long. Bring joy to your servant, Lord, for I put my trust in You."
Psalm 86:1-4

How often do we stop and think about how wonderful our Lord is? He is always with us, loving us and wanting to help us, but often we don't even think about Him. We just do it our way.

He wants us to trust Him, and then He will fill us with joy.

Because God is forgiving and good, we can go to Him at any time with any problem. We never have to be alone.

We are never unloved.

He is never too busy because He loves us.

He is "abounding in love to all who call" to Him.

Are we not blessed by a heavenly father who wants us to call to Him?

Have we thanked him for loving us?

Have we told him we love him?

MY PRAYER: *Lord, You are wonderful. You are never too busy for us and always want the best for us. Thank you for Your love. We love you.*

MaryEmma

AUGUST 19

OUR EVER-PRESENT HELP

"God is our refuge and strength, an ever-present help in trouble. Therefore we will not fear, though the earth give way and the mountains fall ...."
Psalm 46: 1-3

When I read these words, my spirit smiled. What a wonderful God we have. It is hard to believe how much He loves us and cares for us. He is our protector and helper, and my spirit said, "Thank You, Lord."

I continued reading the Psalm and verse 10 gave me my direction for the day. In verse 10, He says: "Be still, and know that I am God". We are so busy, that we have trouble with stillness. When are bodies are still our mind is still working on what we need to do. God wants us to stop and enjoy him, relish in his presence, in his peace. That is what God wants for us.

Every year we celebrate the birth of our savior and yet sometimes we get so busy we forget the "reason for the season".

When are we fearful?

Are we trusting God when we have no peace?

Have we talked to God about it?

MY PRAYER: *Lord, thank You for being my refuge and strength. We need your help on a daily basis. Forgive us when we try to take care of things alone without asking you for help. Help us to be still and know that you are Lord. We love you.*
MaryEmma

AUGUST 20

"I will sing of the Lord's great love forever…. The heavens praise your wonders, Lord, Your faithfulness, too, in the assembly of the holy ones… Who is like you, Lord God Almighty?"
Psalm 89: 2,5-6,

We have a mighty God. How often do we thank Him for letting us know Him?

We can't get close to the Queen of England or the President of the United States, but we have the Spirit of God with us always. Have we thanked Him for His presence with us, for His love that He showers on us?

God has done His job in giving us this beautiful world and making us and letting us know Him.

What about our job?

Do we declare His love and faithfulness to others?

The heavens praise His wonders. Do we?

MY PRAYER: *Lord, there is no one like you. You are a mighty and holy God. Forgive us for taking your blessing for granted. We are so blessed to know you and know that you love us. We are blessed by your unconditional love. We ask your forgiveness and thank You for You fellowship.*

MaryEmma

AUGUST 21

THE GOOD NEWS

*"Do not be afraid. I bring you good news that will cause great
joy for all the people. Today in the town of David a Savior
has been born to you; He is the Messiah, the Lord."*
Luke 2:10

The good news is a Savior who brings us peace and joy.

Can we rejoice with the angels and the shepherds? Glory to God in heaven and to us on earth, peace.

What does it mean to me personally? Can I rejoice today for His gift or am I so filled with my likes and dislikes that I only think about myself? What are my thoughts and goals?

He wants to give us his joy and peace and love and many other wonderful gifts. The gifts we give others are just a tiny example of what our Savior has given us.

What gift from Jesus is most precious to us?

What gift are we ignoring?

Are we sharing the good news among our friends?

MY PRAYER: *Lord God, thank you for the gift of peace and joy. Some search the earth for the blessings you have given us and don't know that you are close, wanting and waiting for them to turn to you. Forgive us for not sharing the good news to those who need it.*

MaryEmma

AUGUST 22

THE LORD IS MAJESTIC

"The Lord reigns, He is robed in majesty; the Lord is robed
in majesty and armed with strength.... . Your throne was
established long ago; you are from all eternity.
Psalm 93:1-4

This is a beautiful prayer of praise to our heavenly Father. It is a wonderful prayer to pray back to Him and make it personal.

You, Lord, reign. You are robed in majesty. Can we pick out the phrases that the psalmist uses to describe God and also use them? You, Lord, are strength and eternal. Your strength is greater than nature. You are in control of all the elements.

Whatever our problems, you are in control and you will use them to make us more like Jesus.

He is a marvelous God and a loving Father. He need to show him that we love and cherish him; not just use him.

Do we thank him when we talk to him?

Do we praise him to others?

Do we enjoy him?

MY PRAYER: *Lord, You are robed in majesty and armed with strength. You have established the world and you reign secure. Thank You Lord, for letting us know you. We love you.*

MaryEmma

AUGUST 23

"Then the Lord spoke to Job out of the storm...
Brace yourself like a man; I will question you, and you shall answer me. Where
were you when I laid the earth's foundation? Tell me, if you understand.'"
Job 38:1-4

When I complain, am I telling God He is wrong? When I complain, am I telling God He made a mistake? Do I tell God that He doesn't know what He is doing?

Complaining can become a habit and I have been doing a lot of it lately.
I was convicted as I read these words this morning and I can only pray:
"Lord, forgive me and help me. Make me aware of every complaint and
help me to thank you for the good as well as the bad, as Job did."
Why do I complain?
Am I more interested in myself than my Savior?
Can I complain and be thankful both?

MY PRAYER: *Lord, forgive me for all the times I tell you that you are wrong. I am sorry that I complain. Help us all to trust you with the little details as well as the complicated details. We love you.*

MaryEmma

AUGUST 24

HUMILITY

"Then Job answered the Lord: 'I am unworthy—how can I reply to You? I put my hand over my mouth. I spoke once, but I have no answer—twice, but I will say no more.'"
Job 40: 3-4

Job's reaction of unworthiness and humility is a normal reaction when we realize we are in the presence of God. We think we are so great and then we are aware of God; when we are in the presence of His greatness, we realize who we really are.

I think whoever suggested **ACTS** as a praying guide was so right: **A**doration, **C**onfession, **T**hanksgiving and **S**upplication.

As we adore or praise God we slowly realize His greatness and sovereignty, and at the same time, realize who we are in relation to this great God.

Confession is automatic as Job became aware of God. Only God's grace and love give us life. After confession, our spirit starts thanking God for our blessings He has provided. Then we are ready to do what we call praying: Asking.

Do our prayers resemble **ACTS**?

Do we praise and thank him?

Do we ask that his will be done?

MY PRAYER: *Lord God, we love you and want to enjoy you and please you. Please help us to realize how great you are and spend time with you.*
MaryEmma

AUGUST 25

WISDOM

"Where then does wisdom come from? Where does understanding dwell?
God understands the way to it and He alone knows where it dwells:
Job 28:20,23,

This is the great answer to the question men have searched the world for: What is wisdom? To fear the Lord. What is understanding? To shun evil.

To fear biblically does not mean afraid: it means respect, love, awe, and adoration. And that really doesn't explain the word thoroughly, but it gives us the idea.

Only in God do we find true wisdom and understanding. Only in God do we find peace and joy.

To trust and fear God does not mean we will have no problems in our lives, but it does mean that we will receive the help to get us through the problems. Remember: the only perfect man who ever walked the earth was killed by men jealous about losing their jobs.

Where do we find true wisdom?

How do we gain understanding?

Do we have the peace and joy God means for us?

MY PRAYER: *Lord, I pray that we will spend time with you and receive the peace that only you can give. We need wisdom and we need understanding. Only you are capable of giving it to us. We love you.*

MaryEmma

AUGUST 26

PRAYERS FOR ALL

"I prayed to the Lord my God and confessed:...We have been wicked and have rebelled; we have turned away from Your commands and laws. We have not listened to Your servants the prophet who spoke in Your name...."
Daniel 9: 4-6

This is a prayer of confession from an almost sinless man; a man whom God spoke to and through. Why is he confessing?

This is a community prayer of confession. He has taken the sins of His people as His own sin and is confessing.

There are no 'they sinned', but 'we sinned'. What a lesson for us. Do we pray for all the people in our country? Do we ask God to forgive all our sins?

It has been said, that 'confession is good for the soul', but maybe we should make that 'confession is good for the country'. It is so easy to point our fingers at others, but none of us are perfect.

MY PRAYER: *Lord, Help us to remember to pray for our country and our leaders. Forgive us for not praying for politicians we don't like. We have sinned. We love You.*

MaryEmma

AUGUST 27

WITNESS

"So the King gave the order, and they brought Daniel and
threw him into the lions' den. The King said to Daniel, 'May
your God, whom you serve continually, rescue you!'"
Daniel 6: 16,

Why do bad things happen to good people? Maybe it is as a witness to bring others to faith in the living God. Men were jealous of Daniel because of the wisdom the received from talking to God. They plotted to get rid of him, so they could keep their power. It sounds a lot like the plotting to get rid of Jesus Christ when He was on earth, doesn't it?

Daniel trusted God and because of that faith, the King acknowledged God as the Supreme Being and declared it to all his kingdom. The King recognized Daniel's devotion to his God and admired it, but it took this miracle for him to believe, or at least, order reverence be shown to the God of Daniel. This happened because Daniel stayed close to his God.

Do we trust God during hard times?

Is our life a witness to others?

MY PRAYER: *Lord, I pray that we will stay close to You, so that Your 'living waters' will be able to flow through us to others. You are perfect and You have all wisdom. Thank You.*

MaryEmma

SUCCESS OF PRAYER

"Then King Darius wrote to all the nations... 'I issued a decree that in every part of my kingdom, people must fear and reference the God of Daniel. For He is the living God....'"
Daniel 6:25-26

Daniel witnessed about the power of God to 3 kings. Many in this ungodly country knew about the great sovereign God. How did he do this? Daniel was a man of prayer. Whatever happened, in the lion's den or in his office, he was going to continue intimate communication with his God. He knew who was in control of his life and he trusted God, whether he lived or died.

Daniel and his friends were captured in Jerusalem and taken to a foreign land with foreign gods. They had 2 choices: they could complain and rebel or they could trust God and live in close communication with God. Because they chose God, they had a remarkable influence on this foreign country, from a simple guard to kings.

What do we do when we do when bad things happen to us? Do we complain or trust God? Daniel had deep faith because he spent so much time with God. Three times a day he prayed to God. He did not try to force others to live the way he thought they should, but he concentrated on his personal relationship with his Lord and Savior.

What kind of prayer life we have?

MY PRAYER: *Lord, we want to talk to you and listen for your gentle quiet voice. Help us to change our attitude and desires. Help us. We love You.*
MaryEmma

AUGUST 29

"… God sent His Son, born of a woman, born under the law, to redeem those under the law, that we might receive adoption to son-ship…. sent the Spirit of His Son into our hearts…."
Galatians 4: 4-5

When I read these words I am filled with love and gratitude to my heavenly Father. He went to a lot of work and planning for you and me. Why? Because He loves us. We aren't natural born children, we are chosen. We are adopted by our heavenly Father.

First, He sent His Son, Jesus, to be born of a woman, under the law. Jesus was sent to rescue us from the law and give us grace, to be adopted as His child. And then He sent the Spirit of His Son into our hearts.

Why did He go to so much trouble for us? Because He loves us and wants to fellowship with us, just as our natural parents love us and want to spend time with us. We have His Spirit in our being, so we can freely go to Him and have a conversation. We can tell Him our plans, our hurts and our needs. We can let Him solve our problems. But it is our choice.

Will we allow Him to be our best friend?

MY PRAYER: *Heavenly Father, thank You so much for loving us. Thank you for wanting us. We are not rejected but wanted and loved by you. Thank You. We love you.*

MaryEmma

AUGUST 30

DISCIPLINE

"This is what Cyrus king of Persia says: 'Any of his people among
you may go up to Jerusalem in Judah and build the temple of the
Lord, the God of Israel, the God who is in Jerusalem.'"
Ezra 1:3

God keeps His promises. It has been 70 years, just as God told
Jeremiah, that they were in Babylon. A new king has taken over and they
are allowed to go home. Their job is to build a temple and the King is
providing for them.

Their exile in Babylon was punishment because God's children had
turned away from God and were worshipping gods made with human
hands. But He told them it would be 70 years. That is a long time to sit in
the corner—or not watch TV, as parents today discipline. Many did not
return, but those with a love for God did. They had a mission: to rebuild
the temple of God.

God disciplines us today when we need it.

Do we recognize our problems as homework from God?

Do we ask him what he wants to teach us?

MY PRAYER: *Lord God, help us remember You always keep Your promises to*
us. You are a faithful God. Forgive our unfaithfulness when we don't trust You.
MaryEmma

AUGUST 31

HOW DO WE WORSHIP GOD?

> *"... Administer true justice; show mercy and compassion to one another. Do not oppress the widow or the fatherless, the foreigner or the poor. Do not plot evil against each other."*
> Zechariah: 7:8-10

These are the instructions God gave the people after they returned to Israel to rebuild the temple. They had asked if they should return to fasting and mourning certain months.

God basically said they were just doing empty religious rituals. He gave them these instructions for pure worship.

As I thought about these verses, I realized that we have organized our government to help the needy, but what about us? How do we respond when we see the beggar on the street, or the homeless? They may be in that position because of losing a job or mental illness. What is our reaction to the widow or the fatherless getting welfare checks? How does our heart respond to the foreigner coming here for a better life?

What do our hearts value? I see more reaction to an injured animal on the news than to a mistreated child.

What are our values?

Do we show mercy and compassion to others?

MY PRAYER: *Lord, I am afraid we don't follow Your command to help the weak and needy. We seem to condemn and blame. Give us your wisdom and mercy and compassion. Help us and forgive us for our self centeredness.*

MaryEmma

SEPTEMBER 1

PRAYER OF COMPASSION

> *"I....fell on my knees with my hands spread out to the Lord my God and prayed: 'I am too ashamed and disgraced, my God, to lift up my face to You, because our sins ....."*
> Ezra 9: 6-10

Ezra's prayer was a prayer of confession for the sins of others. When he arrived in Jerusalem after seventy years in Babylon, he discovered that many of the men had married wives with foreign gods. That was the sin of Solomon that began their journey of turning away from God.

Ezra is heart broken and his prayer is full of remorse.

It is not a prayer of self-righteousness but compassion and fear.

Do we pray for the sins of others?

Do we pray for the sins of our country as Daniel and Ezra did for theirs?

We are called a Christian nation, but are we really?

Do we pray for our community of Christians who are not living Christian lives?

Do we pray with the compassion of Ezra?

MY PRAYER: *Lord, I pray for the secret sins in our own heart, and I pray for the sins of our people; our country. Help us to turn back to you and trust and obey you. We love You.*

MaryEmma

SEPTEMBER 2

HUMILITY IN PRAYER

"For some days I mourned and fasted and prayed before the God of heaven. Then I said: 'Lord, the God of heaven, the great and awesome God, who keeps His covenant of love with those who love Him…'"
Nehemiah 1: 4-5,

This is a prayer of praise: he is telling God how great He is, how wonderful He is, before he turns to confession.

Nehemiah is cupbearer to the King. His problem: he had been told that the city of Jerusalem was in bad shape. The walls had not been repaired. Ezra had taken the second group of exiles to rebuild the temple about 14 years earlier.

But the city is still in "great trouble and disgrace". He wants to do something about it, but he needs the King's help, so before he talks to the King, he is talking to God. Getting His advice and help. He is not approaching God with pride and self-confidence, but he is approaching God in humility. He realizes there is sin in his life and his people's lives, and he is asking for help.

Do we pray for God's wisdom before we tackle a problem?

Do we talk to God about the problems and needs of the people in our country?

MY PRAYER: *Lord God, we need your help. We need to reverence you and talk to you with humility. Give us awareness of problems and to take them to you. Forgive us for not praying for our country. Help us all to recognize your power and your love as well as our need as Americans.*

MaryEmma

SEPTEMBER 3

SENTENCE PRAYERS:

*"They were all trying to frighten us, thinking, 'their hands will
get too weak for the work, and it will not be completed.'
But I prayed, 'Now strengthen my hands.'"*
Nehemiah 6:9

We don't have to get down on our knees, in a quiet place to pray. We can pray at any time and any place. Nehemiah is a good model for prayer. He used sentence prayers throughout the day when opposition raised its ugly head. Nehemiah and his people are trying to get the gates up in the city wall, and opposition continued. He prayed for help.

What do we do when opposition turns on us?

There are times when others try to discourage us at work, or in relationships. What are we to do? Fuss and fume, or talk to God and get His wisdom?

Sometimes opposition comes from within with negative thoughts. What do we do? Ask God to give us positive thoughts. Have a Bible verse handy in our minds, so we can praise God. Bible verses are my armor against negative thoughts. There will always be opposition in our lives.

How will we handle it?

MY PRAYER: *Lord, thank you for your help every day, any time of the day. We just need to remember you, to trust and obey you. We love you.*

MaryEmma

SEPTEMBER 4

STIFFNECKED

"They stood where they were and read from the Book of the Law…
in confession and in worshiping the Lord their God.….
Nehemiah 9: 2-3

The walls and the gates are up and they have come together to give thanks to the Lord for helping them. This prayer starts with praise and thanks for all God has done through the centuries, but they don't gloss over their sins.

They confess their sins and the sins of their ancestors for not obeying—for turning away from their God.

They confessed they turned their backs on God even though God warned them through his prophets. They admitted he was patient but they paid no attention to him.

This God is our God. We also become stiff-necked at times and want our own way instead of God's way.

The beauty of our God is that when we confess, He forgives.

Do we recognize our sins?

Do we confess them?

Do we believe God will forgive us?

MY PRAYER: *Lord, thank you that you are a forgiving God, gracious and compassionate always loving us and wanting the best for us. You are wonderful. We are so blessed to know you.*

MaryEmma

SEPTEMBER 5

ONE FAMILY

"Therefore Israel will be abandoned until the time when she who is in labor bears a son, and the rest of his brothers return to join the Israelites. He will stand and shepherd his flock ....
Micah 5: 3-4

The exiles have returned to Jerusalem, the temple rebuilt, the walls and gates are up. They are home, and there is silence from God's prophets for about 400 years, but they are left with this word: A son will be born.

God is sending His son to "shepherd His flock in the strength of the Lord". He will be born in Bethlehem.

They were looking for an earthly king, but they received a spiritual king. He would bring us Gentiles into his kingdom as well as his favored people, the Jews. He would be the light in a dark world!

Their problem and our problem is that we are interested in earthly things: our possessions, but they are temporary.

God provides eternal possessions: Eternal life: True peace, joy and love.

Where is our focus?

Is it on the eternal or the temporary?

MY PRAYER: *Lord, Help us to focus on you instead of the 'wants' of the world around us. We love you and want to honor you. You bless us and bless us. You are worthy of all honor and we are unworthy and we thank You.*

MaryEmma

SEPTEMBER 6

REMINDER

"...to turn the hearts of the parents to their children and the disobedient to the wisdom of the righteous —to make ready a people prepared for the Lord."
Luke 1:16-17

John the Baptist was born in preparation for the birth of our Jesus Christ. He was to lead the way to prepare people's heart to receive Jesus as Savior. He would bring many people *back* to the Lord their God.

It is so easy to get involved in our family and activities and we push our Lord to the back burner. There are days when we go to church, but our mind is not on God but on what we are going to do, or what we did. We need to help ourselves to bring us "back to the Lord our God".

What can we do? Could we squeeze 10 minutes before we leave for worship to pray to God? Could we get up 10 minutes earlier in the morning so that we could spend that time talking to God?

Do we need a reminder of the Lord?

Do we need to write a Bible verse on a card for a reminder?

What does it take to remind us to talk to you? Trouble?

MY PRAYER: *Lord, we need to talk about our personal worship time with you. We need to turn our hearts back to you. Show us what you want us to do. We want to please you. We love you.*

MaryEmma

BELIEVE

> *"... John saw Jesus coming toward him and said, 'Look, the Lamb of God, who takes away the sin of the world!'... 'I saw the Spirit come down from heaven as a dove and remain on Him'"*
> John 1: 29, 32

John the Baptist was chosen by God to prepare people to believe Jesus. His job was to make them realize their sinfulness and their need of a Savior. When Jesus appeared, John introduces him as the Sacrificial Lamb who will take away their sins.

All we have to do is to believe in Jesus. When we believe, God baptizes us with His Spirit, His Holy Spirit, and it's through His Spirit that He lives in us and enables us to understand God's will.

How blessed we are to know God intimately through His Spirit!

Do we think of God as a faraway God?

Do we think of him as gentle and forgiving?

MY PRAYER: *Lord God, thank You for Your gift. You not only gave us eternal salvation, but you also have given us your Spirit to live in us and guide us according to your will. Your gifts are priceless. They cost you much, but are free to us. Thank you. We love you.*

MaryEmma

SEPTEMBER 8

BELIEVE AND UNDERSTAND

"They replied, 'it has taken 46 years to build this temple, and you are going to raise it in three days?' But the temple He had spoken of was His body.
John 2:20

Jesus spoke plainly and clearly to His disciples and to those who believed, but to those who did not believe, He spoke in riddles, because they did not want to know the truth.

When our heart is open and we want to fellowship with our Lord, the Spirit helps us to understand God's message. It is an advantage we had that the disciples did not have.

Will we spend time in God's word today?

Will we talk to God first and ask Him to help us understand His message for us?

Do we believe that God loves us and wants the best for us?

MY PRAYER: *Lord, thank you for the faithfulness of disciples, even when they did not understand. Thank you for your Spirit with us to help us understand and helps us to obey.*
We love you.

MaryEmma

SEPTEMBER 9

OUR EXAMPLE

"By myself I can do nothing; I judge only as I hear, and my judgment is just, for I seek not to please myself but Him who sent me."
John 3: 30

This is the reason that Jesus, the Son, spent time in prayer. So He could do what God, the Father wanted Him to do.

When He had a busy day, He got up early to pray, or late at night, He went out on a mountain by Himself to pray—to talk to God. This is the example he gave to us. We need to make God our priority.

We are blessed to be able to have a conversation with our Lord and Savior at any moment.

Do we think we are too wise to need God's wisdom?

Should we talk to God any less than Jesus?

Do we take advantage of this wonderful blessing?

MY PRAYER: *Lord, it is so wonderful that we can just visit with you at any moment. We can tell you our concerns and ask you what to do but we can also just enjoy your presence and your words of love and remember your promises. Thank you.*

MaryEmma

SEPTEMBER 10

WE SEE GOD EVERYWHERE

> *"The heavens declare the glory of God; the skies*
> *proclaim the work of His hands."*
> Psalm 19:1

God can be seen everywhere: from nature around us to the great buildings God gave man the wisdom to build. God may be invisible, yet we see His influence everywhere we look. We can look at his nature growing around us and see his love.

He loves us and He wants the best for us. He gives us beauty to look at. He gives us protection and guidance.

Even when "bad" things happen, He makes it work out for our good. We have a wonderful Lord and Savior. Let's praise Him.

When we look at the skies, do we say 'thank you?'

Do we see his glory in the sunshine, in the rain and beautiful Spring flowers?

MY PRAYER: *Lord, thank You. You are wonderful. We see your power everywhere whenever we take the time to look. You are always with us, guiding us and teaching us. We love You.*

MaryEmma

DELIGHTS TO SHOW MERCY

"Who is a God like You, who pardons sin and forgives the transgression?
You do not stay angry forever but delight to show mercy."
Micah 7: 18

Sometimes it is good to just stop and think about our God. What a wonderful God we have. He wants to be the Lord of our life and to guide and direct us.

He wants to love us and forgive us, not punish us or be angry with us.
I like thinking that He "delights to show mercy". When I
read those words, I can only say, "Thank You Lord."
Do we thank him for loving me so much?
Do we say "thank you that you delight to show me mercy?"
Will we enjoy his presence today?

MY PRAYER: *You are a wonderful God. You are perfect but you forgive us when we sin. You do not stay angry with us, and instead of punishing us as we deserve, you show us mercy. Thank you for loving us so much.*

MaryEmma

SEPTEMBER 12

PURE JOY

"Consider it pure joy, my brothers and sisters whenever you face trials of many kinds, because you know that the testing of your faith produces perseverance."
James 1:2

I cannot say that joy is my first reaction when I have problems. When it is over, I can say, 'thank You Lord, for getting me through this', but that is not my first attitude.

Later I can see how God blessed me during that time.

I can see how my faith grew as I hurt and God helped me.

If we believe God is in control of all things, we can believe God has a reason for allowing trials to happen.

When problems occur, we have two choices. We can trust God will help us through, or we can be angry and turn our back on God. I pray that we will keep our eyes on God and let His perfect will be done. That is when He will give us that joy.

Are we trusting God?

Do we reflect God's joy?

MY PRAYER: *Lord God, we need you when we have trouble, but we also need you when things are going good. We need you always because you are guiding and teaching us to become more like your son. Thank you for always being with us.*
MaryEmma

WHERE ARE OUR EYES?

"Lift up your eyes and look to the heavens: who created all these?"
Isaiah 40: 26

There are times when we need to just stop and look up. Take our eyes off ourselves and ours, and see God. We like to concentrate on this verse instead of ourselves. What wonderful things God does for us.

But we need to think about God Himself. May we look up today and see His majesty. May we look around at the beautiful buildings and realize that it is our God who gave men the wisdom to build them.

When we see a beautiful park to whom do we give credit?

Do we thank him for the beauty of the trees and grass?

MY PRAYER: *Lord, You are a wonderful loving God. You bless us with so much. Thank you for the beauty of the world we live in. We love You and thank You and praise You. You are the greatest!*

MaryEmma

SEPTEMBER 14

MERCY IS LOVE

*"For I desire mercy, not sacrifice, and acknowledgment
of God rather than burnt offerings."*
Hosea 6:6

It has been said that it is "easier to do, than to be". We fall into that trap and that was the problem with the children of Israel. They had turned away from the living God, and were worshipping idols, but they still continued the habits of their true religion, but their heart and minds were not involved. God is a jealous God, He is the One and only God but their idol worship was more fun.

Could this be true for us today? We don't worship wood and stone figures, but where are our hearts and emotions?

"To do, or to be" is the question.

Jesus said that he was vine and we are the branches. We are to stay attached to the vine or we die spiritually as the branch would. Sometimes we like to separate from the vine and follow our own ideas. When we are connected to the vine, we will show mercy to God's other children, and we will acknowledge God to others. This is what God wants from us. This isn't a lot different than "Love God and love others as ourselves" is it?

MY PRAYER: *Lord, we like to do things for you instead of with you. It takes a lot of time to cooperate with you and we have to forget about ourselves to humble ourselves to hear your voice. It is easier to do our own thing. But we miss out on your blessings and create stress for ourselves. Forgive us. Help us.*

MaryEmma

HE CARES

"The Lord is good, a refuge in times of trouble.
He cares for those who trust Him."
Nahum 1:7

This is a 'feel good' verse, but what is so amazing about this verse are the verses around it.

Nahum consists of 3 chapters of God's anger; how He will destroy wicked people. It is as though He suddenly remembers the people who love him, and he gives reassurance to those who trust Him.

Sometimes we feel as if we are surrounded by people who do not know God and don't want to know God. This verse reminds us of God's love. He has prepared a refuge for us, a place for us to go in times of trouble. "God cares for those who trust Him".

MY PRAYER: *Lord, You are good and you are a refuge for us when we turn to you. Thank you for helping us trust you and receive your love and protection. We love you.*

MaryEmma

SEPTEMBER 16

MY STRENGTH

"Surely God is my Salvation; I will trust and not be afraid. The Lord, the Lord Himself, is my strength and my defense; He has become my salvation."
Isaiah 12:2

Why do we worry and fret? Why are we afraid of what might happen? Is it because we do not trust God? Could it be that we do not know Him well enough to trust Him? Do we believe that God wants the very best for us? Sometimes we may need extra time with Him to understand His hand in our lives.

God is our salvation and we need to trust Him. He is our strength and our defense.

Do we trust Him or do we trust ourselves? It is a decision we need to make to have peace in a sinful world. God has chosen us.

Do we choose to trust Him?

MY PRAYER: *Lord God, thank You for choosing us to be your children. Thank you for Your love, your strength and your protection. You are wonderful and we love you and trust you.*

MaryEmma

THE LORD REIGNS

"The Lord reigns, let the earth be glad; let the distant shores rejoice....
Light shines on the righteous and joy on the upright in heart. Rejoice
in the Lord, You who are righteous, and praise His holy name."
Psalm 97:1,12

Do we love the Lord for who He is, or for what He does for us? That's a good question to ponder.

The Psalmist describes Him in such beautiful ways. Do we rush by those descriptions to get to where He gives us joy and shows His love to us? We have a wonderful loving God.

Do we praise Him?

Do we see him in around us in our world?

MY PRAYER: *Lord, You are mighty and powerful. You love us and help us live in the world. Help us remember to thank You and praise You and not take You for granted. We love You.*

MaryEmma

WILL WE TRUST?

"Whoever dwells in the shelter of the Most High will rest in the shadow of the Almighty. I will say of the Lord, 'He is my refuge and my fortress, my God, in whom I trust. Surely He will save You."
Psalm 91:1-2

How blessed we are to rest in the 'shadow of the Almighty'. He is close to us to protect us and keep us safe. We trust Him. But sometimes things will happen that make us fearful. Our fear and trust struggle for supremacy. Which will win?

If trust wins, we snuggle under the feathers of His wings, and we are comforted.

Do we struggle to submit our will for God's perfect will?

Do we remember that God is our shield?

Do we allow his feathers to comfort us?

MY PRAYER: *Lord God, You are wonderful to love us so much and want to bless us. Thank You for Your feathers that we can snuggle under and feel safe and protected. We choose to trust in you.*

MaryEmma

SELF CENTEREDNESS

"He wanted to die, and said, 'It would be better for me to die than to live.'
But God said to Jonah, 'Is it right for you to be angry about the plant?'
'It is,' he said. 'and I am so angry I wish I were dead.'"
Jonah 4: 6-9

This is my favorite verse in Jonah because I can relate to it. God can bless me so much and then I get upset over little things. I don't appreciate what God has done for me. Jonah didn't want to witness to Nineveh, he wanted them all to be condemned and it took a great fish to swallow him to convince him to witness. Then he was angry because they repented.

His skin surely was raw and tender after being in the great fish, and he wanted shade and protection from the sun, but he didn't care for the one hundred and twenty thousand people who didn't know God. He wanted God's blessing for himself only.

Do we recognize the wonderful things God does for us?

Do we see His loving hand when He disciplines us and tries to teach us?

MY PRAYER: *Lord God, forgive us our self-centeredness. Forgive us for wanting our way instead of Your way. Help us to love others as You love us.*

MaryEmma

PRAISE HIM

"Praise the Lord. Praise the Lord from the heavens; praise Him in the heights above. Praise Him, all His angels; praise Him, all His heavenly hosts....
Psalm 148:1

We are to praise our Lord. This Psalm tells us that nature praises God. Are we humans are the only creation of God that doesn't continually praise Him?

As I meditated on this Psalm, I thought about Psalm 144, wondered why my heart was moved by reminding me of what God does for me, more than just being reminded of how is to praise God. Is my God too small? Can I only relate to Him when I think about how He helps me, rather than how great He is?

I think I need to make this a matter of prayer. We are to praise God for who He is, not for what He does for us. He is a glorious wonderful God. He shows us how to love others. He makes the world beautiful for all to see.

Do we see God's greatness in nature?

Do we hear him through that 'small quiet voice' within us?

Do we see his love in others?

MY PRAYER: *Lord, you are great, help us see your work around us today and be reminded to praise You. We love You.*

MaryEmma

PEACE DURING TROUBLE

"The angel said to them, 'Do not be afraid, Mary; You have found favor with God. You will conceive and give birth to a son, and you are to call Him Jesus"
Luke 1:30

Mary agreed, but would she be able to handle the gossip in her village?

Looking back in history, this sounds wonderful for Mary: a young Jewish girl chosen to be the mother of the Son of God. But will Mary be able to convince the people in their village that she had conceived by the Holy Spirit? Will there be a scandal? Will they blame Joseph for being impatient and not waiting?

She had to accept the bad along with the good.

In our lives, we often have bad times before the good times arrive. Can we trust God to lead us through the valley when we can barely see the top of the mountain?

Mary trusted God's wisdom and plans. Do we?

MY PRAYER: *Lord God, Help us accept the plan you have for our lives. Forgive us for complaining. Help us to recognize your peace among the trouble. We love you.*

MaryEmma

SEPTEMBER 22

FAITH AND TRUST

"Then he fell to the ground in worship and said....
"The Lord gave and The Lord has taken away; may the name of The Lord
be praised.' In all this, Job did not sin by charging God with wrongdoing."
Job 1:20-22

Why do bad things happen to good people? Job had just found out that all his children had been killed and all his wealth had been destroyed.

Could anything be worse than this?

Was Job wicked? No, he was faithful in his trust of God. Why did God allow this terrible thing happen to one of His people?

We know, but Job never did. Even his friends accused him of doing wrong things that caused it. Job questioned why, but he never questioned God faithfulness.

We have bad things happen in our lives and we wonder why. Job never knew why this happened, but he trusted God.

That is our job: To trust God.

Do we believe that Jesus will give us peace during trouble?

MY PRAYER: *Lord, I pray that as we have bad times that we will spend the necessary time with you. Help us accept and have the peace with you that you promised us. We love you*

MaryEmma

SEPTEMBER 23

DOUBT OR TRUST?

"But Mary treasured up all these things and pondered them in their heart."
Luke 2:19

Do you think maybe Mary was wondering if an angel really spoke to them? Was Joseph doubting the dream? Was it just an upset stomach? Were shepherds really seeing a host of angels who spoke to them? Mary and Joseph were human and young. They needed confirmation and God sent it.

First the shepherds, then a week later, maybe when they were still pondering the message, God sent Simeon and Anna to confirm God's message to them. God doesn't leave us in doubt. He wants us to learn to trust Him in every situation.

I was concerned about a situation this morning and how I would deal with it and when I opened my book, this was the verse: "You shall not go out with haste, for the Lord will go before you, and the God of Israel will be your rear guard."

Why was I upset?

God just reminded me that He is always with me, going before me and guarding me in the rear. My job is to trust Him and act as He guides.

Are we concerned about something today?

Talk to God about it. He is a God of much Grace.

MY PRAYER: *Thank You, Lord, for your help. You are always with us. Forgive us when we forget about your presence and love. We love you.*
MaryEmma

SEPTEMBER 24

LIGHT OF REVELATION

*"For my eyes have seen your salvation, which you have
prepared in the sight of all nations: a light for revelation to
the Gentiles, and the glory of Your people Israel."*
Luke 2:30--32

"A light for revelation to the Gentiles". As I read this phrase this
morning, it sparked a memory of our trip to Turkey.

Our guide showed us 7 different civilizations in Turkey's history. We
saw some ruins of buildings and we also saw their worship places. It was
the Hittites worship area that came to my mind. We know the name from
the Old Testament: Abraham bought the cave he buried Sarah in from the
Hittites. We passed some ruins and wound our way up to the huge top of
the mountain. Here was a formation of rocks and we climbed up to the
peak. Two huge rocks had an opening between them and one of our people
went inside and sang. You could hear her sing as if she were standing beside
us. This was what they worshipped. They were worshiping God's nature,
not the true and living God.

That is an example of the darkness that Jesus' light shines into. We
may not be Hittites, but most of us are Gentiles. Think where we would be
without Jesus birth, death and resurrection: in the darkness of worshipping
nature or man made objects. Jesus said, "I am the light of the world". This
was what Simeon was prophesying when Jesus was 8 days old.

MY PRAYER: *Lord, thank You for being the light in our hearts and mind.
Thank you for showing us our Savior. Thank you for the love you show to us.
Forgive us when we ignore you and thank you for forgiving us.*

MaryEmma

SEPTEMBER 25

FIRST MISSIONARIES

*"And all who heard it were amazed at what the shepherds said to them…
the shepherds returned, glorifying and praising God for all the things
they had heard and seen which were just as they had been told."*
Luke 2: 17-18,20

The shepherds were our first missionaries! They went, they saw, and they shared with others. This is what we need to be doing. Sharing with others what a great Savior we have; sharing what He is doing for us. Christmas season is a wonderful time to be doing this, because we are already thinking about the baby in the manger, but I pray we will not leave Him in the manger.

Jesus came into this world to show us the love and mercy of our heavenly father. He came into this world to die for our sins. He came into this world to show us the resurrection from earthly death to eternal life.

The shepherds returned home overflowing with joy and love; praising and glorifying God.

Do we have the joy of Christmas in our hearts?

Do we share the good news with others?

MY PRAYER: *Holy God, we love you and praise you. We thank you for Your salvation. We thank you for your Spirit within us, to guide and direct us. Bless us today with a greater awareness of your presence, and help us share with others.*
MaryEmma

SEPTEMBER 26

THE HUMBLE IN HEART

"the shepherds said to one another, 'Let's go to Bethlehem and see this thing that has happened, which the Lord has told us about.'"
Luke 2:15

When the angels left, did the shepherds pinch themselves, did they ask another, "Did you see what I saw?' They were filled with wonder. What did this mean? Did they sit on the hillside and think about it? No. No sitting around: they hurried off to see what it was about! What they found was the Christ child, the Savior of the world.

Why did God choose the humble shepherds to be the first to know? They were considered 'not polite society'. They smelled! Maybe after years of being with sheep they didn't have good manners.

But God didn't ignore them. He chose them to be first. God loves the humble in heart, rather than the prideful person, because they are willing to believe. When we are filled with pride, all our attention is on ourselves and not on God.

A question for today: are we so full of ourselves that we can't see the majesty of God around us?

Are we so full of ourselves that we push God away and are not aware of His presence?

Do we need to talk to God about this?

MY PRAYER: *Lord God, we love you and ask your forgiveness for our self-centeredness. Give us a greater awareness of your presence with us and help us understand how you want us to live our lives. Amen.*

Mary Emma

HOW DO WE KNOW?

"...said, 'Joseph son of David, do not be afraid to take Mary home as your wife, because what is conceived in their is from the Holy Spirit.'"
Mathew 1:20

God has a way of giving us assurance when we are confused and upset. Just as He helped Joseph understand and gave him peace, He helps us when we need it. God can speak to us in many different ways. In the Scriptures, it was through visions and dreams. They did not have the written scripture as we do, so God spoke directly.

We are blessed to have the word of God in black and white! I learned years ago 4 ways we can understand what God is telling us when we are confused:

1. Through the scriptures, because God will not tell us anything contrary to His word.
2. Through peace and assurance that God gives in our mind.
3. Through circumstances that fit the situation.
4. Through another person who walks with the Lord.

God will let us know what He wants us to do.
Do we talk to Him and listen with an open mind?
Do we pray until we have peace?

MY PRAYER: *Lord, thank you for giving us peace when we know your will. Help us to trust you and love you and take time to listen to You. Thank you for blessing us in so many ways.*

MaryEmma

September 28

DISAPPOINTMENT

"Because Joseph her husband was a righteous man and did not want to expose her to public disgrace, he had in mind to divorce her quietly."
Mathew 1:19

Who was Joseph? We don't think much about him. He is like the groom at a wedding. All eyes are on the bride and the groom just stands there.

What are his emotions? How is he feeling? He must feel hurt and disappointment. The law says that she is to be stoned publicly. Would he?

Joseph must have been a gentle man: with love and compassion. Maybe the best solution would be to leave her with her family. Her reputation would be ruined, but she would be alive. He was a righteous man—he was right with God. He allowed God to guide him in his decision.

When we are hurt and disappointed, what is our reaction?

Do we take it to God and pray and meditate until God gives us peace?

Do we seek revenge?

Do we keep the resentment in our hearts?

True peace never comes until we turn it over to God and allow Him to handle it.

MY PRAYER: *Dear Lord, we need you. We need your love and grace in our hearts and minds. We need your guidance to help us to do the right thing. We need to confess and allow you to forgive and restore hurt feelings. We love you and thank you.*

MaryEmma

SEPTEMBER 29

REMEMBERING THE GIVER

"And Mary said: 'My soul glorifies the Lord and my spirit rejoices in God my Savior, for He has been mindful of the humble state of His servant.'"
Luke 1: 46

How do we respond when we are really excited?

What do we do when we feel so blessed, so thrilled?

Mary praised God. She was so aware of His blessing that praise just poured out of her mouth. 'My soul glorifies the Lord, my spirit rejoices in God my Savior".

How do we react when we are excited? Is thanking God our first thought? Or do we only think of ourselves?

MY PRAYER: *Lord, we rejoice in you. You are mighty and great. You are also loving and gentle. Thank you for your love and your blessings. Help us to better appreciate what You give us. We love You.*

MaryEmma

SEPTEMBER 30

CHRISTIAN SUPPORT

"At that time Mary got ready and hurried to a town in the hill country of Judea, where she entered Zechariah's home and greeted Elizabeth. When Elizabeth heard Mary's greeting, the baby leaped in her womb...."
Luke 1:39-40

Why would Mary immediately make the long trip from Nazareth to the hill country? Was she afraid? Was she confused? Did she need to talk to someone who would understand? Mary was obedient, but it doesn't mean that she wasn't fearful.

How would she explain to their family about her pregnancy?

Elizabeth could understand and rejoice with her. God puts godly people in our lives when we need them. We are fearful sometimes when we enter a new situation. That doesn't mean God isn't with us.

Do we turn to Him in prayer and talk to Him?

Do we look for assurance in His word?

Do we spend time with Godly people who can help us?

MY PRAYER: *Lord, help us to trust you. Help us to be obedient even when we are fearful and help us to see the help you are providing. Thank you for loving us and helping us over the rough paths of life. We love you.*

MaryEmma

OCTOBER 1

CONDITION OF OUR HEART

"'I am the Lord's servant,' Mary answered. 'May your
word to me be fulfilled.' Then the angel left her."
Luke 1: 38

Did Mary know what she was getting into? She accepted the angel's words. Did she realize the problems, the whispers, the heartaches she would have because she was obedient to God?

The angel told her that she was chosen by God, and she was obedient. She said, "I am the Lord's servant. May your word to me be fulfilled." Maybe this is the reason that she was chosen from all the other virgins because of the condition of her heart. Maybe this is the reason she was picked, even though she was not educated, not from a wealthy family or a great city, but because of the condition of her heart.

Mary's heart condition was to obey and trust.

What does God see when He looks into our heart?

Does He see love and mercy?

Does He see resentments and greed?

I asked God this morning and this was my answer: "You like to help people, but only when it doesn't inconvenience you".

Do I ignore this answer and pretend I didn't hear it?

Do I make it a matter of prayer, so God can change my heart?

MY PRAYER: *Lord, I need you to help me truly love others. I want to please you. Purify the emotions in our hearts. Help us to put you first in our lives and let you take care of everything else. Thank you for this example of Mary's obedient attitude.*

MaryEmma

OUR GIFTS

"… you, my child, will be called a prophet of the Most High; for you will
go on before the Lord to prepare the way for Him, to give His people
the knowledge of salvation through the forgiveness of their sins."
Luke 1:76-77

This child was John, the Baptist. He was to prepare the way for Jesus ministry. His ministry was calling for repentance, to make people aware of their sins, of their need of a savior.

We all have different ministries. We all have different gifts and talents. What gifts has God given us to use for Him?

We have different personalities. How do we use them to glorify God?

God has a plan for our life. We need to talk to Him and ask Him His plan for us.

What gift has God given us?

Are we using it for his glory?

Do we need to talk to God?

MY PRAYER: *Father God, bless us with an awareness of your presence. Help us to see you in our circumstances. Show us how you want us to react to the different people we encounter today. Show us how we can glorify you. We love you. Thank You.*

MaryEmma

OCTOBER 3

GOD'S PLAN

"'How will this be,' Mary asked the angel, 'since I am a virgin?'
the angel answered, 'The Holy Spirit will come on You, and
the power of the Most High will overshadow You.'"
Luke 1: 34- 35

Mary was bewildered. How could she conceive a baby without a man? What was this angel saying? It wasn't

Possible. It was impossible.

All things are possible with God. God had a plan. God helps us to understand, one step at a time. First He gave the law, to prepare us. He knew we couldn't keep the law perfectly but it would make us realize we were sinful and in need of a Savior.

The innocent perfect lamb that was sacrificed at Passover was an example of the Savior yet to come. His next step was to send God His Son to earth as a baby to show us love and then die for our sins as the lamb did.

It is the perfect gift. That is one reason we give gifts at Christmas, to remember the greatest gift of all.

MY PRAYER: *Thank You, our heavenly Father, for the greatest gift of all times: Salvation. We thank You and love You.*

MaryEmma

OCTOBER 4

PATH TO PEACE

"Mary was greatly troubled at His words and wondered what kind of greeting this might be. But the angel said to her, 'Do not be afraid, Mary; You have found favor with God.
Luke 1:29- 30

We don't know what angels look like, or how they sound, but every time one appears to a person, they are frightened.

They listen carefully to the angels' words. Mary was totally confused—troubled at his words. What did they mean?

Mary was the chosen one; the one to give birth. She was told it would be a boy, she was told what to name the baby. She was told He would be great. Did she understand all that was happening to her?

We don't understand all the circumstances God allows in our lives. We don't understand how God will use them to bring us closer to Him. We don't understand everything we read in the Bible, but as we pray and meditate, God helps us to understand. We either accept what He is doing or we fight God and tell Him He doesn't know what He is doing. Our job is to listen and cooperate with God:

Do we ask him to help us understand?

Do we trust him to lead us through the situation?

This is the path to peace.

MY PRAYER: *Lord God, help us understand what you want us to do. Help us to love you and trust you. Give us guidance so we can become the person you created us to be. Teach us to listen. We love you.*

MaryEmma

OCTOBER 5

WHY?

"The virgin's name was Mary. The angel went to her and said,
'Greetings, You who are highly favored! The Lord is with You.'"
Luke 1: 27-28

WOW!!! That is my reaction when I read this. What made Mary so special? Why did God pick her? She wasn't highly educated, she wasn't from a wealthily family, and she didn't live in an important city. Why did God pick Mary?

God told Samuel when He chose David to be king that God does not look at the outward man, but at the inward man.

God looks into our thoughts and our attitudes. He knows if there is love and compassion in us. He knows our character and if we can handle difficult situations.

What does God see when He looks into our inward person?

Does He see love and joy and mercy?

Does He see trust and faith directed at Him?

Does He see a desire to please Him above all else?

MY PRAYER: *Holy Father, when you look into our hearts, you aren't always pleased, are you? We are selfish, we are greedy, we want our own way. Help us, Lord, to become the person you created us to be, full of love for you and others.*
MaryEmma

OCTOBER 6

PEACE

"For to us a child is born, to us a son is given, and the government will be on His shoulders. And He will be called Wonderful Counselor, Mighty God, Everlasting Father, Prince of peace."
Isaiah 9:6

The prophet Isaiah prophesied of the birth of Jesus centuries earlier. He would reign forever and He would be called "Prince of Peace."

What does peace mean? People are searching for it. Governments are searching for peace. Peace starts in our hearts and minds. Peace starts by trusting God.

Peace starts when we allow God to be in control of our lives.

Do we have peace in our hearts?

Do we spend enough time with you to understand what you want us to do and be?

Do we need to talk to you about our free time?

MY PRAYER: *Lord, we want peace. We want you to give us peace, but I am not sure that we want You to be in control of our lives. Too often we say, "I can do it myself". Give us the faith to will allow you to rule our lives, to be our Wonderful Counselor. We love You.*

MaryEmma

OCTOBER 7

PEACE IN A TROUBLE WORLD

"I have told you these things, so that in me you may have peace. In this world you will have trouble. But take heart! I have overcome the world."
John 16: 33

This is the final week of Jesus life and He is preparing His disciples. He is preparing them for the shock of despair at His death and He is also preparing them for the shock of delight at His resurrection!

They heard the words, but they didn't understand. They were still expecting an earthly kingdom instead of a spiritual kingdom. His 33 years on earth was finished. He was returning to His Father. What would they do?

In this world, we have trouble. In our families, we have trouble. In our jobs, we have trouble. But in our God, our Savior, we have peace offered to us, but we must stay connected to the Vine, to him. He is the source of our peace and our strength.

How do we handle troubled times?

Do we go to the Father for help?

Do we allows his Spirit to direct us and give us peace?

MY PRAYER: *Lord Jesus, help us to stay connected to you today. Give us an awareness of your presence. Help us to trust you instead of ourselves when trouble rears its ugly head. Give us your peace and teach us how to maintain your peace in our hearts.*

MaryEmma

OCTOBER 8

HIS PERFECT WILL

*If You remain in me and my words remain in You, ask
whatever You wish, and it will be done for You."*
John 15:7

Jesus promises to answer our prayers, but there is a condition given. His words must be in our hearts and minds. We have to be close in fellowship with Him. Then we will know Him so well, we will be able to ask for the right things that will improve the situation.

Another place the scriptures say that if we "ask according to His will", whatever we ask will be done. Just as any loving parent wants the best for their child and they will not say yes to something that isn't good, God won't say yes to things that will hurt us.

We must remember when we talk to God that He knows the situation better than we do, and He also knows the past and the future.

We need to trust God. Share our needs and our wants with Him, but allow Him freedom to give us the best. Sometimes He says, 'wait, this isn't the right time.' We must stay connected to the vine or we will wither away and be good for nothing.

Do we trust God?

Do we share our concerns with him?

MY PRAYER: *Lord, help us be more aware of your presence. Help us be aware of your love for us and I pray that you will guide us through this day in fellowship with your Spirit.*

MaryEmma

OCTOBER 9

GOD PRUNES

"I am the true vine, and my Father is the gardener. He cuts off every branch in me that bears no fruit, while every branch that does bear fruit He prunes so that it will be even more fruitful."
John 15:1-2

Pruning hurts. The gardener doesn't want to prune. He would like all the branches to grow together and be beautiful and healthy. But some branches grow in the wrong direction, away from his fellow branches. So they get clipped!

God prunes us. We are beautiful in God's sight but when we grow the wrong way, He prunes us to keep us beautiful. God prunes because He loves us, for the same reason we send our children to school. The teacher prunes through homework and tests until the children know the subject.

When we hurt through the pruning we know that God is there with us, showing us His love and teaching us the next step in our lives.

MY PRAYER: *Lord, when you prune us, help us to recognize it is your hand and understand what you want us to learn. We love you and thank you.*

MaryEmma

OUR HOME

"Jesus replied, 'Anyone who loves me will obey my teaching. My Father will love them, and we will come to them and make our home with them .'"
John 14:23

Is there a more beautiful thought anywhere than "The Father and I will make our home with you"? Jesus is reassuring His disciples. He told them He was leaving, but He wasn't going to leave them all alone. He was sending His Spirit back to help them.

He called His Spirit an 'Advocate, the Spirit of truth'. In verse 17 He tells us he will both live in us and with us.

Now He adds that He and His Father will make their home with us. What a tremendous blessing?

He loves us and lives with us.

What does that mean in our lives?

Do we visit with our boarder?

MY PRAYER: *Lord Jesus, thank you for living in us in the form of your Holy Spirit. Thank You that we are never alone, that you are always with us because you live in us and with us. Thank you for making your home with us. Help us to love and obey your teachings. Help us to trust you and please you. Thank you for your love.*

MaryEmma

GIVE THANKS

"Give THANKS in all circumstances; for this is
God's will for you in Christ Jesus."
1 Thessalonians 5:18

If we would live by this verse, how blessed we would be.

If it were our motto, we would have wonderful peace and joy in our lives.

Notice it does not say we are to be thankful FOR every situation but IN every situation. We can thank God that He is with us, and helping us through the hard times in our lives, as well as the good times.

When I start thanking God for things He has given me, and things He has done for me, I become so aware of His presence and His love. This is a wonderful reason to thank Him. It also helps me to keep my patience and my temper when things are not as I would like. We feel God's strength and love as we thank Him for His help, for giving us wisdom and knowledge.

Have we thanked Him for today?

Have we thanked him when we were depressed?

Did we thank him when our world seems to fall apart?

Thanking him gives us his strength.

MY PRAYER: *Lord God, I thank you for your presence, for our love. I thank you for the sun and the moon that you put in place. I thank you that You chose me to be Your child. I love you.*

MaryEmma

WITH THANKSGIVING

"Do not be anxious about anything, but in every situation, by prayer and petition, WITH THANKSGIVING, present your request to God."
Philippians 4:6

God says, "Don't worry. Trust me! Tell me what is bothering you and thank me in advance and I will take care of it because I love you. I may not handle it as you would like, but I know the past, present and future, and you do not. I have a purpose in your life. Thank me."

We want peace in our lives. The way to peace is through trust and thankfulness. When I can't get my mind off myself and my wants, I can start thanking God and there is an immediate transformation in my inner self. Fear and anxiety are signs God gives us to remind us to turn to Him.

What do we do when we can only think of our pain?

What is the answer to depression?

Do we bring God closer by thanking him for his blessings?

He is waiting for us to turn to him.

MY PRAYER: *Lord, I love you and I do want to trust you in every situation. Increase my faith and my awareness of your presence. I want to please you. Thank you for your love.*

MaryEmma

MUSIC IN OUR HEARTS

"Sing and make music from your heart to the Lord,
ALWAYS GIVING THANKS TO GOD the FATHER
for everything, in the name of our Lord Jesus Christ."
Ephesians 5:19b-20

I learned a little song when I was a child at camp that sometimes just pops into my head and heart:

'Thank you, Lord, for saving my soul,
Thank you, Lord, for making me whole.
Thank you, Lord, for giving to me
thy great salvation, so rich and free.

When I am not alone, I can sing it in my heart. When I am alone, I can sing it aloud. It brings joy and peace into my mind.
Are we thanking our Lord and Savior?
Have we praised him today?
Do we make music in our hearts to him?

MY PRAYER: *Thank You, Lord, for the power of music to remind us of you. Thank you for saving my soul and making me whole. You are wonderful. We love You.*

MaryEmma

OCTOBER 14

THE LORD IS GOOD

*"Know that the Lord is God. It is He who made us, and we
are His; we are His people, the sheep of His pasture.
Enter His gates with thanksgiving and His courts with
praise; give thanks to Him and praise His name.*
Psalm 100:3-4

The Lord is good. What is our reaction to that statement? Do we think about him through the day when things are going good or do we only think about him when we know that we need him? Do we think about to all that God has done for us?

Do we fix our eyes on Jesus think of all the blessings He has provided?

His love for us is as great as the heavens are above the earth. We may want more things, but we can thank Him for what He has given us.

We are the sheep of His pasture, and we stray, but He brings us back to Himself. He goes searching for us.

Why does He go searching for us? Because He loves us. What more could we ask for in a Savior? He has given us himself, his Spirit, his love. Our God is good!

How much do we love Him?

How much time do we spend with him?

Do we center our mind on him or ourselves?

MY PRAYER: *Thank you, Lord, that we are yours. We are your people, your sheep. We are unworthy of you but you love us so much you made us worthy through the sacrifice of your blood. We praise you and thank you.*

MaryEmma

OCTOBER 15

HIS SPIRIT--OUR GUEST

"...Counselor to be with you forever—the Spirit of truth. The world cannot accept Him, because it neither sees Him nor knows Him. But you know Him, for He lives with you and will be in you."
John 14:16-17

These words fill me with peace and confidence. God promises us we will never be alone. He has given us His Spirit to be our Counselor.

There are days when we feel alone, but it is just our emotions, not the truth. We can turn to John 14 and 15 and read about his love and what he plans for us.

Jesus was preparing His disciples for His departure and He wanted them to know the Spirit of God would be with them.

When He was on earth, He could only be in one place at one time. Now His spirit can be everywhere. This promise extends to us when we believe.

Do we listen to his Spirit?

Do we thank him for sending his Spirit back to us, to teach us?

Do his words comfort us?

MY PRAYER: *Lord God, You have given us Your spirit to live with us and help us understand what you want us to do. When we are hurt or confused your Spirit, our Counselor is here with us to teach us and guide us. Thank you. We love you.*

MaryEmma

OCTOBER 16

PEACE OR FEAR?

"Do not let your hearts be troubled. You believe in God, believe also in me."
John 14:1

This has been a favorite verse since I was a child. When I read it, it is just like a river of peace flowing through me. I loved it so much that I memorized the first 6 verses and would repeat them to myself at times when I needed reassurance.

Jesus had just told His disciples that He was going away and they were upset. He also told them He would return, but they didn't hear that. Only that He was leaving. We have selective hearing! We hear something bad and ignore all the good things that were also said.

He said "I am going to prepare a place for You, I will come back and take you to be with me." They didn't hear this.

Bad things happen to us in life, but God is always there to make it right. I can look back on the things I considered 'bad' and I see how God blessed me because I went through them with Him.

If something 'bad' is happening now, take it to God and let Him show You the 'good' He is creating for you.

How often do we read his words and not hear them?

How often do we dwell in our own fears instead of his word?

Have we accepted his promise of peace?

MY PRAYER: *Thank You Father, that you want us to have your peace and not be troubled. Thank you for your words of reassurance and love. We love you.*
MaryEmma

OCTOBER 17

GOD'S PLAN

"...The King will reply, 'Truly I tell you, whatever you did for one of the least of these brothers and sisters of mine, you did for me.'"
Mathew 25: 40

This is quite a message! It makes me feel very inadequate. But it does explain Jesus words, "to love our neighbor as ourselves".

How do we show our love for God? By showing love to his children.

We want to do something special for God, so we force ourselves into rigid rules. We try to obey the commands of God without the sweet fellowship of God who will help us.

God has a plan for each of our lives. He gave us all different gifts and that includes interests in different aspects of his service.

Have we asked Him how he wants us to use our gift?

Have we asked Him what His plan for us is today?

Have we asked Him to help us bless another today?

MY PRAYER: *Lord, show us your will for us. We admit that we are selfish and we want to choose who we will help and who we will show love to. We ask you to change our self-centered thoughts and give us your love to show to others.*
MaryEmma

OCTOBER 18

THE END OF THE STORY!

"Jesus said to her, 'I am the resurrection and the life.
The one who believes in me will live, even though they die,
and whoever lives by believing in me will never die.'"
John 11:25-26

This is wonderful news. Jesus just told Martha the end of the story! If we know how things are going to end, we can handle the present better. We are going to live forever.

We have two lives: A physical life and a spiritual life. We know the physical life is temporary. We will die—everyone else does eventually! But our spirit never dies.

We can live eternally with our glorious Lord and Savior by simply believing. We don't have to climb mountains or swim the oceans—we just believe.

Martha believed! She didn't understand but she believed. It is so simple and easy to believe. Why don't we?

We will have hard times in this world, but we can handle them when we know the end of the story.

Do we believe we will live forever with our Lord.

Do we remember the end of the story during fearful times?

Do we trust him with both lives?

MY PRAYER: *Thank You, Lord, for the peace you give us. and for eternal life. Thank you we don't have to work for it. We just have to love you and enjoy you.*
Mary Emma

OCTOBER 19

WORSHIPPING TOGETHER

"Then Thomas (also known as Didymus) said to the rest of the disciples, 'Let us also go, that we may die with Him.'"
John 11:16

"Unless I see the nail marks in His hand... I will not believe."
John 20: 25

Thomas is so human! I can relate to him. He spent 3 years with Jesus. He was passionate about going to Jerusalem with Jesus, even though he thought they would all die there.

But after Jesus was killed, he gave up. He had believed for no reason! He was depressed and in his self-misery he did not gather with the others on the evening of 'that first day of the week'.

When he was encouraged by his fellow disciples he joined them. When he gathered with them later, he was blessed.

Do we gather with other Christians?

Are we are blessed and encouraged as Thomas was when we join them? Why or why not?

MY PRAYER: *Lord, we have doubts even though we love you. We give in to self-pity when we are disappointed. Thank you for providing other Christians that we can gather with and be encouraged. We love You.*

MaryEmma

OCTOBER 20

LOVE IS THE ANSWER

"He answered, 'Love the Lord your God with all your heart
and with all your soul and with all your strength and with
all your mind' and 'love your neighbor as yourself.'
'You have answered correctly,' Jesus replied. 'Do this and you will live.'"
Luke 10:26-28

Have we ever thought what it means to love God in this way? What would happen if we only loved God with all our mind? Would there be a change in us? Would that change be noticeable to those around us?

What if everything we thought of was only of God and God directed as Jesus was. There would be no arguments, there would be peace, it would be a perfect world. But we cannot love God this way. We cannot love each other as we love ourselves. We have all tried and failed. It is humanly impossible! That is reason Jesus came to earth to show us the way. That is the reason He died on He cross for our sins. That is the reason He was resurrected and returned to heaven so He could send the Holy Spirit back to us to help us.

Have we put our faith in Jesus?

Has our love for him made a change in us?

What will enable us to love as Jesus directs?

MY PRAYER: *Lord, Thank you for Your help. Thank you for Your Holy Spirit that helps us obey You. Cleanse our minds and purify our hearts, please. We love you.*

MaryEmma

OCTOBER 21

MUCH PRAYER

"After Jesus had gone indoors, His disciples asked Him privately, 'Why couldn't we drive it out?' He replied, 'This kind can come out only by prayer.'"
Mark 9:28-29

God impressed these words on me when I was a young adult, only I remember it as 'much prayer'. I wish I could say that I immediately improved my prayer life, but at the time, 3 minutes took care of my prayer time and I only knew to ask.

But when God impresses us with a message, He helps us understand. Step by step, I learned more about how to talk to God. Prayer is not just asking for help, prayer is a conversation with God. It is a time of fellowship with Him. I talk and He guides me with ideas, impressions and guidance, just as our mind does when we visit with a friend. I have a letter from Him (Bible) that I can read to get to know His character and His wishes, and that helps me communicate with God.

We can pray at any time and any place, but I love the quiet of the early morning when I have no distractions in my mind. That is when I Spirit allow his Spirit to fill me.

I also do panic prayers as I did this morning when I spilled my coffee— 'Please help me clean my carpet! Please help me get the stain out!' And He did.

MY PRAYER: *Thank you for teaching us to pray. Thank you for wanting to spend time with us. We love you and we love the peace and comfort we receive when we spend special time with you.*

MaryEmma

WHERE ARE OUR EYES?

*"Then Peter got down out of the boat, walked on the water and
came toward Jesus. But when he saw the wind, he was afraid
and, beginning to sink, cried out, 'Lord, save me!'"*
Mathew 14:29-30

This is what happens when we take our eyes off our Lord, and look at
the situation around us. We start to sink, spiritually and emotionally. This
is the time to call for help.

We joke about Peter's lack of faith, but he is the only one who tried.
He didn't just step out of the boat onto the water, but he "got down out of
the boat". That took some effort.

He had complete faith in His Lord until he took his eyes off His Lord
and saw the wind and the waves. How quickly our emotions change when
we concentrate on the situation instead of God.

I love the diagram for prayer where we keep our gaze on God and only
glance at our requests. This is true prayer. We focus on the One who can
help and not on the problem.

Do we step out in faith with Jesus?

Would he say to us, "Oh you of little faith"?

Are our eyes on Jesus or on us?

MY PRAYER: *Lord, thank You that you are always with us, helping us when
we need it. Even when we are unconscious of you, You are faithful. Thank you.
We love you.*

MaryEmma

OCTOBER 23

THE GIFT

*"He made Him who knew no sin to be sin for us, that we
might become the righteousness of God in Him."*
2 Corinthians 5:21

Jesus did His part. He took our sins on Himself so we could become the family of God.

What is our part? It is a gift and as any gift we have to accept it or reject it. We can enjoy it or we can set it aside and go on our way, and ignore it. Our part is to enjoy God. We have fellowship with him by talking, by listening to Him, by reading His word.

There will be hard times in our lives. God doesn't prevent them, but He helps us through them. He is not only our savior, but our best friend, too.

How do we treat our best friend?

Do we talk and share and spend time together?

Is this how we treat our Lord?

MY PRAYER: *Lord Jesus, You are so wonderful to love us and help us. You took on our sinfulness so that we might have the righteousness of God in us. Thank you. We love you.*

MaryEmma

OCTOBER 24

LUKEWARM?

"I know your deeds, that you are neither cold nor hot. I wish you were one or the other! So, because you are lukewarm—neither hot nor cold—I am about to spit you out of my mouth."
Revelation 3:15-16

I think my biggest sin is taking God for granted.

I get into a routine with Bible Study or church and it becomes mechanical. I don't have the love and joy in my heart. I am simply going through a routine. I like my coffee either hot or iced cold. I won't drink it lukewarm. This must be how God feels about us when we take Him for granted.

We had a beautiful example when we were in Turkey. We were in the area of Laodicea and a park had a pump where you could pump out the water. I tried it. It was lukewarm! (They probably did it for us Christians who visit, but it worked. I was thrilled!)

But He does not kick us out of His family when we become lukewarm. He counsels us and encourages us. He encourages us to come and have fellowship with him. He loves us and wants to spend time with us.

Are we lukewarm in our relationship with Jesus?

Do we spend quality time with him?

Are we hot or cold or lukewarm?

Do we need to talk to Jesus about this?

MY PRAYER: *Thank You, Lord Jesus, for Your encouragement and Your love. We need You always. We love You.*

MaryEmma

OCTOBER 25

THANKSGIVING IS THE KEY

"Rejoice always, pray continually, give thanks in all circumstances;
for this is God's will for you in Christ Jesus."
1 Thessalonians 4:16-18

This is confession time for me. The trip home from Turkey was long (21 hours with 2 changes) and I woke up with a sore throat that morning that progressed all day long. In other words, I was physically miserable, but what bothered me was that God seemed to be far away. I did not have His peace and joy in my spirit. I was just unhappy in body and spirit.

I kept trying to talk to Him and to pray but peace and joy never came. I read His word, but it seemed dry and uninteresting. Since I have been home, I have been pondering this and trying to decide why I couldn't be miserable physically and enjoy God at the same time. This morning during my prayer time, the answer came. I had asked and I had complained to Him, but I had not been thanking Him for His presence.

My sore throat changed my attitude. I should have been thanking Him for the trip, all the wonderful things I saw and learned and from the lovely people on the trip. But I just concentrated on me!!!! I have said before that this verse is backward. First, we have to give thanks whatever--which is prayer and then joy comes. We might remember that in the fruit of the Spirit list, love and joy come before peace.

God finally gave me my answer this morning, which I hope I never forget again and I wanted to share it.

MY PRAYER: *Lord, thank you for Your answer. Forgive me for not thanking you for all your blessings. Bless us today with your peace and joy.*

MaryEmma

OCTOBER 26

PRAYER IS THE WORK

"...and he will be filled with the Holy Spirit even before he is born. He will bring many of the people of Israel to the Lord their God...."
Luke 1: 15

This is what the angel told John the Baptist's father before his birth. Our parents are not usually told what is the plan for our lives, but God has a plan already for us. Do we know what it is? Ephesians says that we were "created in Christ Jesus to do good works, which God prepared in advance for us to do".

How do we know? Prayer is the first step. Just ask God.

We are all created differently. Some of us are mouths or we may be ears to listen. Some may be a finger, which does nothing by itself, but in cooperation with other fingers becomes essential. We might be the liver, which no one ever sees or thinks about, but is essential for life.

Prayer is the greatest work, which is available to everyone. Prayer gives us spiritual strength and grows our faith. Prayer makes God our friend and personal counselor. He has a plan for our lives.

Have we asked Him what His plan for our life is?

Are we developing the gift God has given us?

Are we using our gift to glorify God?

MY PRAYER: *Lord, thank you for providing a way for us to talk to you and discern your plans for us. Guide us through this life. We love you.*

MaryEmma

OCTOBER 27

MY REDEEMER LIVES

"I know that my redeemer lives, and that in the end He will stand on the earth. After my skin has been destroyed, yet in my flesh I will see God...."
Job 19: 25-26

This is the most wonderful, beautiful statement of faith in the whole Bible. Job is in great pain, physically and emotionally, but he knows His Lord and Savior. He doesn't understand why he is going through all this, but he knows and trusts His God. Life on earth may be hard, but we have this hope, this promise of eternal life with our Lord.

Jesus gave us an example to teach us this truth. Isaiah 53 foretells His death and in the gospels we see how it happened. But physical death was not the end; He came back after 3 days in the grave to visit and reassure His disciples before He departed into heaven to sit at our Father's right hand.

Do we know that our Redeemer lives?

Do we trust him with our plans?

Are we sure we will see him in our eternal life?

MY PRAYER: *Lord, we thank you that we will see you and be with you in eternity. Help us to be as faithful as Job was and love you as You deserve.*

MaryEmma

"For no one is cast off by the Lord forever. Though He brings grief, He will show compassion, so great is His unfailing love, for He does not willingly bring affliction or grief to anyone."
Lamentations 3:31-32

Jeremiah is trying to make sense of all the troubles his people are having. He knows that most have sinned and turned away from God, but he also knows that some have stayed faithful to God, and they are being punished also. They are being killed and removed from their homes and mistreated just like the wicked ones.

He is reassuring them that God is faithful, and He will show compassion and love and give good things.

The scriptures remind us that it rains on both the faithful and unfaithful. When bad things happen to us, it may be because of the sins of people around us.

Can we trust God during hard times?

Do we look for his compassion or concentrate of the grief?

Do we thank him for his presence with us?

MY PRAYER: *Thank You, Lord, for wanting the best for us. You allow grief and affliction to bother us, but you also give us much compassion and love with it. We trust and love you.*

MaryEmma

OCTOBER 29

A NEW HEART

> *"I will give you a new heart and put a new spirit in you; I will remove from you…And I will put my Spirit in you and move you to follow my decrees and be careful to keep my laws."*
> Ezekiel 36: 26-27

This is what happens to us when we accept Jesus as our savior. He puts His spirit in us, so that we can know God personally. It requires repentance and submission to God. We acknowledge that God is Lord of our life and we want Him intimately involved in our life. This is when we receive his new heart and new spirit. It enables us to be obedient.

God is spirit and He can be anywhere and do anything. But the most amazing thing of all is that this great and holy God loves us and wants to be a part of our lives. We can talk to Him.

Do we use this gift to talk to him?

Do we listen for His still, quiet voice?

Do we spend time with him?

MY PRAYER: *Father God, when we loved you and accepted you, we are given a new heart and a new spirit in us. Your Spirit is your Holy Spirit that your son sent back to us to teach us and help us live the way you want us to. Thank you for all that you do for us. We love you.*

MaryEmma

OCTOBER 30

THE WAIT

"'I have heard you,' replied Jeremiah the prophet. 'I will certainly pray to the Lord your God as you have requested; I will tell you everything the Lord says and will keep nothing back from you.' Ten days later the word of the Lord came to Jeremiah."
Jeremiah 42:4,7

If we had to wait 10 days for an answer to our prayers, we would think God had forgotten us! We expect instant answers and get discouraged when we don't get them.

Why would God wait so long before answering? After all, we are commanded to "not be anxious, but to pray".

Maybe we aren't ready for the answer. Maybe we need to think more seriously about the request. Maybe God is growing us in faith and patience. We don't know! We just trust.

It is necessary for our spirit to talk to the Lord often. We don't always need an answer; we may just need the closeness of talking to God. He is not Santa Claus and He is not a magician. He is our heavenly Father who loves us and wants the best for us.

Do we talk to Him often?

Do we continue to spend time with him when he seems quiet?

Do we trust that he will give us the right answer?

MY PRAYER: *Lord, when you take a long time to answer our prayers, help us remember you have a good reason. Silence isn't always no. You want us to trust you as well as love you. Give us your gift of discernment that we may know you better.*

MaryEmma

OCTOBER 31

HOPE IN HIM

'The Lord is good to those who hope is in Him, to the one who seeks
Him; it is good to wait quietly for the salvation of the Lord."
Lamentations 3:25-26

We have another choice to make. Do we wait quietly for the Lord, or do we rush ahead and do our own thing?

If God is our portion, our hope and our savior, why do we rush?

We have been taught that a day with the Lord is as a thousand years and a thousand years is as a day. God has a different timetable than we do.

We like microwaves. They are quick, but God knows us and he knows what we need. He knows if we need to change our thinking or attitude before he answers us. He is our teacher and he knows if we learn quickly or slowly.

Can we wait quietly to hear His still quiet voice?

Do we put our hope in our God?

What is our choice?

MY PRAYER: *Lord, we are impatient people. Forgive us. Help us to wait patiently for your answer. You know what is best for us and whether to say yes, no or wait until later. We trust and love you. We want to please you.*

MaryEmma

NOVEMBER 1

THE NEW COVENANT

"This is the covenant I will make with the people of Israel
after that time," declares the Lord. "I will put my law in their
minds and write it on their hearts. I will be their God,
And they will be my people."
Jeremiah 31: 33

This future promise made to Jeremiah by God is repeated in Hebrews to encourage them and make them remember the blessings they had under the new covenant. It was the new covenant that Jesus gave us after his death and resurrection. It was first demonstrated in the book of Acts.

This new covenant gives us grace and mercy. This gift allows us intimate fellowship with Jesus and our Holy Father. Not by keeping external rules do we have a relationship with our God, but by his Spirit when we accept Jesus as our Savior. What was received at Pentecost we still have 2,000 years later.

Don't we have a wonderful God?

Have we thanked him for his gift today?

Do we allow his Spirit to flow into us?

MY PRAYER: *Jesus, our Lord and Savior, we love and thank you. You have put your laws into our hearts and minds with the presence of your Spirit. You teach us and forgive us. You are a wonderful Savior and Lord.*

MaryEmma

NOVEMBER 2

A RIGHTEOUS BRANCH

"'The days are coming,' declares the Lord, 'When I will raise
up for David a righteous branch, a King who will reign
wisely and do what is just and right in the land....'"
Jeremiah 28: 5

When we read this verse, we know that it is Jesus, the Son of God, who is our Lord and Savior. The religious leaders have led the people astray and they are being exiled from their country, but at the same time God is allowing this to happen, He is comforting them with the promise to bring them back home. He even tells them the number of years they will be gone. Long enough for their hearts to turn back to Him.

He also is telling them about the more distant future, when He will send his son, the Messiah, to be born of a virgin, conceived by the Holy Spirit, to live as man-God on earth for 33 years, to teach us about God. He was tempted early to decide if He would live for His glory on earth, or to live for God's glory. He chose to live in constant communication with God, His Father. He also chose to die on the cross, so His blood could cover our sins instead of the blood of a lamb killed every year.

Have we thanked God for His son, Christ Jesus?

Are we following Jesus example in talking to our heavenly Father?

Do we trust him to take care of us?

MY PRAYER: *Lord, Our Righteous Savior, we love you. You make our life good. Without you; we are nothing, we are unworthy. You are the One who made it possible for us to enjoy God and feel his love and presence. Thank you.*

MaryEmma

November 3

CALL TO ME

"This is what the Lord says... 'Call to me and I will answer you and tell you great and unsearchable things you do not know.'"
Jeremiah 33:2-3

"Call to me", the powerful God who made the whole world wants to hear from us! Who are we to be worthy of such a great blessing? We are God's children that He loves.

When should we call? When we are making our plans for the day, when we have question about what to do. We call when we just want to visit with Him and enjoy His presence with us.

Do we need to get out of our spiritual routines and 'call' Him?

Do we have a desire to talk to him?

Do we allow him access?

MY PRAYER: *Lord, God, thank You for the honor of being able to call on You at any time. We don't need an appointment. We don't have to be an important person. We just have to be Your child and we are welcome at any moment. You are wonderful. Thank You. We love You.*

MaryEmma

NOVEMBER 4

SEEK HIM

"Then you will call on me and come and pray to me, and I will listen to you. You will seek me and find me when you seek me with all your heart."
Jeremiah 29: 12-13

What a wonderful reassurance we have that God listens when we call. He wants us to talk to Him. He promises to listen. He wants us to look for Him. He does not want us to be lost and lonely and afraid.

There are times when it seems that God seems far away, but we know that we are the ones that have moved, not Him. When we are going through a dry spell it seems that we can't pray. We just say familiar words and phrases but they are coming from our head and not our heart.

That may be the time we need to call to Him for help: to admit we have let problems come into our lives and pushed Him away. God is continually telling His people that it is heart religion He wants, not head religion. He wants our heart and our love, just as human parents do.

Does God seem distant?

Do we seek his presence?

Do we call on the Lord often?

MY PRAYER: *Lord, thank you that you want us. You want us to talk to you, to call for you. Thank you that we are special to you and you always accept us, wherever we are in our Spiritual life. You are great.*

MaryEmma

NOVEMBER 5

GOD'S PLANS

"For I know the plans I have for you,' declares the Lord, 'plans to prosper you and not to harm you, plans to give you hope and a future.'"
Jeremiah 29:11

We have a wonderful loving God, who wants the very best for us. Sometimes we wonder if that is true when things aren't going right in our lives, and we feel like the student who doesn't like homework and tries to avoid test day. We forget that God is an intimate part of our lives and is guiding us

He wants to help us avoid mistakes. He wants us to have the best life possible. He wants us to have hope.

When we have lost hope and are discouraged, we need to remember God's plans for us.

> God was talking to people He had just sent into captivity for
> 70 years. They were ruining their lives and He interceded.
> He changed their location and told them to "build houses and
> settle down; plant gardens and eat what they produced."

Even in punishment he was with them, teaching, loving and guiding. A wonderful God we have!

What are God's plans for us?

Do we know?

Do we believe he is with us now, helping us?

MY PRAYER: *Lord God, You want to prosper us and give us hope and a future. You don't want to harm us but do we sometimes force you to discipline us? Forgive us when our hearts are not in tune with you. Forgive us when we want our own way and not your way. Thank you for your promise to bless and protect us. We love you.*

MaryEmma

DISCIPLINE

"I will build them up and not tear them down; I will plant them and not uproot them. I will give them a heart to know me, that I am the Lord."
Jeremiah 24:7

God disciplined His children in a very hard way. He sent them as captives to a foreign land because they loved things of the world instead of Him, but this is what discipline is: a form of teaching. God wants the very best for us, and sometimes the discipline is harsh, but notice His love! His eyes will watch over them for their good. He knows that by the time 70 years have passed "they will return to me with all their heart."

This isn't just Old Testament teaching: We are also taught in the New Testament that God disciplines us because He is our parent. A parent who loves, disciplines and teaches His children. God uses many methods to teach us. Only He knows the right form of teaching to make our heart right with Him.

What is God teaching us?

Do we have a heart to know him?

Do we trust him?

MY PRAYER: *Lord, even when you are disciplining us, you are loving us and blessing us. Thank you for building us up and giving us a heart to know you. We love you.*

MaryEmma

NOVEMBER 7

VISITING

"I thank and praise You, God of my ancestors; You have given me wisdom and power, You have made know to me what we asked of You."
Daniel 2: 23

This is a beautiful prayer of praise and thanksgiving. I like to change the 'He' to 'You' when I am praying this prayer as Daniel did in V 23, when he started thanking God. It just makes me more aware of God's presence with me. Daniel and his 3 friends were taken from Judah and entered the King's court as wise men. But the King was angry when he tested the wise men with insisting they tell him his dream as well as interpret it. He ordered all of them killed. When Daniel heard this, he asked for time to interpret it. He first went to His three friends and urged them to pray with him, to plead for mercy. During the night he received the vision of the dream. This prayer of praise and thanksgiving is his response.

Prayer is not just to get answers; prayer is to visit with God. Prayer is to become one spirit with God, so that we can know Him better and know what He wants us to do and to be.

Do we pray for guidance during decision time?

Do we talk to God just to thank him?

Do we pray just to enjoy God?

MY PRAYER: *Thank You, Lord, for teaching us to pray. You want to spend time with us so you can teach us what you know we need to know. You are a wonderful God.*

MaryEmma

GOD IS IN CHARGE

"But the pot he was shaping from the clay was marred in his hands; so the potter formed it into another pot, shaping it as seemed best to him...He said, 'Can I not do with you, Israel, as this potter does?'"
Jeremiah 18:4-5

When I read these words, I remembered singing a song that asks God to mold us into the person he wants us to be. Do we submit our will to God, or do we try to get Him to do our will?

I was reminded this morning that 'this is God's will for me in Christ Jesus" when things didn't go my way. Instead of self-pity or anger or resentment, I needed to remember that God is in control of my life and that is really what I want. I just need that reminder sometimes! And sometimes it hurts when He reshapes us!

Are our prayers instructions to God?

Do we pray to get his guidance?

Do we trust what he is doing in our lives?

MY PRAYER: *Lord, we thank you for caring for us and wanting the best for us. Sometimes your best is not what we want and we rebel. Forgive us and help us to understand your viewpoint; what you know is best for us. We love you.*
MaryEmma

'THE LORD SEARCHES

"I, the Lord, search the heart and examine the mind, to reward each person according to their conduct, according to what their deeds deserve."
Jeremiah 17:9-10

The prophet Jeremiah asked and he received an answer from God. God searches our heart and examines our mind. But He does more than reward or discipline. He teaches us and guides us into the right decisions when we allow Him.

The little nagging worries that we are doing the right thing is an indication that it is time to talk to God about it. If circumstances don't seem right and things aren't coming together is an indication that we need time with God to discuss it with Him.

Remember Philippians 4: If it is a concern, a worry, we need to talk to God about it. God loves us and he wants to help us to the right thing.

When God searches our hearts, what does He find?

Does he find dissatisfaction?

What quality of love does he find?

MY PRAYER: *Lord God, search our heart and make us aware of what is not worthy of you. Purify us and help us to trust you. You know what is right and what we need. We are unworthy of you, but you love us anyway. Thank you.*
MaryEmma

THE DROUGHT

"But blessed is the one who trusts in the Lord, whose confidence is in Him. They will be like a tree planted ... It has no worries in a year of drought and never fails to bear fruit."
Jeremiah 17:7-8

Who does the Lord bless? The one who has confidence in Him, who trusts in Him.

We are like a tree planted by the water. Hard times come, but we make it through because of our faith. Everyone in Oklahoma knows about a year of droughts. That is when the grass is brown and the leaves turn brown and fall off, but the tree planted by the water stays green.

This is a beautiful picture for us. We all have dry spells; disappointments and pain. With God's help we manage. Just like the water for the tree, He gives us encouragement as we pray and rejoice and thank Him through the difficult times.

How do we handle the hard times?

Do we fear when the drought comes?

Can we thank him in dry periods?

MY PRAYER: *Lord, You protect us and love us. You are our water and when we stay close to you, we are safe. You nourish us through your word and encourage us through your Spirit. Thank you. We love you.*

MaryEmma

OUR THOUGHTS

"Yet, You know me, Lord; You see me and test my thoughts about You."
Jeremiah 12:3

What are our thoughts?
Are they pleasing to God?
Are they filled with love for those around us?
Are they full of pride? Anger?
Are they resentful? Or trusting, Joyful?
Are they full of "thank You, Lord, for this experience"?
Hebrews tells us to "fix our thoughts on Jesus".
Colossians tells us to "set our mind on things above, not earthly things."
Is it time to have a talk with God about our thoughts?

MY PRAYER: *Lord, we have trouble with our thoughts. There is so much of the world in them. Our thoughts are often just about us, and how we can get what we want. Too often they are not filled with you. Forgive us and bless us with your thoughts.*

MaryEmma

GREAT AND MIGHTY!

"No one is like You, Lord, You are great, and Your name is mighty in power. Who should not fear You, King of the nations?....
Jeremiah 10:6-7

I think we can all say this from our heart. There is no one like our Lord. There is no other power that can do what He can do. There is no greater wisdom than what He has and He gives to us as we need it. We worship the greatest of all powers, the creator God that in spite of His power, loves each one of us and is very concerned about us.

Jeremiah was a prophet during the time of Isaiah and he continued trying to get God's people to turn away from their idols. Shapes that other men made.

Do we have idols in our lives?

We don't worship images, but do we worship the gold and silver?

Do we worship a child or a car or a job?

It is so easy to move God out of first place in our lives.

Do we?

MY PRAYER: *No one is like You, Lord. You are the greatest power; you have love and concern for us. We don't deserve your love, but we thank you. We love you.*

MaryEmma

FORGIVENESS

"In his distress he sought the favor of the Lord His God and
humbled himself greatly before the God of his ancestors.
And when he prayed to Him…
Then Manasseh knew that the Lord is God."
2 Chronicles 33:12-13

This is a beautiful illustration of how we can never be too bad or move from God so far, so that when we repent and seek God, He forgives us.

Manasseh was the son of Hezekiah, one of the great kings who worshipped God, but he must have been too busy for his son, because he was one of the worst of all kings. Verse 2 says: He did evil in the eyes of the Lord" and even put an image in God's temple, and the people followed him.

But God wouldn't let him get away with it, He sent the King of Assyria to take him prisoner and put him in shackles. This discipline woke him up and he prayed, and God forgave him. He got rid of the foreign gods and restored worship to the one and true and living God.

Some wander away from God and think they can never be forgiven, but the story of Manasseh teaches us differently.

God welcomes anyone that humbles themselves and asks for forgiveness. Will we make our God the Lord of our life?

Do we ask for forgiveness when we realize we have sinned?

Do we believe God forgives when we repent?

MY PRAYER: *Lord God, thank you for your forgiveness. Help us remember you are always listening when we confess. Thank you for your love. We love you.*
MaryEmma

THE POTTER

"Yet You, Lord, are our Father. We are the clay, you are the potter; we are all the work of your hand."
Isaiah 64:8

This is a wonderful thought for us to remember when we get upset. God is in control of our lives. He is the potter we are soft and pliable in His hands. He makes us and molds us, but sometimes we try to get away from Him and remake ourselves. The result? We are upset and angry and unhappy with life.

One of the biggest sins we struggle with is pride. We forget that we are the clay and the honor goes to God. When we struggle with life, we need to pray.

What is our attitude?

Are we filled with His love?

Do we want his perfect will in our life?

MY PRAYER: *You are the potter, Lord and I am the clay. I am the work of your hand. Make me and mold me according to your perfect will. We love you.*

MaryEmma

NOVEMBER 15

A RIGHTEOUS GOD

"There is no God apart from me. A righteous God
and a Savior; there is none but me.
Turn to me and be saved, all you ends of the earth;
for I am God and there is no other..."
Isaiah 45:21-22

This is what God said to the children of Israel to convince them to turn back to worshiping Him instead of the world, but He is also saying it today to all of us.

There is only one true and living God. We are to worship Him and honor Him. He alone can save, he alone can truly help us.

Do we honor and worship Him?

Who is the Lord of our heart?

Who is the God in our thoughts?

Only in him is deliverance and strength.

Do we turn to Him for guidance?

Do we wait until we are in trouble to go to Him?

MY PRAYER: *Lord God, You are the only God and you are a righteous God. We thank you are saving us and we praise you. You alone are God in all of the universe. We love you.*

MaryEmma

THE GREAT HELPER

"Do not fear, for I have redeemed you; I have called you by name; you are mine. When you pass through the waters I will be with you; and when you pass through the rivers, they will not sweep over you."
Isaiah 43:1

This verse has been very comforting to me when I have had to do something new and I have been fearful. As I repeat it to myself, I am reminded that God knows my name and I belong to Him. I feel His love and presence.

I just need to remember that He is the Lord my God. Isaiah, the prophet, has been trying to get God's children to stop worshipping idols and turn back to Him. Now He is trying to prepare them for captivity. Because even though they have turned against Him, He still loves them and although He is punishing them, He plans to restore them when they repent.

This is an example for us today. Even though we sin and others around us sin, God will teach us; He is the loving parent who loves us wants us to learn by our mistakes and return in love to Him.

Have we thanked Him today for these blessings?

Do we trust him to help us through difficult times?

Do we turn to him for help or trust ourselves?

MY PRAYER: *Thank you for redeeming me. Thank you that you know me well enough that you can call me by name. That means you know me in addition to all your other children. Lord, we want to please you and show you our love. You are the greatest. You are my God and Savior.*

MaryEmma

NOVEMBER 17

RIGHTEOUS RIGHT HAND

"So do not fear, for I am with you; do not be dismayed,
for I am your God. I will strengthen you and help you; I
will uphold you with my righteous right hand."
Isaiah 41:10

I love this verse. God is with me and He is helping me to live my life, to help me make my decisions, He is guiding me through difficult situations.

When I make a mistake, He is here to help me up and strengthen me. With a God like we have, the one true and holy God, we don't have to be afraid and upset.

Why do we become afraid? I don't know. Is it because we don't really trust God? Is it because we forget and ignore God? That is why I pray that I will be aware of God's presence as I go through my day. "So do not fear, for I am with you; do not be dismayed, for I am your God".

Why do we forget He is our helper?

Why do we forget He loves us?

Will we trust Him?

MY PRAYER: *Lord, You are my protector and my Savior. You are my lover and my counselor and my hope. Thank you for helping us. Thank you for loving us. We love you.*

MaryEmma

HOPE

"But those who hope in the Lord will renew their strength.
They will soar on wings like eagles; they will run and not
grow weary, they will walk and not be faint."
Isaiah 40:31

Hope is not a wishy-washy want, as we use the word today. We hope we win the lottery; we hope it doesn't rain tomorrow.

Hope means trust and assurance. I looked in the dictionary and it means "joyful and contented expectation". We can have our hope in the Lord or in us or in another person.

Those who hope in the Lord will not be discouraged or feel hopeless. When we hope in the Lord we have a special strength from our Lord and Savior to do His will. But the hope is in Him, not in ourselves and not in our abilities.

Where do we place our hope?

Is our hope in money?

Is our hope in Jesus?

MY PRAYER: *Lord God, thank You for your strength, thank you for your protection, thank you for giving us hope. With hope in you we don't need to despair and give in to weariness. You are the One who gives us strength and holds us up. We love you.*

MaryEmma

NOVEMBER 19

THE CREATOR

> "...Creator of the ends of the earth. He will not grow tired or
> weary, and His understanding no one can fathom. He gives
> strength to the weary and increases the power of the weak."
> Isaiah 40: 28-29

Sometimes we take God for granted. We forget how great and holy that He is. Sometimes we even forget what He wants to do for us.

He is ready to give us strength when we are discouraged. He wants to help us be the person He created us to be.

We need His help, but too often we don't ask for help.

We forget to ask for guidance.

Isaiah is still trying to get the Israelites to turn from their idols and worship God. Why don't they listen?

We have our little idols too. We need to identify our idols and trust the one and true and living God. He is the One who give us strength.

Why don't we listen?

Why don't we trust Him/

Who or what is our idol?

MY PRAYER: *Lord, thank you for giving us strength. Thank you for helping us through difficult days. Thank you that you never desert us and we can count on you. You are dependable. We love you.*

MaryEmma

OUR SHEPHERD

"He tends His flock like a shepherd: He gathers the lambs in His arms and carries them close to His heart; He gently leads those that have young."
Isaiah 40:11

When I am feeling down or hopeless, I can feel Jesus holding me in His arms close to His heart. On difficult days, I like to remember this verse and feel His love flowing into me from His arms. I feel his love when I picture this in my mind. The scriptures often depict our Lord as having His arms wide open, inviting us to come into His arms. He is not a remote God, but a loving God who wants us to be close to Him.

Isaiah is encouraging his people now so that when bad times come, they will remember God's love. God is going to discipline them by sending them into captivity, but He will restore them at just the right time. We need to remember that He is a loving God, but also a just God.

Do we think of our Lord as our shepherd?

Do we turn to Him when we feel hopeless and lost?

Do we trust Him?

MY PRAYER: *Lord, you love me and I am so thankful. You hold me up when I am too weak to stand. You protect me from the enemy and teach me how you want me to go. Thank you. I love you. You are a wonderful God of love.*

MaryEmma

NOVEMBER 21

WHO DO WE TRUST

"Woe to those who ... rely on horses, who trust
in ... and in the great strength... but do not look to the
Holy One of Israel, or seek help from the Lord."
Isaiah 31:1

Who do we trust? Where do we look for help?

Good questions to ponder.

Our God is so gracious and loving. Do we seek His guidance? Do we spend enough time with Him to recognize His gentle quiet voice?

Abraham went down to Egypt twice and both times he got into trouble. We also get into trouble when we trust horse and chariots, or when we trust our money, our guns, or our jobs instead of Him.

He loves us.

How do we respond?

Do we ignore Him until we have a crisis?

Do we talk to him first?

MY PRAYER: *Lord, thank you for being with us, wanting to help, waiting for us to talk to you and trust you. Forgive us for not trusting you and putting you first in our lives. Help us to recognize your hand moving in our lives. We need your peace and love.*

MaryEmma

GOD IS FAITHFUL

"In that day—'Sing about a fruitful vineyard; I, the Lord, watch over it; I
water it continually. I guard it day and night so that no one may harm it.'"
Isaiah 27:2-3

There are days when we feel empty, alone and not sure about what is
going to happen.

Does God really love us and care of us? Isaiah answers that question.
He promises to guard us.

We are God's children; His vineyard, and this is our reassurance. He
protects us and He nurtures us.

He is the mighty and great God!

How can we not love Him and praise Him?

Do we trust him?

Do we talk to him?

MY PRAYER: *Lord, you are faithful. You guard us day and night so that no*
one can harm us. Yet we try to escape. We want to do our own thing; to please
ourselves. Forgive us for not trusting you. We love you.

MaryEmma

NOVEMBER 23

PRIDE OR HUMILITY

"But Hezekiah's heart was proud and he did not respond to the kindness shown him; therefore the Lord's wrath was on him.... Then Hezekiah repented of the pride of his heart"
2 Chronicle 32:25-26

This is the King Hezekiah that followed God, consulted him and God blessed him.

What a lesson to us that our fellowship with God can shift until we think we are doing it. Moses did it when he struck the rock instead of speaking to it.

God is the great and Holy God. He blesses us and teaches us, but it is up to us to respond and be humble instead of proud.

Pride is a terrible sin, because it means we are trusting ourselves instead of God. We are giving ourselves the credit. The hardest part of a Christian's life is to trust God with ourselves. We want to make the decisions instead of spending the necessary time with God to allow Him to work.

Is our heart proud?

Do we take credit for a good deed?

Do we thank God for helping us do the good deed?

MY PRAYER: *Lord, we don't want to be proud, we don't mean to. Help us appreciate what you do instead of claiming we did it. Thank you for your teaching and for your forgiveness. We love you.*

MaryEmma

OUR RESPONSE"

"In that day you will say: 'Give praise to the Lord, proclaim
His name; make known among the nations what He has
done and proclaim that His name is exalted
Isaiah 12:4

Give praise to the Lord! Do we? Why don't we?

Isaiah 11 is a beautiful little example of what God does for us and how we are to respond. He forgives us, He comforts us, and He saves us. He is our strength and defense. That is what God does for us. What is our response to Him? Isaiah tells us how we are to respond to God's goodness to us.

We are to praise Him: to others, yes, but also to ourselves; in our quiet time we need to praise Him. We are the ones blessed as we praise Him because it helps us remember His greatness, what He does and who He is. As we become more aware of Him, our trust and love grow, and we can handle the bad times as well as the good times.

Our Lord and Savior never moves away from us.

Do we praise him for his strength?

Do we praise him for who he is or only what he does for us?

Do we erect a barrier between us and our Savior?

MY PRAYER: *Lord, You are wonderful. You are mighty. You are magnificent. We love you and praise You.*

MaryEmma

"In that day you will say: 'I will praise You, Lord. Although You were angry with me, Your anger has turned away and You have comforted me.'"
Isaiah 12:1-2

"In that day", when God has reclaimed the world and there is not sin, everything will be perfect. But now we have to co-exist with sin and God is our protector and lover.

My desire is to please God, but there are times when I don't. That is when I have to go to God with repentance in my heart and He comforts me.

He helps me to know what to do. He is our counselor in an imperfect world.

Are we afraid?

Do we trust Him?

Do we praise Him often?

MY PRAYER: *You are my God; you are my salvation. I love you and praise you. You are my strength and my defense. I will not be afraid.*

MaryEmma

THE SPIRIT OF WISDOM

"A shoot will come up from the stump of Jesse... The Spirit of the Lord will rest on Him-the Spirit of wisdom and of understanding, the Spirit of counsel and of might, the Spirit of the knowledge and fear of the Lord"
Isaiah 11:1-3

This is the promise of Jesus, the Christ, the Messiah coming into our lives to help us live the life God wants us to have. This is a description of Jesus Christ when He was on earth.

We know that when we have trouble around us we can trust God to guide us and help us and give us peace. The prophet Isaiah was trying to get God's children to return to Him and see what their sinful life was costing them. Some in the 10 tribes have already been taken into captivity and if they don't change, they will also.

Between His messages of doom and gloom, He gives messages of hope. This is the future—in that day—when you return to the one true and living God.

We receive wisdom and understanding and His counsel, so that we can please our heavenly Father. This is a message of hope given during hard times, and it is a message of hope for us today.

Do we ask for wisdom to please him?

Do we study his life to understand how we are to live?

Do we thank him for being in our lives?

MY PRAYER: *Lord, help us to delight in you. Help us to know and trust you. Help us to understand if we put you first in our lives, we will have your love and joy and peace to guide us. We love you.*

MaryEmma

TRUST

"Do not call conspiracy everything this people calls a conspiracy;
do not fear what they fear, and do not dread it.
The Lord Almighty is the One you are to regard as holy,
He is the One you are to fear...."
Isaiah 8:12-13,

Who do we trust? Is it the wisdom of the world, or God? People come up with some weird ideas, and we can become afraid and trust them instead of God.

Why are we afraid? Our Lord and Savior is not a remote God, He is with us always. Jesus said " if you believe, my Father and I will make our home with you." The Holy Spirit of God resides with us. Isn't that a wonderful thought? We are never alone!

He has taught us to trust Him and listen to Him for guidance and direction in our lives.

Are we afraid? Then we need to spend time with God?

Have we learned to listen and trust?

When bad things happen, do we turn to God?

God is always with us, helping us, loving us and guiding us. He is faithful. Are we?

MY PRAYER: *Lord, there are times when we are afraid. Those are the times when you seem far away, and we can't reach you. Help us remember that if someone has moved, it is us, not you. Give us the faith to remember and trust you. We love you.*

MaryEmma

REMEMBERING GOD

> *"But you brought my life up from the pit, O Lord my God.*
> *When my life was ebbing away, I remembered you, Lord,*
> *and my prayer rose to you, to your holy temple."*
> Jonah 2:4

This is the prayer of Jonah as he thought he was dying.

He was inside the great fish and he was there because he was angry and disobedient.

Isn't it interesting how God's discipline gets our attention? Jonah was only thinking of himself, but when he was in distress, his thoughts turned to God: "In my distress I called to the Lord".

And God answered him as He does us when we call to him. The question is: why do we wait until trouble to call? Why don't we seek His advice first?

Do we trust him?

MY PRAYER: *Lord, we love you but we are weak. We think of ourselves first. We like to make our plans and leave you out. We don't ask for your advice. Forgive us and help us remember as long as we seek you, you will give us success.*
MaryEmma

CHECK-UP

"Surely the arm of the Lord is not too short to save, nor His ear too dull to hear. But your iniquities have separated you from your God; your sins have hidden His face from you, so He will not hear."
Isaiah 59:1-2

Does it seem that God is not answering our prayers? Could it be that we have been disobedient?

Many times I don't recognize my sins until I specifically ask God, "have I sinned?" and the answer is always yes, with a reminder of what I have done. It may be a thought or a word. Usually it is an attitude.

I love these verses because they make me chuckle.

It is almost "tongue in check."

Is His arm too short to reach?

Is God hard of hearing?

I don't expect that in the Bible, but it does get the point across that it is not God, but we that need a checkup.

Have we asked Jesus to show us our sins?

Are we willing to confess to him?

Do we believe he truly loves us or that we are too bad?

MY PRAYER: *Lord, You are so patient with us. We blame you for the problems we encounter, but our sins have created a barrier between you and us. Help us remember you are with us always and we need to confess to you the sins we have committed. You know them but sometimes we don't recognize them because we are used to them and just call them bad habits. Show us where we need your help.*
MaryEmma

NOVEMBER 30

HIS LIGHT

*"Because I have sinned against Him, I will bear the Lord's
wrath, until He pleads my case and upholds my cause.
He will bring me out into the light; I will see his righteousness."*
Micah 7:8-9

Our God never deserts us. When we sin, we move away from God, but He is always near, waiting for us to repent.

Israel had sinned as we do today, with empty worship and making other things our gods. God is going to punish them, but He will forgive them when they turn back to Him.

This is a picture of how He treats us today. He wants us to walk humbly with Him, so He can teach us mercy and love, but we like to 'do our own thing' without Him. We go through rough times, because of our sins, or the sins of others, but we can have comfort because we have hope in the Lord.

Because He loves us, He never gives up on us. He is always available to guide us and help us.

Do we put our hope in the Lord?

Do we wait patiently for him to hear and answer our prayer?

Do we see his righteousness?

MY PRAYER: *Holy God, thank you for bringing us back into your light after we have sinned. Thank you for your love and mercy. Thank you for not treating us as our sins deserve. We love you.*

MaryEmma

WHITE AS SNOW

"'Come now, let us reason together,' says the Lord. 'Though your sins are like scarlet, they shall be white as snow; though they are red as crimson, they shall be like wool. If you are willing and obedient....
Isaiah 1:18

Isaiah was a prophet who condemned Judah for their sins and was trying to get them to return to the one true and living God. They had turned away from God and were worshipping idols. But God still loved them and this is His plea: even though your sins are red as scarlet, if you return to Me I will remove them and make you white as snow.

These words show how wonderful and loving our God is. He is a forgiving God; He is a receiving God who opens His arms wide for us when we repent.

We don't think we sin much, but we need to ask God if he is displeased with us. It can be an action or it can be an attitude. We are good at hiding our real self from others but God see our attitudes. He wants to forgive us and restore us.

Do we recognize our sins?

Do know when we stray from his presence?

Do we believe God can change us from scarlet to white?

MY PRAYER: *Lord, thank you for blotting out our sins. Thank you for making us pure as snow after we confess. You are wonderful and we love and thank you.*
MaryEmma

DECEMBER 2

REAL SUCCESS

"King Uzziah did what was right in the eyes of the Lord...
As long as he sought the Lord, God gave Him success."
2 Chronicles 26: 4-5

When I read this, I thought: that is what is wrong with our lives today. We don't seek the Lord's advice. It is the secret to success.

God wants to be in our lives, just as any parent does. He wants to guide us in our ventures. He wants to give us good advice. So why do we use our common sense or our emotions to make our decisions, and leave Him outside, looking in? We don't have to spend our lives on our knees. God is always with us. We only need to acknowledge Him. God wants to help us with our business, our families and leisure time. We are His "royal priests"!

Do we consider ourselves his priest?

Are we are special to God?

Have we learned the secret of real success?

MY PRAYER: *Lord, we want to serve you. We want to please you. Help us to seek you for the help we need instead of trusting our common sense. Thank You. We love You.*

MaryEmma

DECEMBER 3

HOLY AND HOLY

"Above Him were seraphim ...and they were calling to one another: 'Holy, holy, holy is the Lord Almighty; the whole earth is full of His glory.'"
Isaiah 6:2-3

We think of God as our Father, as our friend and as our helper, and He is; but how often do we think of Him as holy? The angels in heaven know how great and wonderful He is, but do we just think of Him as our Santa Claus?

He is wonderful and He blesses us and loves us, but we need to remember how holy and special He is and treat Him with love and respect and awe, as well as having the confidence to approach Him on His throne. It is hard to get our mind around how great and marvelous He is.

As I was praying for my family this morning, I realized how important it was that we recognize His holiness and not take Him for granted.

Do we respect his holiness?

Do we share our needs and concerns with him?

Are we aware of his holiness?

MY PRAYER: *Lord, you are holy and awesome. Help us to remember your greatness and holiness as we enjoy your fellowship. We can trust you with anything and your grace blesses us. You are special! We love you.*
MaryEmma

December 4

RESTORATION

"I will repay you for the years the locusts have eaten—"
Joel 2:15

I think this is one of the sweetest verses in the Bible. We have all made mistakes; some that seem worse than others, but all move us away from God.

But God doesn't keep a grudge. He forgives! Verse 12 said "return to Me with all your heart...rend your heart, not your garments".

He loves us so much and wants to forgive us and restore us. He will restore the blessings we have missed when we turned away from Him: when our heart changes and we cry out to Him for help.

Do we believe that God forgives and restores?

Do we keep grudges?

Can we forgive?

MY PRAYER; Lord God, we are so blessed to know you and call you our Lord. Continue to teach us and restore us as we confess. You are wonderful and we love you.

MaryEmma

DECEMBER 5

GOD OF SECOND CHANCES

*"Rend your heart and not your garments. Return to the Lord
Your God, for He is gracious and compassionate, slow to anger and
abounding in love, and He relents from sending calamity."*
Joel 2: 13

The prophet Joel is begging His people to turn their heart back to God. Even though Judah has been more faithful to God than Israel, they have also turned to man made idols to worship.

It is hard for us to believe that they would turn away from wonderful loving God who wants only their best, and turn to idols of wood and stone and worship them. But we need to stop and think of the priorities in our lives.

Remember that our Lord is gracious and compassionate, loving and not easily angered.

What do we think about?

Who do we worship?

Where do we spend our money?

MY PRAYER; Lord, You are special. You are so gracious, so full of compassion and forgiveness. Help us remember that you are a God of second chances. We love You.

MaryEmma

PRIDE PROBLEM

"Elisha sent a messenger to say to him, 'Go wash yourself seven times in the Jordan, and your flesh will be restored and you will be cleansed.' But Naaman went away angry...."
2 Kings 5: 10-11

Naaman had a pride problem.

How often do we lose a blessing from the Lord because of our pride? How often do we tell Him, "I'd rather do it my way " or "let someone else do that"?

Naaman was an important man in his country and he expected to be treated in a special way. A message given by a servant was beneath his dignity! But his servants finally persuaded him to go to the dirty Jordan and he was healed.

God wants us to be humble and loving, and treat others as he treats us. We cannot bless another with God's grace if we are thinking only of our self. We cannot bless another if we are full of pride and anger. We must be wiling to humble ourselves to receive his blessings.

Do we have a problem with pride and anger?

Do we consider God our servant or our Lord?

Do we spend enough time with God so that we can hear His gentle quiet voice?

Lord God, You are holy and perfect, we are weak and selfish. Help us to listen for Your gentle quiet voice today. Remind us when we are full of pride and anger and replace it with Your humility and love.

MaryEmma

DECEMBER 7

HOW DO WE RESTORE PEACE?

"After they had finished eating and drinking, he sent them away and they returned to their master. So the bands from Aram stopped raiding Israel's territory."
2 Kings 9: 23

Elisha showed us how to treat the enemy. He showed us how to restore peace.

Elisha showed God's power by their capture and then he showed God's kindness and compassion. What a way to treat the enemy! He took them to the King but recommended that he show kindness instead of death.

What was the result? The enemy stopped raiding Israel.

Jesus told us to love our enemy. Love is not a new idea in the Bible. God's love is shown throughout the scriptures and because we love Him, He can teach us to love others.

Do we return love for hatred?

Do we use God's power to help those who want to hurt us?

Do we recommend mercy instead of justice?

MY PRAYER: *Lord Jesus, you have shown us love and mercy in our lives. You gave us the example of perfect living by your example in the gospels. You showed us how to treat others with love. You and the Father were in perfect communication with each other. Help us to be one with you as you were with our Father. We love you.*

MaryEmma

DECEMBER 8

PEACE COMES FROM TRUST

"... 'those who are with us are more than those who are with them.' ...Then the Lord opened the servant's eyes, and he looked and saw the hill full of horses and chariots of fire all around Elisha."
2 Kings 6: 16-17

The King had chariots, but God has chariots of fire! The servant saw only the enemy's army around them, and he was afraid. But God had His army surrounding him and Elisha: an army of horses and chariots of fire surrounding them.

It is a beautiful picture of God's invisible protection around us. Our vision is limited, but with prayer we can see and feel God's invisible protection that He provides with love. We become fearful so easily and forget that we want God's perfect will in our lives. God is in control of our lives. He uses the experiences that come into our lives—through our fault or others —to teach us. We never get out of school. God is the greatest teacher; His homework and tests are designed especially for us, to make us into the people He created us to be.

Are we fearful?

What frightens us?

Can we trust God in our fear?

MY PRAYER: *Holy God, you are great and marvelous. You never leave us alone. Nothing can happen to us that you can't make good, because you love us. Thank you.*

MaryEmma

FEAR

> *"'I am the only one left, and now they are trying to kill me too.'*
> *'...I reserved seven thousand in Israel—all whose knees have not*
> *bowed down to Baal and whose mouths have not kissed him.'"*
> 1 Kings 19:15,18

Elijah is still having a bit of a pity party. He just saw one of the greatest miracles in the Bible, but one woman made him lose all confidence in God!

Isn't it amazing how we can be so close to God one minute and totally consumed with ourselves the next? But isn't it wonderful that God does not give up on us. He follows us to wherever we are, emotionally or physically. God challenges us to recognize our emotions and look at the facts. God says, "get over your self-pity and get to work. Go, this is your next assignment".

How can a God so powerful be so loving and gentle? Because He is God! Our wonderful Lord and Savior.

Do we listen to the Lord?

Do we trust him to help us through difficulty?

Do we trust God's love and power or the circumstances?

MY PRAYER: *Lord, you are perfect and powerful; we are weak and lowly. We need you and when problems come, we call out to you for help. Forgive us when we show lack of faith. Forgive us when we try to run away from the situation instead of talking to you about it. We need you and love you.*

MaryEmma

DECEMBER 10

GENTLE WHISPER

*"The Lord said, 'Get out and stand on the mountain in the
presence of the Lord, for the Lord is about to pass by.'
And after the fire came a gentle whisper."*
1 Kings 19:11-12

We expect God in big powerful events. We expect Him to make
Himself obvious, but He appeared to Elijah in a gentle whisper.
*Do we ignore God because he is quiet instead of noisy? Our
God is gentle and loving. He doesn't shout, but invites us in.
He stands at the door and knocks; he says "come unto me."*
He issues an invitation without demanding. He loves us and wants our
companionship. He wants us to trust him.

This is what God was telling Elijah in the middle of his big 'pity party'.
This is what He is saying to us. "Come unto me." Listen for the gentle quiet
whisper of our Lord and Savior.

Are we weary?

Are we loaded down with worry?

Will we listen for his gentle whisper?

MY PRAYER: *Lord God, thank you for your gentleness, and for your love.
You want us to slow down so we can hear you and fellowship with you. You are
wonderful. We love you.*

MaryEmma

DECEMBER 11

I HAVE HAD ENOUGH!

*"Elijah was afraid and ran for his life...he came to a broom
tree, sat down under it and prayed that he might die. 'I
have had enough, Lord,' he said, 'Take my life....'"*
1 Kings 19: 3-4

This is the great prophet, Elijah. He had just defeated 450 Baal prophets with such a great miracle from God, so that the people fell prostate and cried, "The Lord—He is God." But because the evil Queen Jezebel threatened his life he ran in fear.

We are so human! God does great things for us and then one little thing can take our eyes off God and onto our own strength or lack of it. We turn away from God, but he doesn't turn away from us. He sent an angel to feed Elijah. God is always near, helping us with our self-doubt. God loves us so much. He wants to take care of us, but He also gave us self will, so the choice is ours.

Do we trust God, or do we trust ourselves?

Do we take our troubles to our Lord?

Do we allow him to minister to us?

MY PRAYER: *Lord, you never give up on us. You let us run ourselves to despair and then You show us Your strength and your love. You never desert us, You are always near, waiting for us to call to You. We love You.*

MaryEmma

DECEMBER 12

REJOICE ALWAYS

"Rejoice always, pray unceasingly, and in everything give thanks, for this is God's will for you in Christ Jesus."
1 Thessalonians 5:16-18

This is not a new verse. Sometimes we just need to go back to our roots, and remember the important stuff.

Rejoice: we are to have joy in our hearts and minds. The Spirit of God lives with us and He produces joy when we allow it.

We can have that joy by praying. We are not to spend our lives on our knees praying, but to be in an attitude of prayer. As we go through the day we need that awareness that God is with us and helping us and loving us.

In everything, we are to be thankful. Not FOR everything, because bad things happen, but in the situation, we can thank God that He is with us, and helping us through that situation. He has promised us that He will "make everything work for our good". We can thank Him for that as well as His presence. If we never have difficult times, we never need to learn to trust Him.

Are we aware of God's presence with us today?

Are we joyful?

Why don't we thank him?

MY PRAYER: *Lord Jesus, thank you for blessing us and reminding us of what we need. We need you and we become more aware of you when we talk to you and thank you for all that is happening to us. When we do that, we receive your peace and your joy. The joy you put in our hearts is a mighty force. Thank you.*
MaryEmma

DECEMBER 13

WHAT DO WE FORGET?

...'Asa then took all the silver and gold that was left in the treasuries of the Lord's temple and of his own palace. He ...sent them to the King of Aram who was ruling in Damascus. 'Let there be a treaty between me and you.....'"
I Kings 15:18-19

King Asa was so human! In spite of his blessings from God and being told "If you seek Him, He will be found by you; but if you forsake Him, He will forsake you" He forgot. In spite of winning great battles with God's power and not his army's power, he forgot. He forgot that God is supreme and can do all things. He forgot to trust God and trusted his own common sense. Isn't that just like us today?

We love our Lord, we trust Him and obey Him and receive His blessings and then all of a sudden, we are afraid. We forget God and trust a human strength. King Asa became angry when he was scolded.

What have we forgotten when we get angry?

Why do we trust the world instead of our God?

Are we like Asa and become angry when shown our sin?

MY PRAYER: *Lord, you are so great and loving. I pray that we will remember that your eyes are on us. Strengthen us whose hearts are committed to you. You are our Lord and Savior who wants to bless us. Help us to make the right choice.*
Mary Emma

DECEMBER 14

"About midnight Paul and Silas were praying and singing hymns to God, and the other prisoners were listening to them. Suddenly there was such a violent earthquake ...."
Acts 16:25-26

Two men in prison were praising God by singing and praying. God responded with the force of nature. God had a mission for these two men and this was part of His plan to increase their influence.

When we praise God by spending time in prayer, it doesn't always change our circumstance outwardly, but it always changes our heart and our attitude. It increases our faith. It renews our hope. It gives us the assurance God can and will take care of us.

They had been beaten and were in pain. Pain is terrible, but the feeling of being alone in pain makes it worse. An awareness of God's presence with us and His comfort and His guidance makes it better. Praying and singing to God keeps our thoughts on our Lord.

How do we handle pain?

What is our attitude when problems happen?

Do we turn to God in prayer and song?

MY PRAYER: *Lord God, help us remember you when in trouble. Help us to focus on you, fix our eyes and thoughts on you during pain and allow your presence to bring us to peace. We love you.*

MaryEmma

DECEMBER 15

GOD HAS A PLAN

'Sirs, what must I do to be saved?'...The jailer took them into his house and set a meal before them; he was filled with joy because he had come to believe in God—he and his whole household."
Acts 16:30,34

If this were a fairly tale, the prince would have rescued the princess from the dragon and they would lived happily ever after! In a way that is what happened. They shared the word of God with the jailer and his family and they were removed from eternal death into eternal life! God had a plan: He kept changing Paul's plans on destinations, He allowed them to be beaten, put in prison—into the darkest deepest part of the prison, all to bring a man and his family to know our Lord. Who knows what happened in the lives of the prisoners who listened! God had a plan!

He has a plan for our lives also. Sometimes we hurt; sometimes we are stretched; but God has a plan.

What is His plan for our life?

Will we trust Him and cooperate with Him?

Do we share the good news?

MY PRAYER: *Lord we don't understand your ways, but we know that you know what you are doing. Sometimes we have to hurt to grow in faith, but you are always with us, holding our hands. Help us to pray and sing praises to you instead of complaining. We love you.*

Mary Emma

DECEMBER 16

AWARENESS OF GOD

"...'Woe to me!' I cried. 'I am ruined! For I am a man of
unclean lips, and I live among a people of unclean lips, and
my eyes have seen the King, the Lord almighty.'"
Isaiah 6: 5.

This is a normal reaction when people see the Lord or one of His angels in the Bible. This is a normal reaction for us when we are in prayer and our spirit becomes wholly aware of God's spirit.

The "ACTS" recipe for prayer is so natural for me because when I am really in fellowship with God's spirit, I am filled with awe and despair at the same time. When I become aware of the holiness of God, I immediately am aware of my sin, my mistakes, my failures, and confession follows, and then thanksgiving is automatic when I understand how blessed I am. I go from adoration to confession and then to thanksgiving, because He is so great.

God blessed and cleansed Isaiah by sending a seraphim with a live coal to touch his mouth and said "See, this has touched your lips: your guilt is taken away and your sin atoned for." This is a beautiful picture of what God has done for us. He sent His Son to die for us and His blood cleanses us from all sin and we are adopted into the family of God.

Has our heart been cleansed?

Have our lips been cleansed.

Do we worship with thanksgiving?

MY PRAYER: *Lord, we confess that we think too much of ourselves instead of you. When we are aware of your presence and forget about ourselves, we are so blessed. Thank you for being with us. We love you.*

MaryEmma

DECEMBER 17

THE PERFECT GIFT

*"She will give birth to a son, and you are to give Him the name
Jesus, because He will save His people from their sins."*
Mathew 1:21

The angel gave Joseph more information: It would be a boy and the
name: Jesus. I am sure Joseph was in shock.

He went from considering a quiet divorce to discovering he was going
be the stepfather of the promised Messiah. He knew the scriptures, a virgin
would conceive, and they would have a great King like David. But this
wasn't the way he thought it would happen!

The name would be Jesus. That is the Greek version of Joshua, which
means—the Lord Saves. This is the 'real reason' for Christmas. We like
to think of a sweet little baby, but He came into the world for a purpose.
That purpose was to "save His people from their sins".

He would show us how to live: communicating with His heavenly
Father and only doing and saying what the Father told Him. Then He would
die on the cross, to become the sacrificial lamb because sacrificing animals
was not enough to save us from our sins. Jesus' death and resurrection
would give us the access to God that we need for salvation from our sins.

Do we remember the "reason for the season"?

Are we too concerned with decorations and gifts?

Is Jesus celebrated in our family?

MY PRAYER: *Lord, help us to truly worship you, to remember your love and
to show your love to those we encounter, even to those who are unpleasant. Thank
you for your perfect gift.*

MaryEmma

OBEDIENCE

"When Joseph woke up, he did what the angel of the Lord had commanded him and took Mary home as his wife. But he did not consummate their marriage ... . he gave Him the name Jesus."
Mathew 1:24-25

Joseph was obedient to God. He did not argue, he didn't try to bargain with God. He simply obeyed. He didn't say he wanted his own child, he was willing to wait to make love to his wife. He simply obeyed. He didn't try to tell God what God should do. He simply obeyed.

Now we can understand why Joseph was chosen to be the earthly father of Jesus.

God rarely speaks to us directly, but we read His words and know how He wants us to live and act. We have wonderful examples of love and obedience in Mary and Joseph.

Do we argue with Him, or bargain, or try to tell Him what to do?

Do we think we know best?

Do we trust him when it is inconvenient?

MY PRAYER: *Lord, forgive us when we argue with you, forgive us when we want our will instead of yours. Help us to love as you love. Thank you for your wonderful blessings. Thank you for this season when we worship Your gift.*
MaryEmma

DECEMBER 19

FAITHFUL

"In those days Caesar Augustus issued a decree that a census should be taken of the entire Roman world.... Joseph went there to register with Mary, who was pledged to be married to him and was expecting a child."
Luke 2:1,3-5

We have another example of the obedience of both Joseph and Mary; obedience to the government. It was not convenient to travel. Mary was 'big with child' at this time and it was a 10 days journey. They could have hidden out in their village and not gone. Others would have protected them, but they obeyed Caesar. And they would have missed a wonderful blessing had they not obeyed the law!

The prophet Micah, had prophesied centuries earlier that the Messiah would be born in Bethlehem. Because of their obedience, even though it was a great inconvenience they were blessed by fulfilling God's prophesy.

Do we obey God and the laws?

Do we decide what to obey and what to ignore?

Do we miss blessings because we do it our way?

MY PRAYER: *Lord God, thank you for the wonderful blessing of your son coming to earth and showing us the way to you. Make our hearts right with you and help us to be a blessing to others this holiday season. We love you.*
MaryEmma

DECEMBER 20

NO GUEST ROOM

"While they were there, the time came for the baby to be born, and she gave birth to their firstborn, a son. She wrapped Him in cloths and placed Him in a manger, because there was no guest room available for them."
Luke 2:6-7

Why did God choose to have His son born in a manger? He could have just as easily been born to a wealthy virgin?

Could it be that He wanted all of us relate to Him. To know that He came for all of us, not just the wealthy and well-known?

There were no adoring grandparents around, but the angel did notify the poorest and least respected people, the shepherds. God sent His son for all of us, from the poorest to the richest. We don't know what day on the calendar He came to earth, but it doesn't matter. What matters is that He came and we worship Him.

There is nothing magical to celebrate about December 25, but there is about the Christ Child!

Do we celebrate Jesus?

Do we focus on gifts?

Do we spend our time and energy on the world's customs?

MY PRAYER: *Lord, this is the Christmas season and we are busy getting ready for our family and friends to help celebrate. I pray, Lord, that we will celebrate you in our hearts and mind as we go through this day. I pray that our love will show as we spend time with friends and relatives and we will be blessed with an awareness of your presence. .*

MaryEmma

DECEMBER 21

PRAISE

"Suddenly a great company of the heavenly host appeared
with the angel, praising God and saying,
'Glory to God in the highest heaven, and on earth
peace to those on whom His favor rests.'"
Luke 2:13-14

Angels give messages, and they also praise God.

They acknowledge God with love and adoration.

How often do we tell God how wonderful He is? We need to take time to think about who He is as well as what He has done. If there are "hosts" of angels praising Him, shouldn't we also praise Him? Praising God brings peace and thankfulness and love into our spirit.

Scripture is full of praises to help us: The Lord's prayer, Isaiah and Psalms and many place in our Bible.

Some of my favorite praise verses are in Revelation, thumb through and see all the praises of the angels. It reminds us how great He is.

We need to spend more time in praising our great God. We will be blessed because it increases our faith and stirs up our love for him.

Do we make it a practice to praise Him?

Do we start our prayer time by telling Him how great He is?

Do we make an effort to praise Him when we are discouraged?

MY PRAYER: *Lord, help us to understand how wonderful you are. Help us to be aware of your presence in good times as well as bad. We love you and praise your holy name.*

MaryEmma

DECEMBER 22

OUR ROCK

"The Lord lives! Praise be to my Rock! Exalted by God my Savior!
Therefore I will praise You among the nations, O Lord.
I will sing praises to Your name."
Psalm 18: 46,49

David calls God his Rock; big and unmovable, his protection.

As He thinks about how God has helped him, he breaks out in praise. And then he tells God, his Rock, that he will sing praises to all nations. He will tell everyone how wonderful his God is.

Isn't this a wonderful example for us?

Do we acknowledge God?

Do we take credit ourselves for the blessings we receive?

MY PRAYER: *Lord, help us to be more aware of you. Help us to look for your presence as we go through our day. We love you and praise you.*

MaryEmma

GIFT OF GRACE

"Out of His fullness we have all received grace in place of grace already given. For the law was given through Moses; grace and truth came through Jesus Christ.
John 1:16-17

We celebrate Christmas each year to remember the great gift we have received from God. Moses gave us the law so we would know what to do and what not to do, but we had trouble obeying.

We needed extra grace, so God sent His Son to be our sacrifice. His blood covers our sins.

We celebrate the great mystery. God is one and yet He is three: the Trinity.

Jesus Christ came to earth to make God the Father known. When He returned to heaven, God sent His Spirit to be with us at all times. This is the great gift we celebrate so we will remember what we have received from our Lord and Savior: Grace and Truth.

MY PRAYER: *Lord, I pray that we will worship you today as we go through our routines. Help us to remember what you have given us: the greatest gift possible. We love you and thank you.*

MaryEmma

DECEMBER 24

CRYING FOR HELP

"Save me, O God, for the waters have come up to my neck.
I sink in the miry depths, where there is no foothold.
… my throat is parched. My eyes fail, looking for my God."
Psalm 69: 1-3

We have all felt like this at some time in our lives. We are in pain, physical or emotional, and all we can think of is ourselves and how we feel.

David had a rough life and he knew fear, but David lets it all out to God. He tells God exactly what he feels and gradually his mind goes from his own misery to God's greatness.

David starts his prayer with a call for help and then he transitions to praise and love. When we are in the presence of God, the fear recedes and we have a fantastic awareness of His love.

We have a wonderful loving and patient Lord. He listens when we finally concentrate on Him instead of ourselves, and our pain is manageable and our hearts love.

Why do we focus on ourselves instead of Him?

Could pain be a blessing because it makes us aware of the help available in our Lord?

Do we share our needs with God?

MY PRAYER: *Lord, You are wonderful to help us through difficult times. Sometimes it seems that we are in a desert far away from you. All we need to do is to call out to you as David did, and you are here. Thank you. We praise and glorify you.*

MaryEmma

BE GLAD IN HIM

"But may all who seek you rejoice and be glad in you; may those who long for your saving help always say, 'The Lord is great!'"
Psalm 70:4

When we want to know God better, we start by seeking Him. We have the written word for our textbook.

God has told us to talk to Him-about everything and anything that is bothering us.

He has provided the Holy Spirit to guide and direct us.

When we are in agreement with these 3 steps, we will rejoice and God will become more real to us and it will be automatic to praise Him and declare: "The Lord is great".

This one little verse is a wealth of power.

Do we read his word?

Do we talk to him?

Do we allow his Spirit to guide us?

MY PRAYER: *Lord, You are great! Thank you for always being available, for your abundant love and your saving help. We love you.*

MaryEmma

DECEMBER 26

"Since my youth, God, You have taught me, and to
this day I declare Your marvelous deeds. ...
Your righteousness, God, reaches to the heavens, You who
have done great things. Who is like You, God?"
Psalm 71: 17,19

Who is like God? It is a good question.

He is my heavenly Father who loves me.

He teaches me and when I have problems, He guides and directs me through them. He protects me.

He is the great Creator God and yet He loves me as if I were His only child. And He loves **you** as though **you** were His only Child!

Are we declaring His power to the next generation?

Who is like God?

Who is God to me?

Do we look for him?

MY PRAYER: *Lord, thank You for teaching me. Thank You for Your promise never to forsake me. You have done great and glorious things and I praise and thank You.*

MaryEmma

DECEMBER 27

FORGIVENESS

…"this has touched your lips; your guilt is taken away and your sin atoned for.' Then I heard the voice of the Lord saying, 'Whom shall I send! And who will go for us? And I said, 'Here am I. Send me!'"
Isaiah 6: 7-8

What happened to Isaiah when he saw the Lord happens to us when we encounter His presence. We may think we are doing great, but when we become aware of God, all we can think of is how unworthy we are. God wants us to recognize our sin so He can forgive us, but He doesn't want us to continue to feel sinful after forgiveness. When we can't accept His forgiveness, we are rejecting Him. We are telling God that He cannot forgive.

God loves us. He sacrificed His Son for us. He wants us to be in His family. He wants fellowship with us just as our friends and family want fellowship.

Is there some little guilt we are hiding deep into our heart that we have not given to God and accepted His forgiveness? Have we accepted God's love and forgiveness?

Will we trust him?

MY PRAYER: *Lord God, you are holy and mighty; powerful and great. You have all power and yet you love and cherish us. Thank you. We love you.*
Mary Emma

DECEMBER 28

WE ARE HIS

"Shout for joy to the Lord… Worship…come before Him with joyful songs. Know that the Lord is God. It is He who made us, and we are His; we are His people, the sheep of His pasture."
Psalm 100: 1-5

How much do we enjoy our God? Do we worship Him with gladness, or from a sense of duty? He is our Lord, our Savior, our creator. He made us to belong to Him. We are his, we are His sheep, His little lambs that He loves.

He protects us, like the shepherd protects His sheep.

The Lord is good. The Lord's love endures forever.

Do we worship Him?

Do we acknowledge His help and His love?

He is faithful: are we?

MY PRAYER: *Lord God, we love you. Forgive us for not telling you more often. Forgive us for not praising you as you deserve. You are magnificent! You are great and we love and thank you.*

Mary Emma

DECEMBER 29

BY FAITH

*"By faith we understand that the universe was formed at God's command,
so that what is seen was not made out of what was visible."*
Hebrews 11:3

Faith is trusting God when we don't understand what is going to happen but we know that He is in control and He has a purpose in our lives. Every time I feel fear, I am not trusting God, but if I am in tune with God, I recognize it as a precaution and follow his guidance. There are lots of theories on how our world was made, but there is only one true one. That is, God did it. He spoke and it happened. We quibble over details: Was it a 24 hour physical day, was it a "thousand years which is as a day in the sight of God?" Did it instantly appear or was it like a computer birthday card where you see a finger drawing in all the little details?

If God had wanted us to know, He would have given us details. What He wants us to know is that He did it, to accept it on faith, and honor and worship Him as our Creator God. Our God loves us so much He gave us Jesus to cleanse our conscious from sin. He loves us so much He has blessed us with his Holy Spirit. He loves us so much that He is concerned about us each moment of the day and wants to gives us His best.

God loves us. How much do we love Him?

Will we lift our eyes from our trouble and worship him?

Do we believe him?

MY PRAYER: *Lord God, you are so wonderful and you want to give us your best. You give and give and give and we just accept without even thinking that it is you who are blessing us. Forgive us our self- centeredness and help us to lift our eyes and worship you.*

Mary Emma

FAITH PLEASES GOD

"By faith Enoch was taken from this life, so that he did not experience death: 'He could not be found, because God had taken him away.'
(Genesis 5)

For before he was taken, he was commended as one who pleased God."
Hebrews 11: 5

How do we please God? We love him, we enjoy him and we maintain communication with him. There is a children's story about Enoch that I love: "One day God and Enoch were taking a walk, just visiting and enjoying each other's company. Enoch looked at his watch and said, 'I'd better leave. It will be dark before I get home." God answered him and said, 'It is closer to my house than yours. Why don't you come home with me?" And Enoch said, "Yes, thank you, I would like to."

Do we enjoy being with Him so much that we forget the time? God loves us.

Do we love him?

Do we spend special time with Him?

Do we need to talk to God about this?

MY PRAYER: *Lord God, You are wonderful and we do love You. Sometimes we enjoy being with You and sometimes we are impatient to get on with the rest of our lives. Lord, help us remember that You are the rest of our lives. Without You, life is not worth living. Thank You for teaching us that. We love You.*

MaryEmma

ENCOURAGEMENT

"There was also a prophet, Anna…never left the temple but worshiped night and day, fasting and praying. Coming up to them at that very moment, she gave thanks to God and spoke about the child to all who were looking forward to the redemption of Jerusalem."
Luke 2: 36,38

Why would God send 2 people to come up to the young parents with a baby? Could it be that they were feeling overwhelmed with all the events and needed reassurance?

Simeon and Anna affirmed that the baby they carried was God's and he had been given a great mission. It must have been a great encouragement to them.

Are there people around us who need encouragement? Is someone doing a good but difficult job that needs our affirmation? If we are looking for a New Years resolution, maybe this is it. First we must pray each day about it and ask God to remind us to encourage. He may have a special person He wants us to help.

How did Simeon and Anna know this baby was the Christ child? Simeon was righteous and devout. He spent personal time with God. Anna worshiped night and day, fasting and praying. They used their time to develop a personal line to God so that they could understand what He wanted them to do.

Do we need to talk to God about how we use our time?

Do we need to ask God to give us the gift of encouragement?

Do we need to look for ways to encourage?

MY PRAYER: *Holy Father, you are always in control. You allow us freedom to make mistakes, but you are also there with us when we need and want your help. We just need help in opening our spiritual eyes so we can be aware of your presence. We thank you and love you.*

MaryEmma

And One to Grow On!

GIVE THANKS

"Give thanks to The Lord, for He is good. His love endures forever.
Give thanks to the Lord of lords; His love endures forever. To Him,
who alone does great wonders, His love endures forever."
Psalm 136:1,3,4

Give thanks to the Lord for His love! Psalm 135 told us to praise the Lord. Today we are told to thank the Lord.

Sometimes we get confused about the two. We think they are the same. It is the difference in a child saying, "Mom, You are wonderful!" and 'Mom, thank You for breakfast." Is one more important than the other?

We praise God for who He is: Creator, Lord and Master of the universe; He is love. We thank God for what He does for us. He loves us. He blesses us.

Both are important and both make us think of Him in a slightly different role. I pray that we will thank Him today for His love. His love is so great that He gave us only Son to die on the cross to take away our sins and make us pure in His sight.

MY PRAYER: *Thank You Lord, for loving us and helping us. We love You and thank You. Thank you for the sun and the rain. Thank you for your salvation, thank you for your peace you give us.*

Mary Emma

Printed in the United States
By Bookmasters